Peterson's

MASTER CRITICAL READING FOR THE SAT

PETERSON'S

A ⓝelnet COMPANY

PETERSON'S

A **nelnet** COMPANY

About Peterson's, a Nelnet company

To succeed on your lifelong educational journey, you will need accurate, dependable, and practical tools and resources. That is why Peterson's is everywhere education happens. Because whenever and however you need education content delivered, you can rely on Peterson's to provide the information, know-how, and guidance to help you reach your goals. Tools to match the right students with the right school. It's here. Personalized resources and expert guidance. It's here. Comprehensive and dependable education content—delivered whenever and however you need it. It's all here.

For more information, contact Peterson's, 2000 Lenox Drive, Lawrenceville, NJ 08648; 800-338-3282; or find us on the World Wide Web at www.petersons.com/about.

Previous editions published as *New SAT Critical Reading Workbook* © 2005 and *Peterson's Exercises for the SAT* © 2001

Stephen Clemente, President; Fern A. Oram, Content Director; Bernadette Webster, Operations Director; Laura Paul, Editor; Roger S. Williams, Sales and Marketing; Jill C. Schwartz, Production Editor; Ray Golaszewski, Manufacturing Manager; Linda M. Williams, Composition Manager; Scott Johns, CD Quality Assurance

ISBN-13: 978-0-7689-2724-5
ISBN-10: 0-7689-2724-2

Printed in the United States of America

10 9 8 7 6 5 4 3 2 1   10 09 08

Second Edition

OTHER RECOMMENDED TITLES

Peterson's Master Writing for the SAT
Peterson's Master Math for the SAT
Peterson's Master the SAT

Contents

PART IV: TAKE IT TO THE NEXT LEVEL

Top Techniques for Critical Reading

PART V: FOUR CRITICAL READING PRACTICE TESTS

APPENDIX

Before You Begin

HOW THIS BOOK IS ORGANIZED

This book is designed to help you improve your score on the critical reading sections of the SAT. After a broad overview of critical reading and a diagnostic test, you will learn about the various types of questions in the critical reading sections and different strategies for answering each type of question. You will be presented with practice exercises of increasing difficulty along with answer keys and comprehensive explanations. Then you can "Take It to the Next Level" by learning strategies for answering the toughest and trickiest questions on the SAT. Finally, there are four practice tests to measure your improvement.

TRACKING YOUR PROGRESS

This is not an ordinary SAT exercise book. Every test is graded for difficulty so that you can pace yourself according to your needs. Level A questions are slightly easier than actual SAT questions; level B questions are approximately equal in difficulty to real exam questions; level C questions are more difficult; and level D questions are of varying degrees of difficulty. Level D tests have a difficulty level approximately equal to that of a regular SAT.

If the equivalent score on the diagnostic test is below the level required by the college of your choice, you may need to improve your study skills or your understanding of the exam or both. The diagnostic test's answer explanations will help you find out whether your vocabulary and critical reading skills are sufficient. In addition, by studying the test-taking tips in each section, you will become more familiar with the exam format, which will in turn enable you to work on the questions in an efficient, orderly way. Follow the five steps below for maximum results:

1. Take and score the diagnostic test.

2. Analyze your results to see how well you did in each category.

3. Study the advice given, as well as the "Check In" and analysis in each category.

4. Apportion your time for the drill tests according to the amount of trouble you had in each category.

5. Retest yourself periodically between the time you take the diagnostic test and the time you plan to take your SAT. Use the four critical reading practice tests. If, for example, there are eight weeks from the time you took your diagnostic test until your SAT, you should plan on taking the critical reading practice tests in the second, fourth, sixth, and eighth weeks.

Your scores should keep climbing as continued practice gives you confidence and experience.

COMPREHENSIVE ANSWER EXPLANATIONS

For the diagnostic test, all practice exercises, and the four practice tests, comprehensive answer explanations are provided. They explain the correct answer and the reason for it. They also identify traps, explain why the other answer choices are wrong, and teach you strategies for answering the question.

SPECIAL FEATURES

Throughout this book, you will find the following special features:

GOALS

At the beginning of each chapter, your goals and objectives are listed.

CHECK IN

Before beginning the exercises in Chapters 3 and 4, these "pretests" will get you ready to dive into the exercises.

CHECK OUT

At the end of each chapter, you are reminded of your goals for the chapter so you can ask yourself if you have accomplished them.

A HELPFUL WORD LIST

The appendix contains "A Helpful Word List," which is a list of words commonly found on the SAT. Studying these words will increase your vocabulary and prepare you to do your best on the SAT Critical Reading Test.

YOU'RE WELL ON YOUR WAY TO SUCCESS

Remember that knowledge is power. By using *Peterson's Master Critical Reading for the SAT*, you will be studying the most comprehensive preparation guide available for the critical reading sections of the SAT, and you will become extremely knowledgeable about SAT critical reading. We look forward to helping you score higher in SAT critical reading and improve your college prospects. Good luck!

GIVE US YOUR FEEDBACK

Peterson's publishes a full line of resources to help guide you through the college admissions process. Peterson's publications can be found at your local bookstore, library, and high school guidance office, and you can access us online at www.petersons.com.

We welcome any comments or suggestions you may have about this publication and invite you to complete our online survey at www.petersons.com/booksurvey. Your feedback will help us make your education dreams possible.

PART I

ALL ABOUT CRITICAL READING FOR THE SAT

Fundamentals of Critical Reading

1

Your goals for this chapter are to:

- Become familiar with the two types of SAT critical reading questions.

- Learn some test-taking tips for the critical reading sections.

Three of the ten sections of the SAT are critical reading sections. You have twenty-five minutes for two of the sections and twenty minutes for the third section. The experimental section might test critical reading, and although this section is unscored, it is also unidentified. Therefore, it is important you do your best on all sections.

The critical reading sections test critical reading and vocabulary skills.

TYPES OF CRITICAL READING QUESTIONS

The critical reading sections of the SAT test vocabulary, verbal reasoning, and the ability to understand reading passages. These skills are measured by two question types:

1. Sentence completions
2. Passage-based reading questions

SENTENCE COMPLETIONS

This type of question tests your knowledge of the meanings of words and your ability to recognize relationships among the parts of a sentence so that you can choose the word or words that best complete each sentence.

Example:

Conditions in the mine were ----, so the mine workers refused to return to their jobs until the dangers were ----.
(A) filthy .. disbanded ~ to stop sth or sb
(B) hazardous .. eliminated
(C) deplorable .. collated ~ to collect info
(D) conducive .. ameliorated ~ unacceptable
(E) illegal .. enhanced ~ make it easy

The correct answer is (B). The workers wanted the *hazardous* conditions *eliminated*.

PASSAGE-BASED READING

This type of question tests your ability to read and understand passages taken from any of the following categories: <u>humanities</u>, <u>social sciences</u>, <u>natural sciences</u>, and <u>fiction</u> or <u>nonfiction narrative</u>.

Based upon reading selections ranging from 100 to about 850 words, passage-based reading questions may require you to

- Recognize the meaning of a word as used in context
- Interpret specific information presented in the passage
- Analyze information in one part of the passage in terms of information presented in another part of the passage
- Evaluate the author's assumptions or identify the logical structure of the passage

Some reading selections consist of a pair of passages that present different points of view on the same or related subjects. The passages may support each other, oppose each other, or in some way complement each other. Some questions relate to each passage separately, and others ask you to compare, contrast, or evaluate the two passages.

Example:

Private enterprise is no stranger to the American prison. When the United States replaced corporal punishment with confinement as the primary punishment for criminals in the early nineteenth century, the private sector was the most frequent
(5) employer of convict labor. Prisoners were typically either leased to private companies who set up shop in the prison or used by prison officials to produce finished goods for a manufacturer who supplied the raw materials to the prison. The former arrangement was called the contract system, while the latter
(10) came to be known as the piece-price system. In both instances, a private company paid the prison a fee for the use of prison labor, which was used to partially offset the expense of operating the prison. Blatant exploitation of inmates sometimes developed as a consequence of these systems.
(15) Opposition to the use of prison labor from rival manufacturers and from the growing organized labor movement began to emerge in the latter part of the nineteenth century as more and more prisoners were put to work for the private sector. Opposition reached a peak during the Great Depression
(20) when Congress passed a series of laws designed to prohibit the movement of prison-made goods in interstate commerce, thus insuring that these products would not compete with those made by outside labor. Many state legislatures followed suit, forbidding the open market sale or importation of prison-made

(25)   goods within their borders and effectively barring the private
         sector from the prison. As a consequence, prison-based manufac-
         turing operations became state-owned and -operated businesses,
         selling goods in a highly restricted market.

1. Prisons stopped producing readily available goods due to all of the
   following EXCEPT
   (A) laws passed by state legislatures
   (B) laws passed by the Congress of the United States
   (C) opposition from organized labor
   (D) dissatisfaction of the prisoners
   (E) opposition from rival manufacturers

   The correct answer is (D). This question requires you to apply
   information given in the passage. There is no mention of prisoner
   dissatisfaction, so (D) is correct. Choice (A) is mentioned in lines
   23–26, choice (B) is mentioned in lines 19–24, and choices (C) and
   (E) are mentioned in lines 15–19.

2. In the arrangement known as the "contract system"
   (A) companies set up shop inside a prison and used prisoners for
       labor.
   (B) manufacturers supplied raw materials to the prison.
   (C) all of the prisoners signed a contract to produce a certain
       amount of goods.
   (D) prisoners with suitable skills would contact the companies.
   (E) exploitation inevitably ensued.

   The correct answer is (A). This question requires you to
   interpret details. In lines 5–6, the contract system is defined as a
   system in which prisoners were "leased to private companies who
   set up shop in the prison."

3. According to the passage, which of the following was instrumental
   in the development of the private sector in prison?
   (A) Seed money from the federal government
   (B) The replacement of corporal punishment with confinement
   (C) The crudeness of the original prison system
   (D) The constant exploitation of the prisoners by manufacturers
   (E) The piece-price and contract systems

   The correct answer is (B). This question requires you to
   evaluate information. Choice (B) is stated in the second sentence
   of the passage.

4. Which of the following statements can be inferred from the passage?
   - (A) There is no longer any private sector work done in prisons.
   - (B) Legislatures are ready to repeal the previously passed prison laws.
   - (C) Prison systems were once fully supported by the fees paid by the private sector.
   - (D) The Great Depression was caused by excessive prison labor.
   - (E) Piece-price was more profitable than the contract system.

   The correct answer is (A). This question requires you to make an inference. Choice (A) follows from the last sentence of the passage.

VOCABULARY: DOES IT MATTER?
IN A WORD: YES.

Vocabulary *as such* is not tested on the SAT. Until a few years ago, the exam included antonym questions, which required you to pick a word whose meaning was the opposite of some other word. Those questions have been eliminated. So the most direct and obvious form of a vocabulary question on the SAT is no more.

That leaves *indirect* and *hidden* vocabulary questions—of which there are plenty.

1. Reading comprehension passages now include vocabulary-in-context questions. These focus on particular words in the passage and ask you to determine their meaning *in the passage*. Sometimes the words chosen are obviously "hard" words (*latent, replete,* and *eminent,* to name three real examples). More often, they are seemingly "easy" words that are tricky because they have so many possible meanings (*camp, idea,* and *hard,* for example). In both cases, the broader, more varied, and more accurate your vocabulary knowledge, the better your chances are of answering these questions quickly and correctly.

2. The better your vocabulary knowledge, the easier you'll find it to understand both the critical reading passages and the sentence completion items (which are, in effect, mini-passages, each one sentence long). Even an occasional math item is made a little more complicated by the use of a challenging vocabulary word.

Therefore, vocabulary knowledge makes a clear and significant difference in your performance on the SAT. Fortunately, the kinds of words that regularly appear on the SAT, as with so much else on the exam, fall into definite patterns.

The SAT is basically a test of "book learning." It's written and edited by bookish people for the benefit of the other bookish people who run colleges and universities. It's designed to test your ability to handle the kinds of academic tasks college students usually have to master: reading textbooks, finding information in reference books, deciphering scholarly journals, studying research abstracts, writing impressive-sounding term papers, and so forth.

The hard words on the SAT are hard words of a particular sort: scholastic words that deal, broadly speaking, with the manipulation and communication of *ideas*—words like *ambiguous, amplify, arbitrary,* and *arcane.* The better you master this sort of vocabulary, the better you'll do on the exam.

Fortunately, you don't need to find these words on your own. We've done the spadework for you. By examining actual SAT exams from the last several years, we've been able to list the words most commonly used in reading passages and sentence completions, including both the question stems and the answer choices. This list became the basis of the SAT Word List, which can be found in the appendix. It includes about 500 primary words that are most likely to appear in one form or another on your SAT exam. It also includes hundreds of related words—words that are either variants of the primary words (*ambiguity* as a variant of *ambiguous*, for example) or that share a common word root (like *ample, amplify,* and *amplitude*).

If you make yourself acquainted with all the words in the SAT Word List, you will absolutely learn a number of new words that will appear on your SAT. You'll earn extra points as a result.

THE BEST VOCABULARY-BUILDING TIPS FOR THE SAT

STUDY VOCABULARY DAILY

There are some topics you can easily cram. Vocabulary isn't one of them. In general, words don't stay in mind until the fourth or fifth time you learn them. Try to begin your vocabulary study several weeks before the exam. Take 15 or 20 minutes a day to learn new words. Periodically review all the words you've previously studied; quiz yourself, or have a friend quiz you. This simple regimen can enable you to learn several hundred new words before you take the SAT.

LEARN A FEW WORDS AT A TIME

Don't try to gobble dozens of words in one sitting. They're likely to blur into an indistinguishable mass. Instead, pick a reasonable quantity—say, ten to fifteen words—and study them in some depth.

Learn the definition of each word; examine the sample sentence provided in the Word List; learn the related words; and try writing a couple of sentences of your own that include the word. Refer to your own dictionary for further information if you like.

LEARN WORDS IN FAMILIES

Language is a living thing. Words are used by humans, innately creative beings who constantly twist, reshape, invent, and recombine words. (Think of the jargon of your favorite sport or hobby, or the language that has blossomed in cyberspace in recent years.) As a result, most words belong to families, in which related ideas are expressed through related words. This makes it possible to learn several words each time you learn one.

In the SAT Word List, we've provided some of the family linkages to help you. For example, you'll find the adjective *anachronistic* in the word list. It means "out of the proper time," as illustrated by the sample sentence: The reference, in Shakespeare's *Julius Caesar,* to "the clock striking twelve" is anachronistic, since there were no striking timepieces in ancient Rome.

When you meet this word, you should also get to know its close kinfolk. The noun *anachronism* means something that is out of its proper time. The clock in *Julius Caesar*, for example, is an anachronism; in another way, so are the knickers worn by modern baseball players, which reflect a style in men's fashions that went out of date generations ago. When you learn the adjective, learn the noun (and/or verb) that goes with it at the same time.

BECOME A WORD ROOT TRACER

The two words we just discussed—*anachronistic* and *anachronism*—are like brother and sister. Slightly more distant relatives can be located and learned through the "Word Origin" feature you'll find near many of the words in the list. The origin for *anachronistic* connects this word to its source from another language: the Greek word *chronos* means time. Ultimately, this is the root from which the English word *anachronistic* grows.

As you explore the word origins, you'll find that many words—especially bookish SAT words—come from roots in Latin and Greek. There are complicated (and interesting) historical reasons for this, but the nub is that, for several centuries, learned people in England and America knew ancient Latin and Greek and deliberately imported words from those languages into English.

They rarely imported just one word from a given root. Thus, many word roots can enable you to learn several English words at once. The word origin for anachronistic tells you that *chronos* is also the source of the English words *chronic, chronicle, chronograph, chronology,* and *synchronize.* All of these have to do with the concept of time:

- *Chronic* means lasting a long time

- A *chronicle* is a record of events over a period of time

- A *chronograph* is a clock or watch

- *Chronology* is a timeline

- *Synchronize* means to make two things happen at the same time

Learning the word root *chronos* can help you in several ways. It will make it easier to learn all the words in the *chronos* family, as opposed to trying to learn them one at a time. It will help you to remember the meanings of *chronos* words if they turn up on the exam, and it may even help you to guess the meaning of an entirely new *chronos* word when you encounter it.

USE THE WORDS YOU LEARN

Make a deliberate effort to include the new words you're learning in your daily speech and writing. It will help solidify your memory of the words and their meanings. Maybe you've heard this tip about meeting new people: If you use a new acquaintance's name several times, you're unlikely to forget it. The same is true with new words: Use them, and you won't lose them.

CREATE YOUR OWN WORD LIST

Get into the habit of reading a little every day with your dictionary nearby. When you encounter a new word in a newspaper, magazine, or book, look it up. Then jot down the new word, its definition, and the sentence in which you encountered it in a notebook set aside for this purpose. Review your vocabulary notebook periodically—say, once a week. This is a great way to supplement our SAT Word List, because it's personally tailored. Your notebook will reflect the kinds of things you read and the words you find most difficult. The fact that you've taken the time and made the effort to write down the words and their meanings will help to fix them in your memory. Chances are good that you'll encounter a few words from your vocabulary notebook on the exam.

CHECK OUT

Before you go on to the next chapter, can you

- Name the two types of critical reading questions?
- State some test-taking tips for the critical reading sections?

PART II
DIAGNOSING STRENGTHS AND WEAKNESSES

CHAPTER 2   Practice Test 1:
Diagnostic

Practice Test 1: Diagnostic

26 Questions • 25 Minutes

> **Directions:** The incomplete sentences below are followed by five words or pairs of words. Choose that word or pair of words that, when substituted for the blank space or spaces, best completes the meaning of the sentence. Mark the letter of your choice on your answer sheet.

Example:

In view of the <u>extenuating</u> circumstances and the defendant's youth, the judge recommended ----.

(A) conviction
(B) a defense
(C) a mistrial
(D) <u>leniency</u> - relaxing
(E) life imprisonment

Ⓐ Ⓑ Ⓒ ● Ⓔ

✓1. Gregory's face was ---- when he reported the loss of his ship.

(A) vivid
(B) somber
(C) animated
(D) <u>pusillanimous</u> - scared
(E) <u>antiquated</u> - old-fashioned

2. You have a(n) ----; the test has been postponed for a week.

(A) absence
(B) holiday
(C) request
(D) assignment
(E) <u>reprieve</u> - to cancel

3. The sheik's wealth was a matter of ----; nobody had the least idea of how much he possessed.

(A) conjecture - a guesswork
(B) conjunction
(C) <u>divinity</u> - god-like
(D) <u>obloquy</u> - criticism
(E) concern

4. During the 1923 German inflation, there was a ---- of paper currency; it took a wheelbarrow to transport enough money to buy a suit.

(A) shortage

(B) supply

(C) dearth — *lacking sth*

(D) transfer

(E) plethora — *superfluous*

5. Trespassing on private property is ---- by law.

(A) proscribed — *to say sth is forbidden*

(B) warranted

(C) prescribed

(D) eliminated

(E) forgiven

6. Since you have just made a(n) ---- sale, this is a(n) ---- time to ask for a raise.

(A) meager .. excellent   *poor in quality / insmall in quantity*

(B) ostentatious .. precipitous

(C) impressive .. opportune

(D) plausible .. preposterous

(E) pernicious .. reprehensible

7. People are ---- to confess such anxieties for fear of appearing ----.   *harmful   deserving criticisms*

(A) reluctant .. virtuous — *moral*

(B) eager .. recondite — *only known to a few people*

(C) constrained .. derelict — *not used or cared for*

(D) reticent .. weak   *inclined to be silent*

(E) hesitant .. prudent

8. A person who commits a wrong may be required to ---- his property as a penalty.

(A) confiscate — *take away punishments*

(B) destroy

(C) forfeit

(D) assess — *to judge sth or someone*

(E) sell

9. He said he didn't get the job done because he was incapacitated; in truth, he was ---- and slothful.

(A) indigent

(B) indolent — *lazy*

(C) indulgent — *spoiled*

(D) insipid — *having almost no taste or flavour*

(E) incapable

10. The "policemen" turned out to be clowns; the setup was a ----.

   (A) stickup
   (B) mystery
   (C) mix-up
   (D) fracas - ~~~~ fight
   (E) hoax• an act of false persuasion

11. During colonial winters in America, there was a ---- in every ----.

   (A) fire .. hearth- bottom of the stove
   (B) stoker .. pot
       - steamer
   (C) flintlock .. chimney
   (D) tepee .. stockade
   (E) blizzard .. storm

12. Since she was so hardworking, Jillian's parents never had to ---- her for being ----.

   (A) chide .. industrious
       criticize
   (B) ride .. superfluous
   (C) punish .. independent
   (D) chide .. slothful
   (E) commend .. intransigent - stubborn

Directions: Each reading passage below is followed by a set of questions. Read the passage and answer the accompanying questions, basing your answers on what is stated or implied in the passage. Mark the letter of your choice on your answer sheet.

Questions 13–18 are based on the following passage.

Nancy Langhorne was born in the United States in 1879. She moved to England, married Viscount Astor, and became the first woman ever to sit in the House of Commons, a position she held from 1919 to 1945. As Lady Astor, her politics were often questionable—she was among those who sought to appease the Fascists in the 1930s—but her door-opening role for women in politics made her an important figure. The following comments are excerpted from a 1922 address at Town Hall in New York City.

My entrance into the House of Commons was not, as some thought, in the nature of a revolution. It was an evolution. My husband was the one who started me off on this downward path—from the fireside to public life. If I have helped the cause
(5)   of women, he is the one to thank, not me.

A woman in the House of Commons! It was almost enough to have broken up the House. I don't blame them—it was equally hard on the woman as it was on them. Pioneers may be picturesque figures, but they are often rather lonely ones.

(10) I must say for the House of Commons, they bore their shock with dauntless decency. No body of men could have been kinder and fairer to a "pirate" than they were. When you hear people over here trying to run down England, please remember that England was the first large country to give the vote to women

(15) and that the men of England welcomed an American-born woman in the House with a fairness and a justice which, at least, this woman never will forget....

Now, why are we in politics? What is it all about? Something much bigger than ourselves. Schopenhauer was

(20) wrong in nearly everything he wrote about women—and he wrote a lot—but he was right in one thing. He said, in speaking of women, "the race is to her more than the individual," and I believe that it is true. I feel somehow we do care about the race as a whole, our very nature makes us take a forward vision;

(25) there is no reason why women should look back—mercifully we have no political past; we have all the mistakes of sex legislation with its appalling failures to guide us.

We should know what to avoid, it is no use blaming the men—we made them what they are—and now it is up to us

(30) to try and make ourselves—the makers of men—a little more responsible in the future. We realize that no one sex can govern alone. I believe that one of the reasons why civilization has failed so lamentably is that it has had a one-sided government. Don't let us make the mistake of ever allowing that to happen

(35) again.

I can conceive of nothing worse than a man-governed world except a woman-governed world—but I can see the combination of the two going forward and making civilization more worthy of the name of civilization based on Christianity, not force. A

(40) civilization based on justice and mercy. I feel men have a greater sense of justice and we of mercy. They must borrow our mercy and we must use their justice. We are new brooms; let us see that we sweep the right rooms.

13. According to Lady Astor, the reaction of the men in the House of Commons to her being seated was one of

   (A) surprise and horror.
   (B) polite consternation.
   (C) resigned distaste.
   (D) witticisms and good humor.
   (E) amused acceptance.

14. Lady Astor urges Americans to give England its due for

    (A) having a bicameral legislature.
    (B) its tolerance toward women in politics.
    (C) allowing an American into their Parliament.
    (D) both A and B.
    (E) both B and C.

15. Women look forward, according to Lady Astor, because

    (A) the history of sexism makes their past insignificant.
    (B) something may be gaining on them.
    (C) they have made so many mistakes in the past.
    (D) they have no real sense of history.
    (E) men refuse to do so.

16. Lady Astor sees the ideal government as a balance between

    (A) fairness and compassion.
    (B) the past and the future.
    (C) Christianity and force.
    (D) honesty and courage.
    (E) virtue and strength.

17. When Lady Astor refers to "new brooms" (line 42), she means that

    (A) women belong in the home.
    (B) there is now a fresh chance to clean up things.
    (C) the tide of history has swept right by women.
    (D) it is time to sweep men out of power.
    (E) sweeping change is a thing of the past.

18. Lady Astor's attitude toward men seems to be one of

    (A) chilly disapproval.
    (B) lighthearted leniency.
    (C) reverent deference.
    (D) defiant contempt.
    (E) weary indifference.

Questions 19–26 are based on the following passage.

Sun Yat-sen (1866–1925) was a revolutionary who worked to overthrow the monarchy and install a republic in China. He served as president of the republic from 1923 until his death in 1925. This speech, which he gave in early 1924, shows his desire to bring China into the twentieth century and make it a world power.

Although we are behind the foreigners in scientific achievement, our native ability is adequate to the construction of a great material civilization, which is proved by the concrete evidence of past achievements. We invented the compass, printing,

(5) porcelain, gunpowder, and the curing of tea and weaving of silk. Foreigners have made good use of these inventions. For example, modern ocean travel would be impossible if there were no compass. The fast printing machine, which turns out tens of thousands of copies per hour, had its origin in China. Foreign

(10) military greatness comes from gunpowder, which was first used by the Chinese. Furthermore, many of the latest inventions in architecture in the West have been practiced in the East for thousands of years. This genius of our race for material inventions seems now to be lost; and so our greatness has become but

(15) the history of bygone glories.

I believe that we have many things to learn from the West, and that we can learn them. Many Westerners maintain that the hardest thing to learn is aerial science; already many Chinese have become skillful aviators. If aeronautics can be

(20) learned, I believe everything can be learned by our people. Science is only three hundred years old, and it was not highly developed until fifty years ago. Formerly coal was used as the source of energy; now the age of coal has given place to the age of electricity.

(25) Recently, America had a plan for nationalizing the water-power of the country. America has hundreds of thousands of factories. Each big factory has to have a powerhouse, which consumes a tremendous amount of coal. The railroads in the country are busily engaged in transporting coal and have little

(30) time for transporting agricultural products. As a means of economizing coal and lessening transportation, a national central powerhouse is suggested. When such a house is built, the entire nation will receive energy from one central station. The result will be the elimination of enormous waste and the increase of

(35) efficiency.

When we learn from the West, it is evident that we should learn the latest inventions instead of repeating the various steps of development. In the case of the powerhouse, we may well

(40)   learn to adopt the centralized plan of producing electricity, and need not follow the old plan of using coal to produce energy. In this way, we can easily within ten years catch up with the West in material achievement.

The time is critical. We have no time to waste, and we ought to take the latest and the best that the West can offer.

(45)   Our intelligence is by no means inferior to that of the Japanese. With our historical background and our natural and human resources, it should be easier for us than it was for Japan to rise to the place of a first-class Power by a partial adaptation of Western civilization. We ought to be ten times stronger than

(50)   Japan because our country is more than ten times bigger and richer than Japan. China is potentially equal to ten Powers. At present England, America, France, Italy, and Japan constitute the so-called Big Five. Even with the rise of Germany and Soviet Russia, the world has only seven Powers. When China becomes

(55)   strong, she can easily win first place in the Council of Nations.

19. Sun Yat-sen lists past scientific contributions of Chinese inventors (lines 4–6) to show that

   (A)   China deserves more credit for past successes.
   (B)   most important inventions are Chinese.
   (C)   the Chinese have the ability to create and achieve.
   (D)   Chinese inventions have been stolen by foreigners.
   (E)   life would be difficult without scientific exploration.

20. Why has China lost greatness, according to Sun Yat-sen?

   (A)   It has turned inward and lost its place in the world.
   (B)   Its inventions are old and outdated.
   (C)   It cannot turn its inventiveness to good use.
   (D)   The people are not interested in material things.
   (E)   The people's genius for invention has been lost.

21. Sun Yat-sen uses the example of aviation (lines 17–20) to show that

   (A)   the Chinese have the skill to learn from the West.
   (B)   Western inventions are more complex than Chinese inventions.
   (C)   only aeronautics offers a challenge to the Chinese.
   (D)   science is not very old.
   (E)   very few people can become inventors.

22. A vital lesson the West can teach China is the use of

   (A)   centralized electrical power.
   (B)   coal to produce energy.
   (C)   railroads to transport agricultural products.
   (D)   both A and B.
   (E)   both B and C.

23. It is important to Sun Yat-sen that the Chinese learn from the West without

    (A) repeating the West's mistakes.
    (B) having to start from the beginning.
    (C) acting aggressively.
    (D) spending as much as the West has.
    (E) becoming too Western in outlook.

24. Sun Yat-sen compares the intelligence of the Chinese to that of the Japanese (line 45) to demonstrate that

    (A) Chinese spies are just as good as Japanese spies.
    (B) China can become a Power as easily as Japan did.
    (C) with a little education, the Chinese can surpass the Japanese.
    (D) it was not easy for Japan to become a Power.
    (E) it will not be easy for China to compete with Japan.

25. By "critical" (line 43), Sun Yat-sen means

    (A) analytical.
    (B) grievous.
    (C) dangerous.
    (D) picky.
    (E) momentous.

26. A reasonable title for this speech might be

    (A) "How China Lost Its Way."
    (B) "Military Strength."
    (C) "How the West Has Won."
    (D) "Learning from the West."
    (E) "Ten Times Stronger."

STOP

END OF SECTION 1. IF YOU HAVE ANY TIME LEFT, GO OVER YOUR WORK IN THIS SECTION ONLY. DO NOT WORK IN ANY OTHER SECTION OF THE TEST.

ANSWER KEY AND EXPLANATIONS

1. B	7. D	12. D	17. B	22. A
2. E	8. C	13. B	18. B	23. B
3. A	9. B	14. E	19. C	24. B
4. E	10. E	15. A	20. E	25. E
5. A	11. A	16. A	21. A	26. D
6. C				

1. **The correct answer is (B).** When a person loses something as large and important as his ship, his face can be expected to look serious or depressed—not *vivid* (full of life), *animated* (lively), *pusillanimous* (cowardly), or *antiquated* (made to look old). *Somber* (dark and gloomy) is the ideal choice.

2. **The correct answer is (E).** Since the test has been postponed, the students have a *reprieve*—a temporary escape from taking it.

3. **The correct answer is (A).** Since "nobody had the least idea of how much he possessed," apparently one could only make a guess at the amount. *Conjecture* (theory, inference, or prediction based on guesswork) is the best choice.

4. **The correct answer is (E).** If "it took a wheelbarrow to transport enough money to buy a suit," there must have been a superabundance, or *plethora*, of paper currency.

5. **The correct answer is (A).** *Proscribed* means forbidden or outlawed. Choice (B) means justified; choice (C) means recommended; choices (D) and (E) are impossible.

6. **The correct answer is (C).** Both words in the answer choice must be either positive or negative, so choices (A) and (D) are eliminated. Neither choice (B) nor choice (E) makes any sense in the context of the sentence. The correct answer is choice (C): closing an *impressive* sale would be an *opportune* (appropriate) time to ask for a raise.

7. **The correct answer is (D).** A sentence that includes "anxieties" and "fear" has a strong negative connotation, so two negative-sounding words are needed. Only (C) and (D) offer two negative-sounding words. In (C), however, *constrained* (forced or compelled) and *derelict* (irresponsible) make no sense in the context. The correct answer is (D): "People are *reticent* (hesitant) to confess such anxieties for fear of appearing *weak*."

8. **The correct answer is (C).** The key word in this sentence is "penalty." *Forfeiting* one's property is a real penalty. The other answer choices don't fit here.

9. **The correct answer is (B).** "Slothful" means lazy, and the correct answer needs to reflect the same sentiment. Only *indolent* fits into the context of the sentence.

10. **The correct answer is (E).** *Hoax* is another word for joke. The policemen were really clowns, so the word *hoax* fits well into the context.

11. **The correct answer is (A).** The clue word in this sentence is "winter." Use the process of elimination to make sure that only choice (A) makes sense.

12. **The correct answer is (D).** Parents *chide*, or reprove, their children for being *slothful*, or lazy. Because Jillian is a hard-working child, her parents don't have to reprimand her.

13. **The correct answer is (B).** "... They bore their shock with dauntless decency" (lines 10–11), says the speaker. They were shocked, but polite.

14. **The correct answer is (E).** In the end of paragraph 2, Lady Astor commends the English for these two things.

15. **The correct answer is (A).** She is unfailingly polite in her discussion of sexism, but lines 25–27 explain her position.

16. **The correct answer is (A).** This is an accurate translation of "justice and mercy" (line 40).

17. **The correct answer is (B).** The reference is to the adage "A new broom sweeps clean." Lady Astor implies that women, the "new brooms," have the power to change things for the better.

18. **The correct answer is (B).** She thanks her husband for getting her into politics (lines 2–5), and she blames women for making men what they are (lines 28–31). Despite the "appalling failures" of sex legislation, Lady Astor lets men off the hook.

19. **The correct answer is (C).** The point of the opening paragraph is to demonstrate that China once had the power to build and invent and that it may regain this power.

20. **The correct answer is (E).** This is implied by the correlation of clauses in lines 13–15; Sun Yat-sen says that "our greatness has become but the history of bygone glories" because the genius for invention is lost.

21. **The correct answer is (A).** Although aviation is hard to learn, many Chinese have mastered it; therefore, they are up to any task.

22. **The correct answer is (A).** Paragraph 3 is all about this centralization of power.

23. **The correct answer is (B).** Lines 36–38 at the beginning of paragraph 4 state the speaker's desire to learn from the West without repeating all the stages of development.

24. **The correct answer is (B).** China's rivalry with Japan is used here to indicate that China can do anything Japan can do.

25. **The correct answer is (E).** Only *momentous* makes sense in context.

26. **The correct answer is (D).** Most of the speech deals with the fact that China has much to learn from the West if it wants to become a Power.

PART III
PRACTICING CRITICAL READING

Sentence Completions

3

Your goals for this chapter are to:
- Learn strategies for answering sentence completion questions.
- Test your ability to answer sentence completion questions.

WHAT IS A SENTENCE COMPLETION QUESTION?

In each SAT sentence completion question, you are given a sentence containing one or more blanks. A number of answers, or pairs of answers, are suggested to fill the blank space(s). You must select the word or pair of words that best completes the meaning of the sentence as a whole.

Examples:

Through his ---- he managed to cheat his partners out of their earnings.

- (A)   inefficiency
- (B)   ineptness - *no skill*
- (C)   machinations - *a secret & complicated plan*
- (D)   regime - *an unfair government*
- (E)   dealings

The correct answer is (C). Through what (noun) does one cheat? You should be able to answer, "Through unfair play, conspiracy, evil planning, or the like." A look at the five possibilities reveals *machinations* as the only possible choice.

Normally a(n) ---- of dependability, he had let his colleagues down; now he could not face their ----.
- (A)   pillar .. smirks - *evil smile* / *large round stone*
- (B)   besmircher .. titillation - *to sexually arouse sb*
- (C)   paragon .. wrath - *damage one's opinion* / *perfect*
- (D)   bastion .. adulation - *admiration*
- (E)   anathema .. debts - *an opposite belief*

The correct answer is (C). Despite being a what (noun) of dependability, did he let his colleagues down so badly that he couldn't face them? *Paragon, bastion,* and *pillar*—all symbols of strength or virtue—would work; *besmircher* (one who dirties) and *anathema* (curse) would not. Using any of the three that work, focus now on the fact that he had "let them down." What do people show when they are severely disappointed? Certainly not *smirks* (crooked smiles) or *adulation* (praise). *Wrath,* however, is a perfect fit.

HOW TO ANSWER SENTENCE COMPLETION QUESTIONS

READ THE SENTENCE THROUGH FOR SENSE, AND TRY TO ANTICIPATE WHAT WORD WOULD BEST FILL THE BLANK. THEN LOOK FOR THAT WORD IN THE ANSWER CHOICES.

Example:

Alan waited ---- for his turn, relaxing in an easy chair with his eyes closed.

(A)   impatiently
(B)   eagerly
(C)   warily
(D)   calmly
(E)   tensely

The correct answer is (D). When you read the sentence, you might have anticipated that a word like patiently could be used in the blank. Patiently does not appear as an answer choice, but there is one choice that is close to that meaning: *calmly.* None of the other choices is idiomatic; in other words, none has a meaning that is appropriate in the context of the sentence.

This sentence was a fairly easy one. And some of those you encounter on the SAT will be easy. Others, however, will be more difficult. Harder ones will require that you analyze the logical structure of the sentence to see what is required.

DETERMINE WHETHER THE MISSING WORD MUST CONTRAST WITH OR SUPPORT ANOTHER IDEA IN THE SENTENCE.

Although this method will not solve every sentence completion item on the SAT, it is a fairly useful and easy-to-use tool. The idea is that the logic of a sentence requires a certain result, as in the following examples:

> The service at the restaurant was usually very attentive, but on this one occasion the waiter seemed to ---- the diners.
>
> (A) applaud
> (B) urge
> (C) ignore
> (D) restrain
> (E) fulfill

The correct answer is (C). The "but" in this sentence sets up a contrasting idea. The word that fills the blank must contrast with the idea of "very attentive."

> If Peter continues to skip classes and fail to complete homework assignments, he will soon find that he has been ---- the university.
>
> (A) dismissed from
> (B) invited to
> (C) trapped in
> (D) warned about
> (E) reminded of

The correct answer is (A). The logical structure of this sentence requires a completion that shows the logical conclusion of skipping classes and not completing assignments.

WORDS SUCH AS "ALTHOUGH," "THOUGH," "NOT," "BUT," AND "HOWEVER" SIGNAL CONTRAST.

If you spot any of these words in a sentence completion question, you know that you should look for an answer that contrasts with an idea in the sentence.

Examples:

Although the movie was <u>panned</u> by all the major critics, audiences around the country seemed to find it ----.

(A) reprehensible
(B) worthless
(C) <u>subdued</u>
(D) <u>iconoclastic</u>
(E) entertaining

The correct answer here is (E). The "although" signals a reversal of the "panning" or disapproval of the critics: the critics disliked the movie, but the audiences liked it.

The restaurant itself was beautiful and the service excellent, but the food was ----.

(A) outstanding
(B) <u>morose</u>
(C) conclusive
(D) inedible
(E) filling

The correct answer is (D). Here, the "but" signals a contrast between the positive ideas of "beautiful" and "excellent" and an adjective with negative connotations that describes the food. What is a good way of describing bad food? *Inedible* fits best.

WORDS SUCH AS "SO," "FOR," "BECAUSE," "THEREFORE," AND "AS A RESULT" SIGNAL IDEAS THAT SUPPORT EACH OTHER.

If you spot one of these words in a sentence completion question, you know that you should look for an answer that supports an idea in the sentence.

Examples:

Millicent was extremely ---- to be given the award, for she had worked very hard for it.

(A) pleased
(B) open-minded
(C) embarrassed
(D) interested
(E) fruitful

The correct answer is (A). Here, the word that fills in the blank must be something that is consistent with the idea of "working very hard" for something. If you had worked very hard for something, what would be your attitude toward it? You would be proud, or happy, or satisfied. So you can see that choice (A) serves as the best completion.

Throughout his young life, John excelled in sports, and as a result, he decided he wanted to become a professional ----.

(A) chemist
(B) athlete
(C) accountant
(D) sales representative
(E) student

The correct answer is (B). This is a rather simple example of how the logic of a sentence dictates your choice. The phrase "as a result" tells you that John's decision was the logical outcome of his excellence in sports. What is the logical outcome of excellence in sports? A career as a professional *athlete*.

Sometimes the Blank Requires a Word That Restates an Idea Already Mentioned in the Sentence.

Example:

Joan was so abrupt with clients that her supervisor eventually put a letter in her file citing her ----.

(A) enthusiasm
(B) rudeness
(C) lethargy
(D) diligence
(E) patience

The correct answer is (B). Notice that the idea of *rudeness* restates the idea of "abruptness."

SOMETIMES THE BLANK REQUIRES A WORD THAT SUMMARIZES AN IDEA ALREADY MENTIONED IN THE SENTENCE.

Example:

After seeing shocking films of animals maimed and tortured by traps of hunters, Marie concluded that purchasing a new fur coat would be ----.

(A) mandatory
(B) subliminal
(C) glamorous
(D) immoral
(E) redundant

The correct answer is (D). Here, the word that fills the blank must be an adjective that describes a reaction to the shocking torture of animals. The word that best describes such an act is *immoral*.

IF YOU HAVE TO GUESS, FIRST ELIMINATE ALL CHOICES THAT MAKE NO SENSE.

Many wrong answer choices, when inserted into a blank, create a meaningless phrase. Suppose, for example, that you have a sentence completion item that includes as a subpart the element "---- task." Some English words would suitably modify the word "*task.*" You might have an *easy* task, a *simple* task, a *difficult* task, an *arduous* task, or even a *monstrous* task. You could not, however, have a *blushing* task, an *alert* task, a *famished* task, a *determined* task, or an *excitable* task. These are words that just cannot be used to modify the word "task." Therefore, even if you don't understand the overall logic of a sentence, you should be able to eliminate one or more choices that contain words that are unsuitable.

Example:

Professor Martin spent his entire career as a teacher trying to ---- his students to appreciate the beauty of poetry.

(A) alienate
(B) disrupt
(C) encourage
(D) repeal
(E) define

The correct answer is (C). Test each for its suitability in the subpart "---- his students." Using just this part of the sentence, you should be able to eliminate choices (B), (D), and (E). As for (B), you can *disrupt* a class or a meeting, but you cannot *disrupt* a student; as for (D), you can *repeal* an act or a law, but you cannot *repeal* a student; and as for (E) you can *define* the word "student," but you cannot *define* a student. Having eliminated three choices, you can make your guess.

IF YOU HAVE TO GUESS, AS A LAST RESORT, SELECT A DIFFICULT VOCABULARY WORD.

SAT sentence completion items are arranged in order of increasing difficulty. What makes one item more difficult than another? Sometimes it is the logic of the sentence, but other times it is the vocabulary. And for a question to be difficult because it uses difficult vocabulary, the correct answer must be a difficult vocabulary word.

Here is an example of a problem using difficult vocabulary:

Example:

Because the speaker had a reputation for ----, the chairperson warned him to be succinct.

(A) bravery
(B) creativity
(C) lassitude
(D) piety
(E) loquaciousness

The correct answer is (E). Assume that this item is one of the last in a series of sentence completions. Given its position, you know that it is supposed to be a difficult question (remember the order of increasing difficulty). And what makes it difficult is that many test-takers won't know the meaning of the correct answer. Since choices (A), (B), and (D) are likely to be familiar to most test-takers, none of them is a likely candidate for a correct answer. Having eliminated those three, you would guess either choice (C) or choice (E), one of the two difficult vocabulary words. The correct answer is (E); *loquaciousness* means talkativeness.

CHECK IN

Directions: Complete each sentence based on what is directly stated or suggested in each passage. Mark the letter that appears before your answer.

1. The film was completely <u>devoid</u> of plot or character development; it was merely a ---- of striking images.
   - (A) <u>renouncement</u>
   - (B) <u>montage</u>
   - (C) <u>calumny</u>
   - (D) <u>carnage</u>
   - (E) <u>premonition</u>

2. She delivered her speech with great ----, gesturing <u>flamboyantly</u> with her hands and smiling broadly from her opening remarks through her conclusion.
   - (A) <u>candor</u>
   - (B) <u>consternation</u>
   - (C) <u>acerbity</u>
   - (D) <u>verve</u>
   - (E) <u>innuendo</u>

3. As a result of a(n) ---- with her landlord, she was <u>evicted</u>.
   - (A) <u>contusion</u>
   - (B) alternative
   - (C) <u>conflagration</u>
   - (D) <u>altercation</u>
   - (E) aggression

4. It was not possible to set a <u>monetary</u> value on the legal services she provided, so the grateful town had a gold medal struck as a(n) ----.
   - (A) affirmation
   - (B) <u>eulogy</u>
   - (C) <u>exultation</u>
   - (D) <u>elegy</u>
   - (E) honorarium

5. No elected official who remains ---- can play a major role in public life; compromise is the life-blood of politics.
   - (A) <u>obdurate</u>
   - (B) <u>dogmatic</u>
   - (C) pragmatic
   - (D) <u>irrefutable</u>
   - (E) <u>inflexible</u>

6. Contrary to popular opinion, bats are not generally aggressive and rabid; most are shy and ----.

   (A) turgid
   (B) disfigured
   (C) punctual
   (D) innocuous
   (E) depraved

7. The ballet company demonstrated its ---- by putting both classical and modern works in the repertoire.

   (A) versatility
   (B) mollification
   (C) treachery
   (D) dignity
   (E) obtrusiveness

8. Though the concert had been enjoyable, it was overly ---- and the three encores seemed ----.

   (A) extensive .. garrulous
   (B) protracted .. gratuitous
   (C) inaudible .. superfluous
   (D) sublime .. fortuitous
   (E) contracted .. lengthy

9. A good trial lawyer will argue only what is central to an issue, eliminating ---- information or anything else that might ---- the client.

   (A) seminal .. amuse
   (B) extraneous .. jeopardize
   (C) erratic .. enhance
   (D) prodigious .. extol
   (E) reprehensible .. initiate

10. Peter, ---- by the repeated rejections of his novel, ---- to submit his manuscript to other publishers.

   (A) encouraged .. declined
   (B) elated .. planned
   (C) undaunted .. continued
   (D) inspired .. complied
   (E) undeterred .. refused

ANSWER KEY AND EXPLANATIONS

1. B	3. D	5. E	7. A	9. B
2. D	4. E	6. D	8. B	10. C

1. **The correct answer is (B).** A film that has no plot or character development is simply a collection, or *montage,* of images.

2. **The correct answer is (D).** Putting together the gestures and smile yields an impression of enthusiam. *Verve,* a synonym for spirit, is the right choice.

3. **The correct answer is (D).** Eviction is a drastic measure, usually the result of nonpayment of rent or some other negative occurrence. The only possible choice that fits the logic of the sentence is *altercation* (heated argument).

4. **The correct answer is (E).** The context indicates some sort of payment for services but also shows that the amount of remuneration could not be calculated in monetary terms. The correct choice, *honorarium,* according to *Webster's,* is "a payment as to a professional person for services on which no fee is set or legally obtainable."

5. **The correct answer is (E).** The context indicates that whoever does not compromise has no future in politics. The missing word, then, must mean "not amenable to compromise." All choices except (D) describe varying degrees of stubbornness, but only *inflexible* means "a complete refusal to compromise."

6. **The correct answer is (D).** The sentence starts with "contrary," a "thought reverser." So we know that bats are something that is the opposite of "aggressive" and "rabid." *Innocuous,* or harmless, is the opposite of "rabid" and goes nicely with "shy."

7. **The correct answer is (A).** This is basically a vocabulary question. You need to know what noun means "the ability to do more than one thing well." Only *versatility* completes the sentence correctly.

8. **The correct answer is (B).** The "though" sets up a contrast. The concert was enjoyable, but it suffered from some defect. Additionally, the two blanks themselves are parallel, for they complete similar thoughts. Only the words in choice (B) satisfy this condition. The concert was *protracted* (too long), and the encores were *gratuitous* (uncalled for).

9. **The correct answer is (B).** The first blank calls for a word indicating information that a trial lawyer would eliminate because it

is not central to an issue. The only possible choice is *extraneous*. Likewise, a good lawyer would not mention anything that might *jeopardize* (endanger) a client.

10. **The correct answer is (C).** Even though Peter's novel was rejected by many publishers, he was *undaunted* (not discouraged) and *continued* to submit it to others.

EXERCISES: LEVEL A SENTENCE COMPLETIONS

EXERCISE 1

Select the word or pair of words that best completes each sentence. Mark the letter that appears before your answer.

1. Although her lips wore a smile, her eyes wore a ----.
   - (A) veil
   - (B) laugh
   - (C) shadow
   - (D) frown
   - (E) stare

2. Martha's ---- handling of the steaks caused us to amend our plans for dinner and eat out.
   - (A) ingenious
   - (B) ingenuous
   - (C) disingenuous
   - (D) inverted
   - (E) inept

3. The stigma attached to this job makes it ---- even at a(n) ---- salary.
   - (A) enticing .. fabulous
   - (B) unattractive .. attractive
   - (C) attractive .. attractive
   - (D) sybaritic .. meager
   - (E) uninviting .. nominal

4. One man's meat is another man's ----.
   - (A) dairy
   - (B) flesh
   - (C) poison
   - (D) meeting
   - (E) prerogative

5. Joseph's ---- handling of the Thompson account made him the laughingstock of the industry.
   - (A) proper
   - (B) dishonest
   - (C) maudlin
   - (D) humorous
   - (E) incompetent

6. By shrewdly shifting district lines, a party boss can ---- any voting bloc out of ----.

   (A) talk .. registering
   (B) gerrymander .. existence
   (C) shift .. precinct
   (D) cheat .. majority
   (E) gerrymander .. hand

7. The prisoner was in a state of great ---- after three months in solitary confinement with no bathing.

   (A) lassitude
   (B) decrepitude
   (C) solitude
   (D) rectitude
   (E) fortitude

8. He was the chief ---- of his uncle's will. After taxes, he was left with an inheritance of $20,000,000.

   (A) exemption
   (B) pensioner
   (C) beneficiary
   (D) contestant
   (E) winner

9. Don't be ----; I don't have time to split hairs.

   (A) spurious
   (B) childish
   (C) picayune
   (D) erudite
   (E) absurd

10. When his temperature climbed above 104 degrees, he became ----.

    (A) tepid
    (B) discordant
    (C) deceased
    (D) delirious
    (E) presumptuous

11. To climb at another's expense is to ---- yourself morally.

    (A) upbraid
    (B) elevate
    (C) energize
    (D) enervate
    (E) abase

12. We waited patiently for the storm to slacken; it ---- refused to ----.

    (A) persistently .. strengthen
    (B) stoutly .. abate
    (C) wanly .. sublimate
    (D) sternly .. mitigate
    (E) consistently .. perambulate

13. The prince decided to ---- when he found that he couldn't have his love and his throne at the same time; it was 1937.

    (A) prevaricate
    (B) ablate
    (C) alter
    (D) abrogate
    (E) abdicate

14. Although he was not ever at the scene of the crime, his complicity was uncovered; he had ---- and ---- in the robbery by acting as a fence.

    (A) stolen .. sold
    (B) assisted .. testified
    (C) witnessed .. participated
    (D) aided .. abetted
    (E) financed .. mastermind

15. Since his clothes were soaked, his story of falling into the creek seemed ----.

    (A) incredible
    (B) absurd
    (C) predictable
    (D) plausible
    (E) remarkable

EXERCISE 2

Select the word or pair of words that best completes each sentence. Mark the letter that appears before your answer.

1. A person who will not take "no" for an answer may sometimes be classified as a ----.

    (A) salesman
    (B) persistent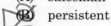
    (C) zealot
    (D) heretic
    (E) notary

2. The children were told that they should be ---- of strangers offering candy.

    (A) weary
    (B) wary
    (C) envious
    (D) considerate
    (E) happy

3. Politicians are not coerced into taxing the public; they do it of their own ----.

    (A) reputation
    (B) appraisal
    (C) graft
    (D) expediency
    (E) volition

4. Elder statesmen used to be ---- for their wisdom when respect for age was an integral part of the value structure.

    (A) known
    (B) venerated
    (C) exiled
    (D) abused
    (E) used

5. The 45-minute sermon is a potent ----; it is an absolute cure for ----.

    (A) astringent .. drowsiness
    (B) aphrodisiac .. celibacy
    (C) soporific .. insomnia
    (D) therapeutic .. malaise
    (E) trial .. lassitude

6. His <u>cynicism</u> was ----; it was written all over him.

  (A) affected
  (B) <u>covert</u>
  (C) infamous
  (D) <u>manifest</u>
  (E) famous

7. Suffering from ----, she was forced to spend most of her time indoors.

  (A) claustrophobia
  (B) <u>anemia</u>
  (C) agoraphobia
  (D) <u>ambivalence</u>
  (E) <u>xenophobia</u>

8. We were not allowed to ---- our appetite until we had <u>tidied</u> up our living quarters.

  (A) fill
  (B) <u>whet</u>
  (C) <u>sate</u>
  (D) <u>flag</u>
  (E) address

9. If you don't <u>badger</u> the child, he may do what you want him to do without ----.

  (A) pleasure
  (B) pain
  (C) pressure
  (D) volition
  (E) waste

10. You must see the head of the agency; I am not ---- to give out that information.

  (A) nervous
  (B) authorized
  (C) programmed
  (D) happy
  (E) <u>avid</u>

11. The magazine is considered a ---- of literary good taste; the stories it publishes are genteel and refined.

  (A) <u>cabal</u>
  (B) credential
  (C) potential
  (D) bastion
  (E) <u>maelstrom</u>

12. The ship was in a(n) ---- position; having lost its rudder it was
subject to the ---- of the prevailing winds.

    (A) inexcusable .. direction
    (B) unintended .. riptides
    (C) untenable .. vagaries
    (D) dangerous .. breezes
    (E) favored .. weaknesses

13. ---- shadows played over her face as the branches above her
danced in the sunlight.

    (A) Transient
    (B) Prolonged
    (C) Swarthy
    (D) Clandestine
    (E) Sedentary

14. Alchemists expended their energies in an attempt to ---- base elements into gold.

    (A) transfer
    (B) raise
    (C) translate
    (D) commute
    (E) transmute

15. Publication of the article was timed to ---- with the professor's
fiftieth birthday.

    (A) coincide
    (B) adapt
    (C) amalgamate
    (D) terminate
    (E) interfere

EXERCISE 3

Select the word or pair of words that best completes each sentence. Mark the letter that appears before your answer.

1. The chariot ---- around the curve completely out of control when Thessalius dropped the reins.
   - (A) trotted
   - (B) competed
   - (C) careened
   - (D) fell
   - (E) caromed

2. Don't ----; stick to the ---- of the issue so that we can take it to a vote.
   - (A) prevaricate .. jist
   - (B) stammer .. meat
   - (C) procrastinate .. promptness
   - (D) delay .. urgency
   - (E) digress .. crux

3. The more the search proved fruitless, the more ---- the parents of the missing child became.
   - (A) disconsolate
   - (B) dislocated
   - (C) disappointed
   - (D) disheveled
   - (E) disinfected

4. When the unpopular war began, only a few citizens enlisted; the rest had to be ----.
   - (A) shot
   - (B) processed
   - (C) pacified
   - (D) reassured
   - (E) conscripted

5. The ---- fumes from the refinery poisoned the air, causing many people to fall ill.
   - (A) superfluous
   - (B) peremptory
   - (C) noxious
   - (D) lugubrious
   - (E) intransigent

6. The upset furniture and broken window silently ---- to the fact
   that the apartment had been robbed.

   - (A) witnessed
   - (B) confirmed
   - (C) attested
   - (D) admitted
   - (E) alleged

7. Although the warrior could cope with blows from swords, he was
   ---- to gunshots; his armor was not ---- to them.

   - (A) reachable .. proof
   - (B) vulnerable .. susceptible
   - (C) vulnerable .. impervious
   - (D) invulnerable .. susceptible
   - (E) invulnerable .. impervious

8. When she addressed the reporters, her beauty, bearing, and
   elegant garb were belied by the ---- words she uttered.

   - (A) untrue
   - (B) uncouth
   - (C) unemotional
   - (D) unfettered
   - (E) unequivocal

9. "A stitch in time saves nine" and other such ---- expressions made
   his speeches insufferable.

   - (A) tried
   - (B) cryptic
   - (C) redundant
   - (D) trite
   - (E) true

10. The new regulations turned out to be ----, not permissive.

    - (A) lax
    - (B) liberal
    - (C) stringent
    - (D) uniform
    - (E) unrestrictive

11. They prefer to hire someone fluent in Spanish, because the neigh-
    borhood where the clinic is located is ---- Hispanic.

    - (A) imponderably
    - (B) sparsely
    - (C) consistently
    - (D) predominantly
    - (E) not at all

12. A dark, cloudy sky is a ---- of a storm.

   (A) remnant
   (B) precursor
   (C) belier
   (D) proof
   (E) constellation

13. The Freedom of Information Act gives private citizens ---- government files.

   (A) access to
   (B) excess of
   (C) redress of
   (D) release from
   (E) no rights to

14. His remarks were so ---- we could not decide which of the possible meanings was correct.

   (A) ambiguous
   (B) facetious
   (C) improper
   (D) congruent
   (E) quiet

15. His performance was ----; it made a fool of him.

   (A) auspicious
   (B) ludicrous
   (C) luscious
   (D) interlocutory
   (E) internecine

EXERCISE 4

Select the word or pair of words that best completes each sentence. Mark the letter that appears before your answer.

1. They are a(n) ---- couple who cultivate many friendships among ---- people.
   - (A) gratuitous .. frivolous
   - (B) indolent .. impeccable
   - (C) gregarious .. diverse
   - (D) insidious .. intrepid
   - (E) solicitous .. laconic

2. When the desk was placed facing the window, she found herself ---- from her work by the activity in the street.
   - (A) distraught
   - (B) destroyed
   - (C) distracted
   - (D) decimated
   - (E) diminished

3. Although no bigger than a bottle cap, the coqui frog emits a ---- screech as looud as a vacuum cleaner.
   - (A) keen
   - (B) malodorous
   - (C) strident
   - (D) subtle
   - (E) reticent

4. Due to destructive fishing practices, such as bycatch, certain seafood populations are in ---- decline.
   - (A) steep
   - (B) temperate
   - (C) voluminous
   - (D) erratic
   - (E) halting

5. The authorities declared an ---- on incoming freight because of the trucking strike.
   - (A) impression
   - (B) immolation
   - (C) embargo
   - (D) alert
   - (E) opprobrium

6. The grade was steep and the load heavy; we had to ---- the oxen in order to arrive home on time.

    (A) rest
    (B) eat
    (C) feed
    (D) goad
    (E) slaughter

7. He was proven guilty; his alibi had been a complete ----.

    (A) attestation
    (B) fabrication
    (C) intonation
    (D) litany
    (E) cementation

8. He claimed to be deathly ill, although he looked perfectly ---- and ---- to us.

    (A) fine .. fettle
    (B) sane .. sound
    (C) hale .. hearty
    (D) hectic .. healthy
    (E) sound .. decrepit

9. Although she had ---- about the weather, she had no ---- about her ability to navigate through it.

    (A) doubts .. confidence
    (B) confidence .. qualms
    (C) qualms .. confidence
    (D) misgivings .. qualms
    (E) reports .. foresight

10. The police department will not accept for ---- a report of a person missing if his residence is outside the city.

    (A) foreclosure
    (B) convenience
    (C) investigation
    (D) control
    (E) guidance

11. Rabbits, elephants, deer, and sheep are ----; they eat only plants.

    (A) omnivorous
    (B) herbivorous
    (C) carnivorous
    (D) ruminants
    (E) pachyderms

12. Foreman and Ali were fighting tooth and nail when suddenly, in the thick of the ----, the bell rang.

    (A) night
    (B) day
    (C) thievery
    (D) fray
    (E) ring

13. The judge ---- the union from blocking the accesses.

    (A) suspended
    (B) ordered
    (C) forbade
    (D) unfrocked
    (E) enjoined

14. The ---- on the letter showed it had been mailed in North Dakota two weeks previously.

    (A) address
    (B) stamp
    (C) postmark
    (D) envelope
    (E) printing

15. It is easy to see the difference between the two photographs when they are placed in ----.

    (A) disarray
    (B) juxtaposition
    (C) composition
    (D) jeopardy
    (E) collaboration

EXERCISE 5

Select the word or pair of words that best completes each sentence. Mark the letter that appears before your answer.

1. We are indeed sorry to hear of your mother's passing; please accept our sincerest ----.
   - (A) adulations
   - (B) congratulations
   - (C) condolences
   - (D) concatenations
   - (E) contortions

2. While on a diet I remained lean, but once off it I became ----.
   - (A) adept
   - (B) remiss
   - (C) corpulent
   - (D) corporeal
   - (E) corporal

3. With his gutter language and vile manner he was positively ----.
   - (A) urbane
   - (B) banal
   - (C) rural
   - (D) liberal
   - (E) boorish

4. The voters show their ---- by staying away from the polls.
   - (A) interest
   - (B) usury
   - (C) apathy
   - (D) serendipity
   - (E) registration

5. Being less than perfectly prepared, I took my exams with ----.
   - (A) aplomb
   - (B) confidence
   - (C) trepidation
   - (D) indifference
   - (E) skepticism

6. Mrs. Crumb has long been considered a ----; she always insists that her students follow her classroom procedures without exception.

    (A) hypocrite
    (B) dilettante
    (C) martinet
    (D) martyr
    (E) sycophant

7. The good-humored joke ---- the tension in the room.

    (A) enervated
    (B) allocated
    (C) dispelled
    (D) cited
    (E) berated

8. When the bomb exploded in front of the building, it destroyed the whole ----.

    (A) cellar
    (B) pontoon
    (C) facade
    (D) facet
    (E) cupola

9. He is expected to testify that he saw the ---- thief fleeing the scene of the crime.

    (A) convicted
    (B) delinquent
    (C) alleged
    (D) offensive
    (E) innocent

10. A child who has not slept well will be anything but ----.

    (A) intractable
    (B) docile
    (C) equine
    (D) bovine
    (E) ill-tempered

11. What we thought was a ---- volcano suddenly erupted.

    (A) deceased
    (B) dactylic
    (C) dormant
    (D) disruptive
    (E) discontinued

12. Cigarette smoking is ---- to your health.
    - (A) disengaging
    - (B) deleterious
    - (C) delectable
    - (D) irrespective
    - (E) irrelevant

13. My uncle hardly ever needed a telephone; his voice was ---- from a distance of half a mile.
    - (A) inaudible
    - (B) audible
    - (C) suspicious
    - (D) visible
    - (E) copious

14. Unlike his earlier paintings, which attracted lukewarm response and were considered ----, his mid-career retrospective has received praise for its energetic originality and complexity.
    - (A) insipid
    - (B) laconic
    - (C) novel
    - (D) prudish
    - (E) profuse

15. The current use of "----" in place of "fat" is a euphemism.
    - (A) overwrought
    - (B) portly
    - (C) insipid
    - (D) obstreperous
    - (E) pugilistic

ANSWER KEY AND EXPLANATIONS

LEVEL A

Exercise 1

1. D	4. C	7. B	10. D	13. E
2. E	5. E	8. C	11. E	14. D
3. B	6. B	9. C	12. B	15. D

1. **The correct answer is (D).** "Although" means "regardless of the fact that." Hence the missing noun must be contrary to the key word "smile." The best answer is *frown.*

2. **The correct answer is (E).** What kind of handling of food would make them decide to forego Martha's cooking? Choice (D) would be meaningless in this context, and (A) would be wrong because such handling would have the opposite effect. Martha's being unworldly, (B), or not unworldly, (C), would become a consideration if a more specific, more narrow adjective, like (E), was not available.

3. **The correct answer is (B).** The word "stigma" indicates that the job puts the jobholder in a disgraceful or unenviable position so that it is *unattractive,* (B), or *uninviting,* (E). But "even" means "in spite of," so the salary must be quite unlike the job. This eliminates (E) and makes (B), with its exact opposite adjectives, the best choice.

4. **The correct answer is (C).** The sentence structure, balancing "one" against "another," suggests contrast and difference. Contrast is not provided by (E), meaning right or privilege, because the first man already has the meat as his *prerogative;* nor by (A), which is another category of food or nourishment; nor by (B), because meat is the *flesh* of mammals; nor by (D), which is only a play on words. But (C) is a contrast, providing not nourishment but harm.

5. **The correct answer is (E).** What kind of management (handling) would make Joseph an object of jokes and ridicule, a fool (laughingstock)? Choice (A) would earn him respect, and (B) would earn disapproval. Choice (D) would make the industry laugh with him, not at him. Choice (C), meaning effusively sentimental, would not elicit ridicule so much as (E), meaning inept.

6. **The correct answer is (B).** To shift district lines in order to separate voters, thus preventing them from exerting all their strength in one district, is, by definition, to *gerrymander.* This is done slyly, not by

confrontation, ruling out (A). It does *cheat* the bloc of its *majority* in its own area, (D), but *majority* would not sound idiomatic here. It does not *shift* the bloc in its entirety but rather cuts it up, ruling out (C), which would also be unidiomatic. Of the two choices using the correct word, *gerrymander,* (E) is relevant ("out of *hand*" meaning at once, immediately, improperly), but (B) completes the meaning more effectively.

7. **The correct answer is (B).** What condition would a man be in after 90 days of solitary confinement? Unlikely are (C), because that's the state he was in and is now freed from; (E), meaning strength of mind; and (D), rightness in intellectual judgment. He could be in a state of exhaustion, torpor, or lethargy, which is what (A) means, but it's most likely that he is in a state of *decrepitude* (B), that is, of weakness, infirmity.

8. **The correct answer is (C).** There is nothing to suggest he has been omitted from the will, (A), or will fight it in the courts, (D). He seems to have obtained his money in one lump sum, not in installments like a pension, (B). Although he may be described as a *winner,* (E), that is not the legal term used for an heir, but *beneficiary* is.

9. **The correct answer is (C).** *Picayune* is the perfect adjective, meaning petty, mean, small-minded.

10. **The correct answer is (D).** High fever can produce a state of mental confusion. (A) and (B) are too mild, and (C) is too severe. (E), meaning exceedingly arrogant or confident, sounds unlikely. But *delirious* is the proper word for someone in the state described.

11. **The correct answer is (E).** The context implies you would be taking unfair advantage of another, and so, in a moral sense, would lower, or *abase,* yourself. There is no indication that you would scold or censure yourself, as (A) would mean, or that it would stimulate, (C), or weaken, (D), you. (B) would be meaningless repetition.

12. **The correct answer is (B).** This is an instance in which you might first try out the second word in each pair. The main idea is that the storm refused to slacken: you must find, for the second blank, a close synonym for slacken. Of the two offered, *mitigate,* (D), meaning alleviate, sounds too affected, but *abate,* meaning diminish or subside, sounds idiomatic. (A) is contrary to what "We waited … for"; (E) would suggest "to travel," which would have a different meaning; and (C) would imply "to weakly refuse to change itself into a more acceptable form," which is remote from the context.

13. **The correct answer is (E).** Which of the five words offered has much to do with deciding between love and the throne? Only (E),

meaning to give up a high position does. Choice (A), meaning to lie, would be the opposite of deciding; (C) wouldn't tell us how or what he would *alter,* or change; (D) wouldn't say which one he would nullify or abolish, which is what *abrogate* would involve; and (B), meaning to vaporize, is ridiculous in this context.

14. **The correct answer is (D).** Choices (A), (B), and (E) can all be ruled out because they do not link idiomatically with "in": a fence would not have *sold, testified,* or *masterminded* in a robbery. Choice (C) does so link (*participated* in) but is still wrong because, we are told, he had not witnessed the crime. Choice (D) does so link *and* makes good sense: a fence, ready to receive and sell stolen goods, can be seen as having *aided* and *abetted* (that is, encouraged, incited) *in* a robbery.

15. **The correct answer is (D).** The soaked clothes make the story believable, or *plausible.*

Exercise 2

1. C	4. B	7. C	10. B	13. A
2. B	5. C	8. C	11. D	14. E
3. E	6. D	9. C	12. C	15. A

1. **The correct answer is (C).** Any person so fanatical and so uncompromising is, by definition, a *zealot.* (A) would make fewer sales if he didn't know when to give up on a customer. Neither (E), a minor official who certifies documents and takes oaths, nor (D), a person of unorthodox views, need necessarily be fanatical. Choice (B) is ruled out because the blank requires a noun, not an adjective.

2. **The correct answer is (B).** The very word "strangers" and the fact that they should be "offering candy" to young people they do not know strongly suggests that the children not be (C), (D), or (E), but rather cautious and watchful, that is, *wary.* Choice (A) is a trap for students who have heard the expression "wary of strangers" but are unable to spell or recapture the exact sound.

3. **The correct answer is (E).** The position taken is that people do things in response either to outer force or to inner will. (B), involving judgment, is close, but (E), meaning the power to will, choose, and decide, is better in context.

4. **The correct answer is (B).** The phrase "respect for age" calls for strong positive regard or reverence for elder statesmen: they were

venerated. (C) and (D) are negative and disrespectful; (A) is too mild and (E) is too matter-of-fact, lacking in feeling.

5. **The correct answer is (C).** The length of the sermon indicates its effect on the congregation: boredom and resultant passivity. Hence the metaphor of the sermon as a *soporific,* a sleep-inducing drug, which would cure *insomnia,* or chronic wakefulness. The other choices repeat the pattern of medicine for a condition but do not account for the emphasis on the 45-minute presentation.

6. **The correct answer is (D).** The last phrase makes it clear that his attitude was obvious, that is, *manifest.* He did not keep it a secret (B), and there is no indication that it was *affected* (A) or that it was either (C) or (E).

7. **The correct answer is (C).** The result of her condition identifies it as *agoraphobia,* or fear of open spaces. (A) would be the opposite: fear of closed places. (E), or hatred of foreigners, can be suffered indoors or out. (D), a state of conflicting emotions, like love and hate for the same person, and (B), a blood deficiency, do not necessarily keep the sufferer indoors.

8. **The correct answer is (C).** Presumably their appetite has already been *whetted* (B), that is, stimulated; (A) is simply not idiomatic; (D) is meaningless in this context; (E), in the sense of facing or acknowledging, would serve if (C), meaning to indulge, was not better.

9. **The correct answer is (C).** The missing word must be a synonym for "badgering," or harrying with persistent chiding or entreaty, pestering. Choice (B) is too strong, (A) is the opposite, (E) is irrelevant in this context, and (D) is wrong because the speaker wants the child to do it on his own *volition.*

10. **The correct answer is (B).** Choice (C) can be ruled out because there is no indication that the speaker is computerized. He is, however, working in a formal relationship to a superior. His own feelings would be inappropriate—(A), (D), (E). *Authorized* would be the factual word for describing what he is and is not allowed to say.

11. **The correct answer is (D).** A magazine that publishes refined fiction might be considered a *bastion* (fortress) of literary good taste.

12. **The correct answer is (C).** A rudderless boat is certainly not in a *favored* position, (E). (C) is the most inclusive and accurate description: the ship is not suitable for occupancy; it is defenseless and subject to the erratic motion of the winds—ideas that are completed with the words *untenable* and *vagaries.*

13. **The correct answer is (A).** If the branches are moving, so are the shadows they cast. Hence (B) and (E), implying "staying in one place," are wrong. The shadows are not *clandestine* or secret, (D), and it would be odd to call them *swarthy,* (C). *Transient,* (A), passing, is the best choice.

14. **The correct answer is (E).** "Into" gives you a clue. (D) is wrong because that would mean substituting one for the other; (A) is wrong because it would mean that the base metal is moved into gold. (C) is metaphoric, and (B) is completely inappropriate. (E), *transmute,* is the perfect word, meaning "to change from one form, nature, or substance into another."

15. **The correct answer is (A).** Choice (E) seems improbable; and (B), (C), and (D) make no sense. (A) only implies that the article was published and the birthday celebrated on the same day.

Exercise 3

1. C	4. E	7. C	10. C	13. A
2. E	5. C	8. B	11. D	14. A
3. A	6. C	9. D	12. B	15. B

1. **The correct answer is (C).** The phrases "out of control" and "dropped the reins" make *careened* the best word: it means moving rapidly and in an uncontrolled manner (swerving). Choice (E) would be appropriate only if the chariot had collided with something and rebounded. Choices (A), (B), and (D) are less specific and less fitting.

2. **The correct answer is (E).** The sentence indicates that the speaker is warning someone not to stray from the main subject, that is, not to *digress* from the *crux,* or heart, of the matter. Choice (A) connotes straying from the truth; (B) involves an involuntary difficulty in speaking; (C) and (D) both involve postponement but are ruled out mainly because "stick to the *promptness/urgency*" is not idiomatic.

3. **The correct answer is (A).** Choices (B), (D), and (E) seem far-fetched; (C) is too mild; and (A) is just right: *disconsolate* means beyond consolation or hopelessly sad.

4. **The correct answer is (E).** If it was an "unpopular war," there was little chance of (C) or (D). On the other hand, because recruits were needed, it is unlikely they would be *shot,* (A), especially since they could be *conscripted.* All the recruits, whether volunteers or draftees, would have to be *processed,* (B).

5. **The correct answer is (C).** If the fumes are poisoning the air, they are surely *noxious,* or harmful.

6. **The correct answer is (C).** The blank requires a verb that is used with "to." Only (C) and (D) are so used. Choice (D) is impossible, so (C) is correct by process of elimination: the state of the house gave testimony, *attested to* the fact, that it had been robbed.

7. **The correct answer is (C).** "Although" alerts you to expect a reversal of results: they will be different for "blows" and "gunshots." *Vulnerable* means susceptible to injury, not sufficiently protected; *invulnerable* means not susceptible, well protected. *Impervious* means incapable of being penetrated or affected. (A) does not fit into the syntax (we don't say "*reachable* to" or "*proof* to"). In (B), *vulnerable* makes sense, but "not *susceptible*" would contradict that. (D) would be wrong in both parts, and (E) would be wrong in its first part.

8. **The correct answer is (B).** The word "belied" tells you that her words contradicted the beauty and elegance of her appearance. The only choice that offers the opposite of beauty and elegance is *uncouth,* meaning crude, rude, and ungraceful.

9. **The correct answer is (D).** Apparently, it's the quality, not the content, of the expressions he uses that makes them "insufferable," that is, unbearable. This rules out (E). Such succinct proverbs are not repetitive or wordy, as *redundant,* (C), would mean, and they are not *cryptic,* (B), that is, they do not contain hidden meanings. However, they are so overused, so overfamiliar, that they no longer command our interest: they have become *trite.* (A) is a trap for the student unfamiliar with the correct spelling and sound of *trite.*

10. **The correct answer is (C).** The phrase "not permissive" rules out *lax,* (A), *liberal,* (B), and *unrestrictive,* (E). Regulations may be both permissive and *uniform,* (D), but (C), meaning severe, makes sense in context.

11. **The correct answer is (D).** Choice (A), meaning incapable of being measured or weighed precisely, is wrong because it is possible to count population; (B) and (E) are wrong because they contradict the need for a Spanish-speaking employee; (C) is incorrect because no neighborhood large enough to have a clinic would be completely made up of any single ethnic group. Choice (D), meaning mainly, makes the most sense.

12. **The correct answer is (B).** Such a sky is neither a *belier,* that is, denier, of the possibility of a storm, (C), nor is it a *proof,* or a guarantee, of a storm, (D). It may be (A), but most likely it's a forerunner,

or *precursor,* (B), of a storm. Choice (E) is a trap for hasty readers who free-associate from sky to stars.

13. **The correct answer is (A).** Judging from the title of the act alone, citizens can enjoy (A), but with no right to correct or rectify information on file, as (C) means. Choice (E) is a contradiction of the title, and (B) and (D) are meaningless in this context.

14. **The correct answer is (A).** "Possible meanings" is your main clue. Any statement with more than one meaning is, by definition, *ambiguous,* (A). (B), meaning flippantly humorous; (C), meaning incorrect; (D), meaning coinciding; and (E) do not necessarily involve different meanings.

15. **The correct answer is (B).** A performance that was *auspicious,* or promising, (A), or one that was *luscious,* sweet and pleasant, (C), would hardly make him a fool. A performance that was *interlocutory,* that is, involving a conversation, (D), or one that was *internecine,* or mutually destructive, (E), would not on those grounds alone be foolish. But *ludicrous,* (B), means laughable, foolish, causing scornful laughter.

Exercise 4

1. C	4. A	7. B	10. C	13. E
2. C	5. C	8. C	11. B	14. C
3. C	6. D	9. D	12. D	15. B

1. **The correct answer is (C).** People who have many friendships are *gregarious* (sociable) and likely to have *diverse* (varied) friends. None of the other answer choices makes any sense.

2. **The correct answer is (C).** A key link is "from": the word supplied must make this connection idiomatically. *Distracted* is the only past participle (used as an adjective) here that is used with "from"; it means, literally, "drawn away, having the attention diverted."

3. **The correct answer is (C).** The question is asking for an adjective that describes the quality of the sound the coqui frog makes. You're looking for a word that deals with sound, and an unpleasant sound at that. Choice (C), *strident,* works, and if you are unsure about its meaning, you can look at the other choices before making a final selection.

4. **The correct answer is (A).** The word you're looking for should be something negative. It might be a word like *dangerous, scary,*

or *depressing,* or it might be an adjective that reinforces the word decline. Answer choice (A), *steep,* reinforces the severity of the decline, and it's the best answer of the lot.

5. **The correct answer is (C).** Choice (A) denotes a physical imprint or psychological effect; (B) is a sacrificial destruction or renunciation; (D) is a warning; and (E) is the state or cause of disgrace. Choice (C) is relevant: an *embargo* is a suspension or prohibition of trade. Memories of *impressment* of seamen might tempt some students to pick (A); the fact that an *alert* can be "declared" might influence some to pick (D); so you should declare a prohibition or an embargo on words that fit neither the context nor the syntax!

6. **The correct answer is (D).** *Slaughtering,* (E), and *eating,* (B), the oxen would never get the load home; *resting,* (A), or *feeding,* (C), them would delay their arrival; so the rationalization leads you to *goading,* (D), them, that is, prodding them with a stick to make them move faster.

7. **The correct answer is (B).** Choice (A) is wrong because he did not affirm, corroborate, or *attest* to the facts; (C) is wrong because the tone of his voice would not be the crucial factor in his defense; (D) is wrong because he was not conducting a liturgical prayer with responses by others; and (E) is wrong because he did not bind or cement anything. Rather he had offered a *fabrication,* a totally false account of where he was at the time of the crime.

8. **The correct answer is (C).** Choice (A) is wrong here because *fettle* is a noun that means condition or shape; it is usually used in a phrase like "in fine fettle" and is incorrectly offered here as an adjective. Choice (B) would be okay only if he had claimed something wrong with his sanity. "Perfectly" *hectic,* (D), and "perfectly" *decrepit,* (E), are both nonsense. So (C) is right, both by process of elimination and by the test of meaning in context: *hale* means whole, free from defect, and *hearty* means vigorous, robust.

9. **The correct answer is (D).** Both words in the pair must be able to link with "about." Only (D) meets this requirement. Beyond that, only (D) requires the "Although …" construction. All the others would make more sense with "and"; for example, (A): "She had *doubts* about the weather and she had no *confidence,* etc."

10. **The correct answer is (C).** Choice (A) is self-contradictory, because *foreclosure* involves barring, hindering, thwarting, or settling beforehand and usually refers to mortgage matters. Choice (B) is not a consideration in this kind of work. Choices (D) and (E) are wrong because the police might conceivably accept such a report for *control* or *guidance,* even though they would not take the responsibility for *investigating* it.

11. **The correct answer is (B).** To be *omnivorous,* (A), they would have to eat everything; to be *carnivorous,* (C), they would eat only meat. Because they eat only herbs, they are (B). Not all of these animals are *ruminants,* (D), that is, cud-chewers, or *pachyderms,* (E), that is, thick-skinned beasts.

12. **The correct answer is (D).** There is no indication of (A), (B), or (C). The bell does identify the scene as a boxing *ring,* (E), but what about "in the thick of"? It has to be "in the thick of" the fight, the heated contest, that is, the *fray.*

13. **The correct answer is (E).** The verb you select has to be one that fits syntactically with "from blocking." This eliminates (B) and (C). Choice (A), too, does not work in context. Choice (D) does not fit at all and is ridiculous in this context, for it means "deprived of the right to practice a profession," like preaching the gospel. Only (E) involves prohibition by legal action.

14. **The correct answer is (C).** True, the information is someplace on the *envelope,* (D), but the envelope is the only thing listed that's NOT "on the letter." Choice (A) indicates the letter's destination, not its origin, and (B) shows denomination and national origin. Choice (E) is too general. Only the *postmark* gives date and local origin.

15. **The correct answer is (B).** Because the photos are placed in some specified order, (A) is wrong: it means a state of disorder. Choice (C) is meaningless, and (D), meaning danger, is ridiculous. As for (E), objects are not "placed in" *collaboration.* Two photos can only be "placed in" *juxtaposition,* that is, put side by side.

Exercise 5

1. C	4. C	7. C	10. B	13. B
2. C	5. C	8. C	11. C	14. A
3. E	6. C	9. C	12. B	15. B

1. **The correct answer is (C).** Only (C), meaning "expressions of sympathy for another person's grief or pain," is relevant. The others are irrelevant because (A) denotes flattery; (B) is recognition of good fortune or outstanding achievement; (D) indicates a series of links or chains; and (E) means the act of twisting out of shape.

2. **The correct answer is (C).** The "but" signals the opposite, and only *corpulent* is opposite, meaning fat. Choices (D) and (E) are traps for people with a vague memory of (C), or vague knowledge that (D)

and (E) have to do with the body. Choice (A) means skillful, and (B) means negligent.

3. **The correct answer is (E).** A rude, impolite person is *boorish.* You might also call him banal, (B), if you believe that such behavior is commonplace and trite. Choices (A), (C), and (D) have nothing to do with manners.

4. **The correct answer is (C).** They show their *interest,* (A), by going to the polls and their lack of interest, or *apathy,* by staying away. Choice (B), meaning excessive interest on loans, does not make sense in this context. In the context of elections, (E) is the act of signing up as a voter. Choice (D) is the faculty of making happy discoveries by accident, something possible only if one shows interest everywhere.

5. **The correct answer is (C).** How did the person take the exams? Certainly not with *indifference* (D), or *aplomb* (A), or *confidence* (B), because lack of preparation tends to undermine any of these forms of self-support. They were not taken with *skepticism,* (E), either, because the doubting that the skeptic does is a way of challenging others' beliefs. This leaves the student taking exams with alarm, apprehension, maybe even some trembling—in short, with *trepidation.*

6. **The correct answer is (C).** Looking at the context, the missing word should be something that indicates strictness and unwavering attitude, based on the description of Mrs. Crumb as a pretty inflexible person. It turns out Mrs. Crumb is a *martinet,* someone very strict about rules.

7. **The correct answer is (C).** Tension in the air is likely to be *dispelled* (driven away) by a joke. None of the other choices makes any sense.

8. **The correct answer is (C).** The *facade* is the front. Choice (D) is a trap for students unsure of the spelling of facade. Choice (B) is unlikely to be found in the front of a building, and (E) is a domed structure surmounting the roof. To be safe, the occupants should have been in the rear of (A).

9. **The correct answer is (C).** If a witness is still to testify against the thief, then the case is still in the trial stage, and he has not yet been *convicted,* (A), or proven *innocent,* (E). Thus, he cannot yet be described as (B) or (D), or even as a thief, but only as an *alleged* thief, that is, as one so accused but not so proven.

10. **The correct answer is (B).** We cannot say for sure whether she will act horselike, or *equine,* (C), or whether she will be sluggish,

dull, and cowlike, that is, *bovine,* (D). But we do know she will be *ill-tempered,* (E), and difficult to manage, that is to say, *intractable,* (A), which is anything but submissive, or *docile.*

11. **The correct answer is (C).** If its eruption was unexpected, then they must have thought it was inactive, or *dormant.* Choice (A) is not a term used for inanimate matter, and (E) is not used for volcanoes. If it had been *disruptive,* (D)—that is, causing disorder and confusion—they would not have been surprised by its activity. Choice (B) refers to a three-syllable foot in poetry.

12. **The correct answer is (B).** Doctors agree that smoking is harmful, or *deleterious.* Choice (C) is certainly inaccurate, and (D) is incorrect usage. Smoking is not *irrelevant,* (E), to health. It's not smoking that should be *disengaging,* (A); it's the smoker who should extricate himself or herself from the habit.

13. **The correct answer is (B).** Suspicious, (C), does not work in this context; a voice cannot suspect. A voice can't be seen, so it's not (D). Because the word *copious,* meaning abundant, is not used to denote vocal power, (E) is incorrect. Because the uncle's voice can be heard from half a mile away, it is by definition *audible*, and not *inaudible.*

14. **The correct answer is (A).** The words *boring, bland,* or *simplistic* would seem to fit in the blank, but are not among the answer choices. So, which of these words is close in meaning to *boring, bland,* or *simplistic?* Choice (A), *insipid,* has similar meaning to *boring* and *unoriginal.*

15. **The correct answer is (B).** A euphemism is an inoffensive term used instead of the offensive truth. In this case, *portly,* (B), which means comfortably stout, is used in place of the blunt word *fat.*

EXERCISES: LEVEL B SENTENCE COMPLETIONS

EXERCISE 1

Select the word or pair of words that best completes each sentence. Mark the letter that appears before your answer.

1. An accident report should be written as soon as possible after the necessary ---- has been obtained.
   - (A) bystander
   - (B) formulation
   - (C) information
   - (D) charter
   - (E) specimen

2. A change in environment is very likely to ---- a change in one's work habits.
   - (A) affect
   - (B) inflict
   - (C) effect
   - (D) prosper
   - (E) rupture

3. With typical diplomatic maneuvering, the State Department used every known ---- to avoid expressing the avowed policy in ---- language.
   - (A) trick .. diplomatic
   - (B) page .. gobbledygook
   - (C) circumlocution .. concise
   - (D) summary .. plain
   - (E) formula .. cryptic

4. The astute attorney asked many ---- questions of the witness in an attempt to ---- the truth.
   - (A) pretentious .. prolong
   - (B) loquacious .. placate
   - (C) nebulous .. mitigate
   - (D) probing .. elicit
   - (E) spurious .. verify

5. The ---- of Santa Ana's forces was the main reason they won at the Alamo.
   - (A) decline
   - (B) felicitation
   - (C) preponderance
   - (D) isolation
   - (E) absence

6. A cloudy suspension may be described as ----.
   - (A) turbid
   - (B) precipitous
   - (C) suspicious
   - (D) auspicious
   - (E) temporary

7. The flamenco dancer stood still, ready to perform, his arms ----.
   - (A) blazing
   - (B) akimbo
   - (C) flailing
   - (D) deadlocked
   - (E) askew

8. The celebrity sued the magazine, claiming that the article ---- his character.
   - (A) demoted
   - (B) deplored
   - (C) defamed
   - (D) implicated
   - (E) whitewashed

9. To be a "joiner" is to be ----.
   - (A) gregarious
   - (B) popular
   - (C) hilarious
   - (D) woodworking
   - (E) singular

10. As a result of constant and unrelenting eating, he changed from slightly overweight to ----.
   - (A) overrun
   - (B) parsimonious
   - (C) oblate
   - (D) obese
   - (E) lilliputian

11. When you have ---- your palate with pickles, you want no more.

    (A) scarred
    (B) satiated
    (C) imbibed
    (D) covered
    (E) palavered

12. To protect the respondents' privacy, names and Social Security numbers are ---- the questionnaires before the results are tabulated.

    (A) referred to
    (B) deleted from
    (C) retained in
    (D) appended to
    (E) computerized in

13. FDA is a(n) ---- for the U.S. Food and Drug Administration.

    (A) homonym
    (B) acronym
    (C) heteronym
    (D) antonym
    (E) pseudonym

14. After the deluge, flood waters ---- the town.

    (A) imperiled
    (B) redeemed
    (C) impugned
    (D) regaled
    (E) traduced

15. To put off until tomorrow what you should do today is to ----.

    (A) prorate
    (B) procrastinate
    (C) preface
    (D) proscribe
    (E) promulgate

EXERCISE 2

Select the word or pair of words that best completes each sentence.
Mark the letter that appears before your answer.

1. New York's climate is not very ----; its winters give you colds, and
   its summers can cause heat prostration.
   (A) sanitary
   (B) volatile
   (C) salubrious
   (D) healthy
   (E) pathogenic

2. One who ---- another is laughing *at* him, not *with* him.
   (A) derides
   (B) defiles
   (C) irks
   (D) buffoons
   (E) harasses

3. To give in to the terrorists' demands would be a betrayal of our
   responsibilities; such ---- would only encourage others to adopt
   similar ways to gain their ends.
   (A) defeats
   (B) appeasement
   (C) appeals
   (D) subterfuge
   (E) treaties

4. It is hard to believe that the Trojans could have been so easily
   deceived by the ---- of the wooden horse.
   (A) tragedy
   (B) stratagem
   (C) strategy
   (D) prolixity
   (E) fetlocks

5. She pretended to be nonchalant but her movements betrayed
   signs of ----.
   (A) greed
   (B) weariness
   (C) worry
   (D) boredom
   (E) evil

6. We can easily forgo a ---- we have never had, but once obtained it often is looked upon as being ----.
   (A) requirement .. unusual
   (B) gift .. useless
   (C) bonus .. unearned
   (D) luxury .. essential
   (E) necessity .. important

7. ---- means an injustice so ---- that it is wicked.
   (A) Iniquity .. gross
   (B) Lobotomy .. inane
   (C) Perjury .. mendacious
   (D) Lobotomy .. pernicious
   (E) Bias .. slanted

8. The navy scoured the area for over a month, but the ---- search turned up no clues.
   (A) temporary
   (B) cursory
   (C) fruitful
   (D) painstaking
   (E) present

9. The ---- assumed for the sake of discussion was that business would improve for the next five years.
   (A) labyrinth
   (B) hypothesis
   (C) outlay
   (D) itinerary
   (E) assumption

10. I wish you wouldn't be so ----; you make faces at everything I say.
    (A) supercilious
    (B) insubordinate
    (C) disconsolate
    (D) superficial
    (E) banal

11. I felt as ---- as a fifth wheel.
    (A) rolled
    (B) round
    (C) superfluous
    (D) axillary
    (E) rotational

12. If we were to ---- our democracy with a ----, there would be no way, short of civil war, to reverse the change.

    (A) contrast .. parliament
    (B) substitute .. constitutional monarchy
    (C) supplant .. dictatorship
    (D) reinforce .. three-party system
    (E) automate .. technocracy

13. A(n) ---- look came into the poodle's eye as a dachshund wandered onto its territory.

    (A) feline
    (B) bellicose
    (C) onerous
    (D) canine
    (E) felonious

14. A few of the critics ---- the play, but in general they either disregarded or ridiculed it.

    (A) mocked
    (B) discredited
    (C) criticized
    (D) denounced
    (E) appreciated

15. The annual ---- in his school attendance always coincided with the first week of fishing season.

    (A) sequence
    (B) hiatus
    (C) accrual
    (D) increment
    (E) motivation

Exercise 3

Select the word or pair of words that best completes each sentence. Mark the letter that appears before your answer.

1. During the Revolutionary War, Hessian troops fought on the British side not as allies, but as ----. They were paid in money, not glory.
   - (A) assistants
   - (B) orderlies
   - (C) valets
   - (D) infantry
   - (E) mercenaries

2. On and on they came, countless as the blades of grass in a field, a ---- of them.
   - (A) myriad
   - (B) dryad
   - (C) dozen
   - (D) multitudinous
   - (E) multiplicity

3. If you find peeling potatoes to be ----, perhaps you'd prefer to scrub the floors?
   - (A) preferable
   - (B) onerous
   - (C) infectious
   - (D) relevant
   - (E) passé

4. The offenders then prostrated themselves and ---- for mercy.
   - (A) entreated
   - (B) applauded
   - (C) begged
   - (D) imprecated
   - (E) deprecated

5. His rebelliousness was ----; it was written all over him.
   - (A) exterior
   - (B) covert
   - (C) implicit
   - (D) contumacious
   - (E) manifest

6. A system of education should be ---- by the ---- of students it turns out, for quality is preferred to quantity.
   (A) controlled .. intelligence
   (B) justified .. number
   (C) examined .. wealth
   (D) judged .. caliber
   (E) condemned .. ability

7. Giving preference to his brother's son for that office smacks of ---- to me!
   (A) chauvinism
   (B) sycophancy
   (C) nepotism
   (D) nihilism
   (E) pleonasm

8. We seldom feel ---- when we are allowed to speak freely, but any ---- of our free speech brings anger.
   (A) angry .. defense
   (B) blessed .. restriction
   (C) scholarly .. understanding
   (D) enslaved .. misuse
   (E) upset .. explanation

9. Although the wind was quite dependable in those waters, the schooner had an inboard engine as a ---- just in case.
   (A) relief
   (B) substitute
   (C) ballast
   (D) generator
   (E) subsidiary

10. Being perfectly prepared, I took my exams with ----.
    (A) aplomb
    (B) pugnacity
    (C) trepidation
    (D) indifference
    (E) resentment

11. Her speech was too ----; its meaning escaped me completely.
    (A) protracted
    (B) concise
    (C) sordid
    (D) circumspect
    (E) abstruse

12. The "life" of some subatomic particles is so ---- it has to be measured in nanoseconds.
    - (A) contrived
    - (B) finite
    - (C) ephemeral
    - (D) circumscribed
    - (E) macroscopic

13. When income taxes are repealed, the ---- will have arrived.
    - (A) apocalypse
    - (B) holocaust
    - (C) millstone
    - (D) milestone
    - (E) millennium

14. Government often seems to regard money as the route to social salvation: a ---- for all the troubles of humanity.
    - (A) provocation
    - (B) panacea
    - (C) standard
    - (D) nucleus
    - (E) resource

15. You'll ---- the day you voted for Zilch; he'll break every promise he's made to you.
    - (A) regard
    - (B) eschew
    - (C) obliterate
    - (D) rue
    - (E) darken

Exercise 4

Select the word or pair of words that best completes each sentence.
Mark the letter that appears before your answer.

1. If he hasn't yet learned the importance of speaking well of others,
   he must be quite ----.
   - (A) loquacious
   - (B) oblique
   - (C) mathematical
   - (D) arcane
   - (E) obtuse

2. Louis XIV was the ---- of ---- elegance; he wore a different outfit
   for practically every hour of the day.
   - (A) paragon .. peripatetic
   - (B) epitome .. sartorial
   - (C) acme .. epicurean
   - (D) architect .. gastronomic
   - (E) root .. European

3. Favoring one child over another will only intensify ---- rivalry.
   - (A) fraternal
   - (B) sororal
   - (C) parental
   - (D) maternal
   - (E) sibling

4. The man ---- the speaker at the meeting by shouting false
   accusations.
   - (A) corrected
   - (B) interfered
   - (C) disconcerted
   - (D) collapsed
   - (E) acknowledged

5. The literal meaning of *astronaut* is "----."
   - (A) space jockey
   - (B) cosmic navigator
   - (C) star sailor
   - (D) space pilot
   - (E) sky pilot

6. If you ---- your energy wisely you will never lack for it; if you ---- it, you'll remain poor.

   (A) burn .. cauterize
   (B) use .. dissipate
   (C) husband .. economize
   (D) expend .. spend
   (E) economize .. alter

7. The only fair way to choose who will have to work over the holiday is to pick someone ---- by drawing lots.

   (A) covertly
   (B) conspicuously
   (C) randomly
   (D) painstakingly
   (E) senior

8. Richelieu achieved eminence under Louis XIII; few cardinals since have been so politically ----.

   (A) retiring
   (B) unassuming
   (C) prominent
   (D) hesitant
   (E) wavering

9. People started calling him a ----; he had broken a law.

   (A) conspirator
   (B) transgressor
   (C) transient
   (D) bystander
   (E) paragon

10. "---- and ----," he said with a smile as he met his class for the new term.

    (A) Warm .. welcome
    (B) Pupils .. colleagues
    (C) Friends .. countrymen
    (D) Hail .. farewell
    (E) Greetings .. salutations

11. I'm glad to see you have ----; patience is a virtue!

    (A) arrived
    (B) decided
    (C) distemper
    (D) time
    (E) forbearance

12. As the fog came ----, visibility dropped to five feet.

   (A) often
   (B) silently
   (C) nigh
   (D) damp
   (E) unopposed

13. A(n) ---- jogger, she could do 15 miles a day.

   (A) reluctant
   (B) indefatigable
   (C) outfitted
   (D) aged
   (E) distant

14. The ---- speech, given on the spur of the moment, received as much publicity as a carefully planned announcement.

   (A) affable
   (B) resilient
   (C) indigenous
   (D) impromptu
   (E) pernicious

15. A week of sun and exercise had a ---- effect; the dark circles under her eyes were ---- and her skin took on a rosy glow.

   (A) peremptory .. reinstated
   (B) salutary .. obliterated
   (C) sentient .. proscribed
   (D) contentious .. deluded
   (E) fulsome .. censured

EXERCISE 5

Select the word or pair of words that best completes each sentence. Mark the letter that appears before your answer.

1. Although she is reputed to be aloof, her manner that day was so ---- that everyone felt perfectly at ease.

    (A) reluctant
    (B) gracious
    (C) malign
    (D) plausible
    (E) arrogant

2. Speeding may be a ----, but fleeing from the scene of a crime is a ----.

    (A) mistake .. nuisance
    (B) faux pas .. crime
    (C) misdemeanor .. felony
    (D) felony .. misdemeanor
    (E) homicide .. fratricide

3. Among his ---- was the skill of escaping from any type of handcuffs.

    (A) strengths
    (B) crafts
    (C) habits
    (D) repertories
    (E) disadvantages

4. His remarks were too ---- to be taken seriously.

    (A) insipid
    (B) crucial
    (C) timely
    (D) pointed
    (E) germane

5. Familiar with the countryside, they were able to ---- the soldiers who pursued them.

    (A) upbraid
    (B) restrain
    (C) elude
    (D) abet
    (E) eschew

6. A(n) ---- lawyer will help her client ---- the law.

    (A) efficient .. abrogate
    (B) honest .. bend
    (C) unscrupulous .. evade
    (D) clever .. elect
    (E) forthright .. obfuscate

7. Your banker may look at you ---- if you admit to not wanting to save money.

    (A) respectfully
    (B) only
    (C) askance
    (D) directly
    (E) subversively

8. The gossip-hungry readers combed through the article for every ---- detail.

    (A) lurid
    (B) common
    (C) nagging
    (D) recurring
    (E) earthy

9. Worshipping her every move, he was her most ---- admirer.

    (A) beneficent
    (B) fatuous
    (C) ardent
    (D) sophisticated
    (E) urbane

10. She was stubbornly persistent; nothing or nobody could ---- her from her self-appointed mission.

    (A) prevent
    (B) slow
    (C) arrest
    (D) pervade
    (E) dissuade

11. To be ---- was her lot; she was destined never to earn enough money to support herself.

    (A) important
    (B) impulsive
    (C) impecunious
    (D) innocuous
    (E) intemperate

12. There was a ---- of food on the table, and no one could finish the meal.

    (A) surfeit
    (B) diatribe
    (C) rancor
    (D) vestige
    (E) remnant

13. Thanks to the state ----, the Arts Center is able to offer the finest in music at prices affordable to all.

    (A) developments
    (B) subsidies
    (C) conventions
    (D) revivals
    (E) clearances

14. The general couldn't attend, but he sent his ----.

    (A) commandant
    (B) commander
    (C) adjutant
    (D) superior
    (E) successor

15. You can depend on a malingerer to ---- his or her duty.

    (A) perform
    (B) pursue
    (C) shirk
    (D) lack
    (E) subordinate

ANSWER KEY AND EXPLANATIONS

LEVEL B

Exercise 1

1. C	4. D	7. B	10. D	13. B
2. C	5. C	8. C	11. B	14. A
3. C	6. A	9. A	12. B	15. B

1. **The correct answer is (C).** Certain kinds of reports do require (E), but not this kind. You do not "obtain" a *bystander,* (A). No *charter,* (D), is required, because such reports are demanded not only by law but also by common sense. *Formulation,* (B), of what? *Information* forms the starting point for any understanding or explanation.

2. **The correct answer is (C).** Choice (E) is far-fetched and unidiomatic. Choice (D), no longer used as a transitive verb, must be rejected also as it suggests only favorable changes when unfavorable ones are also possible. Choice (B) suggests that the change is harsh and brought about by physical assault, another unjustified conclusion. You have to know the difference between the verbs *affect,* (A), and *effect,* (C). Choice (A) means "to have an influence on"; (C), "to bring about, produce as a result," as in, "A change in environment is very likely to *effect* a change in one's work habits."

3. **The correct answer is (C).** Choices (A), (B), and (E) can be ruled out because they are self-contradictory. People guilty of "typical diplomatic maneuvering" are not likely to avoid *diplomatic* language or the bureaucratic jargon known as *gobbledygook* or *cryptic* (secret) language. Choice (B) is also wrong in using *gobbledygook* as an adjective. Choice (D) is half-right: it's *plain* language that diplomats try to avoid, but they don't use a *summary* to do it. Choice (C) is perfect: they used every *circumlocution*—literally, "roundabout expression"—to avoid *concise* expression.

4. **The correct answer is (D).** The reason for asking questions of a witness is to *elicit* (draw out) the truth. To accomplish this aim, the questions must often be *probing* (thorough).

5. **The correct answer is (C).** Choices (A), (D), and (E) are wrong because if Santa Ana's forces had *declined* or been *isolated* or *absent,* they would not have won. The *felicitation,* (B), or congratulation, of his forces must have happened after his victory and could not have influenced the outcome. So both by elimination and by logic, (C) is

correct. What makes the Alamo battle historic is that a small force held out for so long against an army overwhelmingly superior in numbers, that is, a *preponderant* army.

6. **The correct answer is (A).** *Turbid,* a synonym for "cloudy," is defined as "having particles stirred up or suspended." To be described as *precipitous,* (B), it would have to be extremely steep.

7. **The correct answer is (B).** No knowledge of flamenco dancing is necessary to ascertain, by a process of elimination, that (B) is the only word here describing an aesthetic position. When arms are *akimbo,* elbows are bowed outward. Choice (E), meaning crooked, or oblique, would be a vague substitute for (B). The dancer could not be "ready to perform" if his arms were already (C). Choice (D) can describe an argument, but not a physical position. Choice (A) seems to be a trap, a pun on *flame*(nco).

8. **The correct answer is (C).** The celebrity would not sue because his character had been *whitewashed,* (E). He would sue because he believes his character has been blackened, that is, *defamed.* We do not speak of someone's character being *demoted,* (A), or *implicated,* (D), or *deplored,* (B).

9. **The correct answer is (A).** Note the quotation marks. Without them, the word could have a different meaning. By definition, a "joiner" is one given to joining clubs, organizations, causes. She or he is not *singular,* (E), but rather *gregarious,* (A), that is, prone to move with or form a group, to socialize with one's kind. This does not in itself guarantee that one will be *popular,* (B), or *hilarious,* (C). We put "joiner" in quotation marks to show that it's informal English, close to slang, and to distinguish it from joiner without quotes, in formal English. That kind of joiner is a cabinet maker. Choice (D), *woodworking,* is a subtle trap.

10. **The correct answer is (D).** Here the right word is easy, and three of the wrong ones are hard. Choice (B) means stingy, (C) indicates a shape like the earth (a spheroid flattened at the poles), and *lilliputian,* (E), means tiny, like the inhabitants of Lilliput in *Gulliver's Travels.* Choice (A) means exceeding boundaries and is not used to describe a person. *Obese* means extremely fat.

11. **The correct answer is (B).** To "want no more" is, by definition, to be *satiated,* (B). Choice (E) would mean you have flattered or cajoled your palate. Choice (D) would be difficult to do well: the palate is the roof of the mouth. Choice (C) would be even more difficult: to have *imbibed* would mean to have drunk—your palate? Choice (A) is an unlikely result of eating such a soft food.

12. **The correct answer is (B).** Choices (C), (D), and (E) would not "protect the respondents' privacy." The preposition *to* in (A) would not link properly with "questionnaires," to which (because they are not people) nothing could be *referred* anyhow. Only (B) will link properly and "protect … privacy."

13. **The correct answer is (B).** A word made up of the initial letters of words in a phrase (like SAT for Scholastic Aptitude Test) is called an *acronym*. Choice (A) is a word that can have two or more meanings but only one pronunciation: for example, "pool of water"; "let's play pool." Choice (C) is a word that differs in pronunciation when it differs in meaning: "row a boat"; "hurt in a row." Choice (D) is a word's opposite: cold is an *antonym* for hot. Choice (E) is an assumed name: Samuel Clemens' *pseudonym* was Mark Twain.

14. **The correct answer is (A).** Flood waters from a deluge are likely to endanger, or *imperil,* a town. None of the other choices makes any sense in this context.

15. **The correct answer is (B).** The test sentence provides a good definition of the verb to *procrastinate*. Choice (E) means to announce or declare officially, as a decree or a policy; (D) means to denounce or condemn; (C) means to introduce or precede; and (A) means to divide proportionately, for example, half a year's allowance for six months.

Exercise 2

1. C	4. B	7. A	10. A	13. B
2. A	5. C	8. D	11. C	14. E
3. B	6. D	9. B	12. C	15. B

1. **The correct answer is (C).** The climate is allegedly not conducive to good health, or not *salubrious*. Choice (B) means very changeable, which is precisely what New York's climate often is. Climates can be healthful, but only living things can be *healthy,* (D). Choice (A) is too specific and narrow. *Pathogenic,* (E), means disease-causing, but it is not a word you would use to describe a climate.

2. **The correct answer is (A).** *Defiles,* (B), meaning makes filthy, and *harasses,* (E), meaning disturbs, bothers, pesters, are not laughing matters. *Buffoons,* (D), are clowns; the word is never used as a verb. Choice (C) refers to mildly annoying behavior. *Derides* means "treats with contemptuous mirth," definitely laughing *at*.

3. **The correct answer is (B).** To grant concessions to enemies in order to maintain peace is *appeasement.* It is a special kind of *defeat,* (A). Choice (C), meaning urgent requests, and (D), a trick to avoid confrontation, are not the same as "giving in." Choice (E), which refers to open, legal agreements between sovereign states, cannot be made with terrorists, who operate secretly and illegally.

4. **The correct answer is (B).** Even if the wooden beast did have *fetlocks,* (E), projections on the lower legs, that was not what deceived the Trojans. *Prolixity,* (D), or excessive use of language, does not make sense. The whole incident did become a *tragedy,* (A), but that was the result, not the cause, of the deception. It was not a *strategy,* (C), because that is the overall science of military planning. Rather, it was one small part of strategy, a single maneuver or tactic, a *stratagem.*

5. **The correct answer is (C).** She is only pretending to be "nonchalant" (unconcerned), so the answer must be a word opposite in meaning. The only choice that fits is *worry.*

6. **The correct answer is (D).** The word "but" indicates that the words in the two blanks must be opposite in meaning. The best choice is (D): a *luxury* is by definition not an *essential.*

7. **The correct answer is (A).** The words chosen must add up to a wicked injustice. By definition, an *iniquity* is a *grossly* immoral act, a crime against morality. Choice (C) is incorrect; *perjury* is the crime of giving false testimony, automatically ruled out here because an injustice cannot be *mendacious* (untruthful), only a person can. A *bias* is a preference that keeps one from being impartial, and you can rule out this choice because injustice itself cannot be described as *slanted,* (E). A *lobotomy,* (B) and (D), is a controversial brain operation; it may be evil, or *pernicious,* (D), but hardly senseless or silly and *inane,* (B). You would not choose (D) because *lobotomy* does not mean injustice.

8. **The correct answer is (D).** The navy scoured the area for an entire month; the search was, therefore, necessarily *painstaking* (extremely thorough).

9. **The correct answer is (B).** *Assumption,* (E), would be redundant. By definition, a *hypothesis* is a proposition stated as the basis for argument or experiment. Testing (A), (C), and (D) by stripping the subject of its modifying phrases, you find you can say "a *hypothesis* or an *assumption* was that …" but not "a *labyrinth,* an *outlay,* or an *itinerary* was that.…"

10. **The correct answer is (A).** The only adjective listed that is specifically related to facial expression is (A), which suggests being disdainful, raising the eyebrows, looking down the nose.

11. **The correct answer is (C).** Any wheel would be (A), (B), and (E). In the usual four-wheel vehicle, only a fifth would be extra, unnecessary, that is, *superfluous.* Choice (D), a trap, has to do not with *axle* but with *axilla,* the armpit.

12. **The correct answer is (C).** The only irreversible change would be one that abolished the legislature. A *parliamentary,* (A), government is still a legislative democracy, and merely *contrasting* it with our democracy could not lead to irreversible change. Choices (B) and (E), which would create awkward sentences, could still be legislated in and legislated out. Many democracies, including ours, have had at times three or more major parties, (D). Only a *dictatorship* would destroy the mechanism for its own removal.

13. **The correct answer is (B).** *Onerous,* (C), or burdensome, would never describe a look. All dogs look *canine,* (D), that is, doglike. They certainly do not look catlike, or *feline,* (A). Dogs are not subject to legal distinctions, so *felonious,* (E), does not make sense. But the poodle probably does look *bellicose,* (B), that is, warlike, in defense of its territory.

14. **The correct answer is (E).** The correct answer will be the opposite of "disregarded" or "ridiculed." The only possible choice is *appreciated.*

15. **The correct answer is (B).** Both (C) and (D) are wrong because they both involve increase, and it is not possible to increase school attendance beyond the legal requirement, only to decrease it. Choice (E) requires "for" instead of "in" and suggests the unlikelihood that this person was moved to attend only during that week. Choice (A) suggests that the only time this person attended consecutively was that week. *Hiatus,* meaning gap, hence absence, makes sense all around.

Exercise 3

1. E	4. C	7. C	10. A	13. E
2. A	5. E	8. B	11. E	14. B
3. B	6. D	9. E	12. C	15. D

1. **The correct answer is (E).** Soldiers who rent themselves to foreign armies are called *mercenaries.*

2. **The correct answer is (A).** "Countless" calls for *myriad,* an indefinite number that surpasses (C). Choices (D) and (E) are syntactically incorrect. Choice (B) is a wood nymph, here beguiling careless readers with an "-ad" ending like that in *myriad.*

3. **The correct answer is (B).** This task is never *passé,* (E), or out of date, if you don't have the proper machinery. Apparently, the peeler does not find peeling pertinent, suitable, or *relevant,* (D). Hard work is rarely *infectious,* (C), that is, catching. The peeler would not find both tasks *preferable,* (A). But he surely could find undressing spuds burdensome, oppressive, *onerous.*

4. **The correct answer is (C).** *Entreated,* (A), for mercy is not idiomatic, and *applauded,* (B), does not fit with prostration. Choice (D) would involve laying a formal curse on the listener, and (E) means belittled. Choice (C) has the appropriate tone: They humbly asked, or *begged.*

5. **The correct answer is (E).** *Contumacious,* (D), would be redundant; it means obstinately rebellious. Choice (B) is wrong because it means concealed; (C) means evident although unexpressed, which does not fit. Choice (A) is an inappropriate descriptor. *Manifest,* clearly and openly revealed, shows that he wanted his rebelliousness to be perceived.

6. **The correct answer is (D).** The answer is indicated by the phrase "quality is preferred to quantity." *Caliber* is a synonym for quality, and that is how the system is to be *judged.*

7. **The correct answer is (C).** You should pass right over (E); it denotes the use of more words than are necessary; (A) denotes exaggerated patriotism; (B) denotes servile flattery; and (D) denotes anarchism. Choice (C) is just right: *nepotism* is favoring relatives for appointment to high office.

8. **The correct answer is (B).** The word "but" indicates a change in meaning. Speech is not free when it is under *restriction.* Nevertheless, even when free speech is allowed, people seldom feel *blessed* by their liberty.

9. **The correct answer is (E).** From "although," you can infer the engine is "just in case" the wind becomes less dependable and the ship needs an additional source of power—not so much a complete *substitute,* (B), as an auxiliary, a *subsidiary.* Sails don't need (A). Choices (D) and (C) are irrelevant.

10. **The correct answer is (A).** *Resentment,* (E), would be irrational. If (D) were true, why would the speaker have prepared so well? There would be no reason for belligerence or alarm, as (B) or (C) would signify. *Aplomb,* (A), is the poise that comes from self-confidence.

11. **The correct answer is (E).** The speech was difficult to understand, that is, *abstruse.* Choice (B) means the opposite: clear and compact; (A) means drawn out; (C) means vile, filthy; and (D) means cautious.

12. **The correct answer is (C).** All life is (B) and (D), that is, limited. Choice (E) is impossible; a subatomic particle is microscopic, not *macroscopic.* Choice (A) is meaningless in this context, but (C) is perfect: it means *short-lived.*

13. **The correct answer is (E).** At the *millenium,* the world will be filled with peace and good will; even income taxes will disappear. A *milestone,* (D), does not arrive; it is reached and passed. Choice (C) does not arrive either; it is a grinding stone which, speaking metaphorically, can be a burden one carries "around the neck." Choice (A) is a future period prophesied in the New Testament.

14. **The correct answer is (B).** Something that cures all the troubles of humanity is by definition a *panacea* (cure-all).

15. **The correct answer is (D).** You cannot avoid, or *eschew,* (B), a day, especially one in the past. You might blot it out or *obliterate,* (C), it "from your memory," but then you'd have to add those words. There's no sense in (E). You might well, in your disappointment, *regard,* (A), the day with misgivings, but if you are disappointed, you'll remember it regretfully, that is, *rue* it, (D).

Exercise 4

1. E	4. C	7. C	10. E	13. B
2. B	5. C	8. C	11. E	14. D
3. E	6. B	9. B	12. C	15. B

1. **The correct answer is (E).** *Mathematical,* (C), is nonsense. Failing to speak well of others has nothing to do with being very talkative, that is, *loquacious,* (A); being evasive, dishonest, or *oblique,* (B); or being understood only by those with secret knowledge, that is, *arcane,*

(D). But such failure could indicate that one is dull, or *obtuse,* (E), about social life.

2. **The correct answer is (B).** The second clause indicates the kind of elegance and the degree he attained in it. He had elegance in dress, that is, *sartorial* grace, and he is a good representative of it, the *epitome* of it. Other choices are ruled out because they do not relate well to the second clause: (A) deals with elegance in walking; (C) deals with sensuous pleasures; (D) deals with food; and (E) deals with a broad and general category that might work if *root* was not an odd word choice and (B) was not listed.

3. **The correct answer is (E).** What kind of rivalry could there be? (A) would be between brothers; (B) would be between sisters; (C) would be between parents; (D) would be between mothers; and (E) would be between children having the same parents: *sibling* rivalry.

4. **The correct answer is (C).** *Interfered,* (B), would be a natural first choice for meaning, but it does not fit the syntax: it would have to be *"interfered* with." Choice (E) is wrong because such accusations hardly constitute *acknowledgment,* and (A) is wrong because false accusations hardly supply *correction.* Choice (D) is too strong for the facts we have. But *disconcerted* is suitable; it means upset, irked, ruffled.

5. **The correct answer is (C).** The English word is made up of two classical Greek forms: *astron,* star, and *nautes,* sailor.

6. **The correct answer is (B).** *Burn .. cauterize,* (A), is ruled out because to *cauterize* is to burn tissue with a hot or cold instrument; (C) can be ruled out because to *husband* and to *economize* mean the same thing, to conserve; (D) can be ruled out because, in this context, these verbs are synonyms too; and (E) can be ruled out because *alter* is awkward and unspecific in this context. But (B) makes sense, because *dissipate* means squander, waste, expend intemperately.

7. **The correct answer is (C).** "Lots" are defined as "objects used to make a choice by chance," that is, *randomly.* Choices (A), (B), and (D) each describe only one aspect of the process; limiting it, as in (E), defeats its purpose.

8. **The correct answer is (C).** You don't need to know history or biography at all to figure out this type of question: the text yields its meaning to the careful reader. "Eminence" is the word used in the first clause to describe Richelieu. The only adjective offered in the second clause that corresponds to "eminent" is *prominent.*

9. **The correct answer is (B).** A *conspirator,* (A), has not necessarily broken a law; nor has a *transient,* or hobo. A *bystander,* (D), may

have witnessed a crime, but has not taken part. A *paragon,* (E), or ideal, is surely not a criminal. Choice (B) refers to someone who has simply crossed the boundary between legal and illegal activity.

10. **The correct answer is (E).** Choice (B) is out because there's no hint *colleagues* are present; (D) is out because it's not a goodbye; and (C) is out because they are not yet friends, and the class might even include some foreign students. Choice (A) makes no sense at all. Choice (E) fits the occasion: they *greet* each other for the first time and he wishes to *salute* them.

11. **The correct answer is (E).** Because "have" can be either an independent verb taking an object or an auxiliary to a main verb (like *arrived*), (A) seems possible syntactically. But the second clause seems to define the missing word, which should be a noun in the object position: *forbearance,* meaning patience, lenience, restraint, meets these needs. Choice (C), in this context, means ill humor, testiness.

12. **The correct answer is (C).** If the first clause is to explain the second, frequency, (A), sound, (B), and humidity, (D), would all be irrelevant. Only increasing nearness, or *nigh,* (C), would reduce visibility. Lack of resistance, (E), is to be expected.

13. **The correct answer is (B).** If the opening phrase is to help explain the rest of the sentence, a word meaning tireless would do the job best: *indefatigable,* (B), is perfect. If she were (A), she would not make 15 yards, let alone 15 miles; yet being (C) would not be enough. Choice (D) and (E) are unlikely, unidiomatic words in this context.

14. **The correct answer is (D).** *Impromptu* is defined as given on the spur of the moment.

15. **The correct answer is (B).** The beneficial effects described indicate that the sun and exercise had a healthful, or *salutary,* effect. The dark circles under her eyes disappeared, or were *obliterated.*

Exercise 5

1. B	4. A	7. C	10. E	13. B
2. C	5. C	8. A	11. C	14. C
3. B	6. C	9. C	12. A	15. C

1. **The correct answer is (B).** "Although" alerts you to look for the opposite of "aloof," which means cool, distant, uninvolved. The only opposite listed is *gracious,* which means warm, courteous, sym-

pathetic. Choice (A) means somewhat unwilling; (C) means evil, baneful; (D) means seemingly truthful; and (E) means haughty.

2. **The correct answer is (C).** The "but" tells you that the two activities are being put into different categories. The word "crime" suggests that the second is more serious than the first. Choice (A) is much too understated, as is (B): speeding is not a social blunder or false step, which is what *faux pas* means. Choice (E) is greatly overstated, because neither murder generally (*homicide*) nor murder of a brother (*fratricide*) is indicated. By definition, a *felony* is more serious than a *misdemeanor*, so (C) is correct, (D) has them backward, and (C) puts them in the right order.

3. **The correct answer is (B).** You have to put "skill" into an appropriate category. This is easy, because *craft* is a synonym for skill and implies dexterity with the hands. The entire range of his skills and crafts is his *repertory,* in the singular.

4. **The correct answer is (A).** Remarks that are not worth taking seriously are likely to be *insipid* (dull or pointless).

5. **The correct answer is (C).** Familiarity with the countryside allowed them to *elude* (escape the notice of) their pursuers.

6. **The correct answer is (C).** Ruling out (D) because no one can elect the law, you have four choices for the second word that all indicate shady activity for a lawyer: to *abrogate* (nullify), *bend, evade,* or *obfuscate* (confuse, becloud) the law. The first word must then suit this shady activity. The only such choice is *unscrupulous.*

7. **The correct answer is (C).** The banker thrives on people who put money away for him to lend out at a profit, so he will look at you with disapproval, that is, *askance.* He is unlikely to *respect* your decision, (A). Choices (B) and (D) do not make sense here. *Subversively,* (E), is inappropriate.

8. **The correct answer is (A).** What the readers want is information causing shock or horror, that is, *lurid* information.

9. **The correct answer is (C).** "Worshipping her every move" did not of itself make him her kindest, most *beneficent,* (A), admirer, nor did it necessarily prove that he was more worldly and *sophisticated,* (D), more elegant, polite, *urbane,* (E), or more unconsciously stupid, or *fatuous,* (B), than her other admirers. It qualified him only to be called her most devoted, warm, most *ardent* admirer.

10. **The correct answer is (E).** Once you eliminate the only totally irrelevant choice—(D), meaning to spread through—you have four words all expressing some degree of opposition. But only *dissuade,* meaning to discourage by persuasion, fits gracefully into the syntax. To use (A), (B), or (C), you would have to recast the sentence.

11. **The correct answer is (C).** Only one of the five choices relates to money: *impecunious* means lacking money, penniless. The others are irrelevant.

12. **The correct answer is (A).** If people couldn't finish their meals, there was too much food, or a *surfeit*.

13. **The correct answer is (B).** Only state *subsidies,* or financial aid, would enable the Arts Center to provide low-cost programs.

14. **The correct answer is (C).** *Successor,* (E), would make some sense if we knew the general had retired. He can't order his *superior,* (D), to do it; we don't know his relation to (A) or (B)—are they above or below him?—but we do know that his *adjutant,* (C), or assistant, is the logical one for him to tap.

15. **The correct answer is (C).** By definition, a "malingerer" is someone who pretends to be ill, hurt, or otherwise unavailable in order to avoid his obligations. So (C) is the only choice that fits. Choice (D) is a trap: it could be used in a related statement, such as, "You can depend on him to *lack* a sense of duty."

EXERCISES: LEVEL C SENTENCE COMPLETIONS

EXERCISE 1

Select the word or pair of words that best completes each sentence. Mark the letter that appears before your answer.

1. Her selection was kept in ---- pending receipt of response from her references.
   - (A) purgatory
   - (B) abeyance
   - (C) obeisance
   - (D) refrigeration
   - (E) back

2. Scattered around the dead dragon were mementos of the ----: heads, arms, and torsos of its hapless victims.
   - (A) contest
   - (B) relics
   - (C) prom
   - (D) carnage
   - (E) feast

3. The small, prestigious school had very ---- requirements for admission.
   - (A) insidious
   - (B) stringent
   - (C) strident
   - (D) invidious
   - (E) salutary

4. Gold is one of the most ---- elements; it can be hammered into sheets thinner than a human hair.
   - (A) brittle
   - (B) adamantine
   - (C) soft
   - (D) malleable
   - (E) plastic

5. To call a man a coward is to cast ---- on his virility.
   - (A) unkindness
   - (B) aspersion
   - (C) cloud
   - (D) prevarication
   - (E) guilt

6. Noah Webster was famous as a ----; his dictionaries abounded in the English-speaking world.

   (A) lexicographer
   (B) cartographer
   (C) holographer
   (D) journalist
   (E) publisher

7. I don't have time to ---- with you; I'm here on business.

   (A) caucus
   (B) palaver
   (C) brainstorm
   (D) consort
   (E) plunder

8. Propaganda is a(n) ---- of the truth; it is a mixture of half-truths and half-lies calculated to deceive people.

   (A) revision
   (B) perversion
   (C) inversion
   (D) invasion
   (E) dispersion

9. The ---- conflicts of the civil war have cost untold thousands of lives.

   (A) piercing
   (B) hallucinatory
   (C) international
   (D) infinite
   (E) internecine

10. He had a(n) ---- knowledge of photography; he had learned it entirely by experiment, trial, and error.

    (A) esoteric
    (B) intimate
    (C) sketchy
    (D) thorough
    (E) empirical

11. ---- in his income caused both feast and famine.

    (A) Reduction
    (B) Accretion
    (C) Taxes
    (D) Fluctuation
    (E) Amortization

12. The general ---- his order; he had the traitor shot instead of ----.

    (A) reinforced .. hung
    (B) confirmed .. roasted
    (C) rescinded .. hung
    (D) countermanded .. hanged
    (E) reviewed .. canonized

13. Close examination of the ---- and ---- of the island revealed that no new variety of plant or animal had been admitted for at least fifty years.

    (A) rocks .. minerals
    (B) tracks .. trees
    (C) shoreline .. contours
    (D) flora .. fauna
    (E) crustaceans .. mollusks

14. The missionary was determined to ---- the islanders; her aim in life was to bring them into the faith.

    (A) educate
    (B) civilize
    (C) proselytize
    (D) protect
    (E) sterilize

15. The impact of the situation failed to touch him; he remained ---- as a stone.

    (A) oppressive
    (B) reticent
    (C) immaculate
    (D) impassive
    (E) diffident

EXERCISE 2

Select the word or pair of words that best completes each sentence. Mark the letter that appears before your answer.

1. If parole boards functioned properly, there would be less ----; more parolees would remain out of jail permanently.

   (A) criminals
   (B) graft
   (C) plea bargaining
   (D) recidivism
   (E) chauvinism

2. Failure to use the Salk vaccine caused a ---- of polio in isolated communities; many fell ill with it.

   (A) renascence
   (B) recrudescence
   (C) renaissance
   (D) redevelopment
   (E) revival

3. His uncle was the town drunk; the old ---- had never had a sober day in his life.

   (A) lecher
   (B) pensioner
   (C) voyeur
   (D) reprobate
   (E) sadist

4. Never did I see a more ---- crowd than at Neumann's funeral; there wasn't a dry eye in the chapel.

   (A) bellicose
   (B) adipose
   (C) lachrymose
   (D) comatose
   (E) sucrose

5. The Sunday sermon was, as usual, ----; the minister used 4,000 words where 400 would have sufficed.

   (A) finite
   (B) prolix
   (C) prolific
   (D) propounded
   (E) pontifical

6. The battle finally became a ----; neither side could win.

    (A) truce
    (B) stalemate
    (C) fiasco
    (D) rout
    (E) debacle

7. With her tarot cards she made a(n) ---- prediction, but it was so veiled in secrecy and mystery that I couldn't fathom it.

    (A) illicit
    (B) sibylline
    (C) aquiline
    (D) asinine
    (E) bovine

8. No one knows more about the special program than she does; she has been its director since its ----.

    (A) operation
    (B) inception
    (C) culmination
    (D) fulfillment
    (E) disbandment

9. He was ---- as an administrator, forever arguing with the staff.

    (A) unkind
    (B) contentious
    (C) restive
    (D) restless
    (E) accepted

10. The desire for peace should not be equated with ----, for ---- peace can be maintained only by brave people.

    (A) intelligence .. ignoble
    (B) bravery .. stable
    (C) cowardice .. lasting
    (D) pacification .. transitory
    (E) neutrality .. apathetic

11. The couple had been meeting secretly for years at the hotel, but their ---- were rumored among their friends.

    (A) solipsisms
    (B) trysts
    (C) fidelities
    (D) disputes
    (E) gambits

12. That judge is ---- enough to accept a bribe any time.

    (A) obsequious
    (B) venal
    (C) servile
    (D) vilifying
    (E) sanctimonious

13. Don't get involved with ---- politicians; you'll get caught in a(n) ----
    from which you'll never extricate yourself.

    (A) promiscuous .. orgy
    (B) sleazy .. quagmire
    (C) spurious .. counterfeit
    (D) felonious .. prison
    (E) venal .. anathema

14. Algebra I is a ---- for Algebra II; it must be taken first.

    (A) corequisite
    (B) precursor
    (C) prerequisite
    (D) sinecure
    (E) substitute

15. Most of today's students leave school not a(n) ---- wiser.

    (A) atom
    (B) parsec
    (C) inch
    (D) whit
    (E) omega

EXERCISE 3

Select the word or pair of words that best completes each sentence. Mark the letter that appears before your answer.

1. The solution was ----; both parties could live with it.

   (A) friable
   (B) tenable
   (C) reprehensible
   (D) trenchant
   (E) frangible

2. Benedictine was a ---- treat for the count and countess; they enjoyed a glass of it every evening after dinner.

   (A) postponed
   (B) postposition
   (C) posted
   (D) postprandial
   (E) posterior

3. He was considered a(n) ---- on things Russian; he claimed to have read every article written about Russia in the past two years.

   (A) eclectic
   (B) eremite
   (C) authority
   (D) teacher
   (E) source

4. He was ---- as an elder statesman; his colleagues held him in highest esteem.

   (A) venereal
   (B) venerated
   (C) venial
   (D) valetudinarian
   (E) valedictory

5. The ---- of such crimes between midnight and 6 A.M. has been reduced 30% since April.

   (A) threat
   (B) circumstance
   (C) incidence
   (D) graph
   (E) fantasy

6. When she was pursued by the press, the film star sought ---- in her palatial home.

   (A) refuge
   (B) repute
   (C) reserve
   (D) renown
   (E) reference

7. Do not ---- me for giving John a zero in science; it is my ---- to do so.

   (A) chide .. privilege
   (B) thank .. trouble
   (C) fire .. pleasure
   (D) castigate .. prerogative
   (E) distrust .. honor

8. He couldn't tell the truth if he wanted to; he was a(n) ---- liar.

   (A) misguided
   (B) resilient
   (C) prevaricating
   (D) exorbitant
   (E) pathological

9. Their flight to escape persecution was a necessary ----; had they remained they would have been killed.

   (A) escapade
   (B) adventure
   (C) diaspora
   (D) hegira
   (E) genesis

10. Snakebites are not ---- fatal, but they can sometimes cause death if not treated immediately.

    (A) occasionally
    (B) inevitably
    (C) ever
    (D) never
    (E) indubitably

11. The typhoon had ripped every shred of green from the palm tree; it didn't have a ---- left.

    (A) seed
    (B) stalk
    (C) blade
    (D) blossom
    (E) frond

12. A police officer's ---- job is to prevent crime.

    (A) primary

    (B) compendious

    (C) only

    (D) infrequent

    (E) ostentatious

13. The rocking of the boat made him feel ----; he soon felt the onset of an attack of ----.

    (A) oily .. anger

    (B) bionic .. acrimony

    (C) languid .. panic

    (D) queasy .. nausea

    (E) callow .. remorse

14. The soup was served in an antique china ----, which all admired.

    (A) saucer

    (B) platter

    (C) pot

    (D) compote

    (E) tureen

15. The mosque, from the air, appeared to bristle, with its six ---- pointing toward the heavens.

    (A) gibbets

    (B) minarets

    (C) jihads

    (D) staffs

    (E) halberds

EXERCISE 4

Select the word or pair of words that best completes each sentence. Mark the letter that appears before your answer.

1. I could not bear the woodpecker's ---- rhythm; the endless choppy beat aggravated my headache.

    (A) melodic
    (B) staccato
    (C) harmonic
    (D) crescendo
    (E) stentorian

2. She accepted his proposal with alarming ----; she had the "yes" out of her mouth before he finished popping the question.

    (A) joy
    (B) verve
    (C) reserve
    (D) celerity
    (E) acerbity

3. His first novel was ----; in other words, it was dull as well as a waste of time to read.

    (A) topical
    (B) jejune
    (C) historical
    (D) platonic
    (E) narcissistic

4. Despite the judge's ---- to stick to the truth, the defendant perjured herself in her testimony.

    (A) adjuration
    (B) adjudication
    (C) avowal
    (D) determination
    (E) blandishment

5. After the chemical spill, we had to drink bottled water; the well water was no longer ----.

    (A) risible
    (B) potable
    (C) supine
    (D) viable
    (E) tenable

6. An item cannot be sent by first-class mail if it ---- 70 pounds.

   (A) exceeds
   (B) is under
   (C) has over
   (D) holds
   (E) equals

7. The company received a ---- from the government to develop new sources of energy.

   (A) reward
   (B) compendium
   (C) subsidy
   (D) memorandum
   (E) salary

8. Because of her long experience in office management, it was ---- that she was the best person for the job.

   (A) revealed
   (B) assigned
   (C) proved
   (D) assumed
   (E) promulgated

9. For many years slums have been recognized for breeding disease, juvenile delinquency, and crime, which ---- not only the welfare of people who live there but also the structure of society as a whole.

   (A) rebuild
   (B) bolster
   (C) undermine
   (D) disengage
   (E) weld

10. The water just below the falls was sweet, but where it entered the estuary it became ----.

    (A) murky
    (B) brackish
    (C) alkaline
    (D) radioactive
    (E) potable

11. ---- countries almost never seek military conquest; aggression does not seem to be characteristics of self-governing societies.

    (A) Democratic
    (B) Despotic
    (C) Agrarian
    (D) Autocratic
    (E) Plebeian

12. He expressed his displeasure to the mayor in ugly and threat-
    ening terms; as a result, he was charged with sending a ---- com-
    munication to a public official.

    (A) pornographic
    (B) lascivious
    (C) holographic
    (D) minatory
    (E) proscribed

13. You might say that a pupil has ---- to the mind of his teacher;
    after all, he has the privilege of picking his brain.

    (A) resistance
    (B) access
    (C) congruence
    (D) proclivity
    (E) deference

14. As the ----, I have a right to change my own will.

    (A) witness
    (B) peculator
    (C) testator
    (D) testifier
    (E) deceased

15. ---- breathing annoys me; I can't stand snoring.

    (A) Sternal
    (B) Stertorous
    (C) Soporific
    (D) Sublimate
    (E) Salutatorian

EXERCISE 5

Select the word or pair of words that best completes each sentence. Mark the letter that appears before your answer.

1. Commencing with radio in 1928, Buck Rogers was the ---- of all the space jockeys who followed.

   (A) pariah
   (B) prototype
   (C) pilot
   (D) pioneer
   (E) pacemaker

2. Her admirers were ----; her novels were translated into thirty-six languages.

   (A) frenetic
   (B) arcane
   (C) honest
   (D) legion
   (E) erudite

3. Many of the other crew members panicked when the ship ran aground, but she remained ----.

   (A) truculent
   (B) credulous
   (C) amenable
   (D) imperturbable
   (E) incongruent

4. Until recently, *Ars Amatoria* was not studied in high school; the authorities thought it too ----; its more explicit love scenes, ----.

   (A) pornographic .. deleted
   (B) erotic .. taboo
   (C) revealing .. eliminated
   (D) pastoral .. rustic
   (E) traumatic .. depicted

5. His book on smoking was more ---- than ----; it was too "how to" and not enough fire and brimstone.

   (A) inspiring .. instructive
   (B) pedagogic .. academic
   (C) didactic .. inspirational
   (D) prescriptive .. descriptive
   (E) autobiographical .. graphic

6. Juliet, although only fourteen, was able to dismiss her ---- at will, so as to be alone with Romeo.

    (A) stevedore
    (B) students
    (C) confidante
    (D) paramour
    (E) duenna

7. The old ---- had the temper of a she-bear and the vocabulary of a sailor; she was formidable.

    (A) misogynist
    (B) sinner
    (C) knave
    (D) termagant
    (E) tar

8. Don't name Herbert as your ----; I wouldn't trust him with money!

    (A) villain
    (B) friend
    (C) corespondent
    (D) fiduciary
    (E) domicile

9. His net worth was ----; there was no way of computing how much money he had.

    (A) unlimited
    (B) imponderable
    (C) imposing
    (D) waning
    (E) assumed

10. The ten years of ---- didn't mellow him; they made him bitter enough to use his freedom for seeking revenge.

    (A) penance
    (B) incarceration
    (C) penitence
    (D) extortion
    (E) pillage

11. Among the workers there was complete agreement; on the other hand, there was constant bickering on the part of the ----.

    (A) workforce
    (B) antagonists
    (C) enemy
    (D) disenfranchised
    (E) managers

12. Few people are more ---- than some city dwellers I know; they think the world begins and ends within city limits.

    (A) cosmopolitan
    (B) circumspect
    (C) provident
    (D) provincial
    (E) bucolic

13. In city politics, a(n) ---- voice will get you further than an honest heart; loudness is more likely to achieve results than ----.

    (A) earnest .. enthusiasm
    (B) sonorous .. candor
    (C) talented .. action
    (D) silky .. shenanigans
    (E) resounding .. promises

14. If we do identify with an unlikable, evil character in a novel, we probably do so unconsciously, allowing the darker side of our nature to explore evil ----.

    (A) consciously
    (B) deliberately
    (C) vicariously
    (D) conscientiously
    (E) unconsciously

15. The defendant could almost feel the ---- of the hostile crowd.

    (A) eyes
    (B) sympathy
    (C) animus
    (D) detritus
    (E) incubus

ANSWER KEY AND EXPLANATIONS

LEVEL C

Exercise 1

1. B	4. D	7. B	10. E	13. D
2. D	5. B	8. B	11. D	14. C
3. B	6. A	9. E	12. D	15. D

1. **The correct answer is (B).** The very word "pending" suggests her appointment is put into "suspension," that is, temporarily set aside, in *abeyance. Purgatory,* (A), can imply indefinite suspension. Choice (C) is a trap for students who sense that a word sounding like this is right. Choices (D) and (E) can be ruled out as soon as you are sure of the context.

2. **The correct answer is (D).** The evidence is not of a *feast,* (E), or a *prom,* (C), or a *contest,* (A), but of a massive slaughter, that is, *carnage.*

3. **The correct answer is (B).** The school is small and prestigious, so its requirements are likely to be strict, or *stringent.*

4. **The correct answer is (D).** *Plastic,* (E), means capable of being shaped or formed. But (D) is more specific: *malleable* means capable of being shaped by hammering. Choice (A) is the exact opposite, meaning susceptible to breakage under pressure. Choice (B) means hard and inflexible (as a diamond). In the presence of more specific words, (C) is too general; it also works badly in the sentence.

5. **The correct answer is (B).** An *aspersion*—slander, defamation—is always "cast." Only (B) works in this context.

6. **The correct answer is (A).** "His dictionaries" (lexicons, or word-books) and "abounded" suggest the books were not compiled for private use but published. Webster was a writer of wordbooks, that is, a *lexicographer.* He was also a *publisher,* (E), but this was not the basis for his fame. Choice (B) is a mapmaker; (C) is a specialist in laser photography; and (D) is a writer or editor of news to be presented by the media.

7. **The correct answer is (B).** You need a word that denotes something contrary to business. The only such word here is *palaver,* meaning to chatter aimlessly. Choice (A), meaning to assemble; (C), meaning to pool mental resources for quick suggestions; and (D), meaning to

associate with, can all be used to describe facets of business. Choice (E) is nonsensical in context.

8. **The correct answer is (B).** The second clause suggests that the missing word refers to deliberate and evil misuse and misinterpretation, that is, *perversion.* Choice (A) means change, modification, with no evil intention necessarily implied; (C) means a turning upside down; (D) means an attack that involves penetration of enemy territory; and (E) means a scattering, distribution.

9. **The correct answer is (E).** In a civil war, conflicts are *internecine;* they take place between members of a given group or society.

10. **The correct answer is (E).** What he is missing is theory and formal instruction, without which his experience, no matter how extensive, remains empirical. Choices (B) and (D) would suggest knowledge that includes theory, and (A) would suggest advanced knowledge known only to a few. Choice (C) would indicate incomplete knowledge even on the empirical level.

11. **The correct answer is (D).** No special knowledge of economics is needed to see that his income will provide feasts when it goes up, famine when it goes down. Such irregularity is called *fluctuation.* Choice (A) would mean always more famine, and (B) would mean a steady growth and more feasts. If *taxes,* (C), were a factor, they too would have to fluctuate to produce these results. Choice (E) is the process of liquidating a debt by installment payments or writing off expenditures by prorating them over a period of time.

12. **The correct answer is (D).** The listing of both *hung* and *hanged* suggests that proper usage will figure in the answer: pictures are hung, people are hanged. Hence (A) and (C) can be ruled out. Choice (B) is completely nonsensical. Surely he *reviewed* his order, (E), but he has no power to *canonize,* that is, declare a person a saint. Choice (D) makes sense all the way: he does have the right to review, change, or reverse his own command, that is, *countermand* it, and to grant a traitor a soldier's death by firing squad instead of a civilian's death on the gallows.

13. **The correct answer is (D).** The scientific names for plants and animals are *flora* and *fauna,* respectively.

14. **The correct answer is (C).** To bring them into her faith, she would have to do more than *educate,* (A), *civilize,* (B), and *protect,* (D), them; she would have to *proselytize,* or convert them to her religious beliefs. There is nothing to suggest she would want to render them incapable of reproducing, as (E) suggests.

15. **The correct answer is (D).** Here "failed to touch him" means failed to affect his emotions. *Oppressive,* (A), cannot be said of a stone. *Impassive,* (D), gives us the whole story. It means not only devoid of feeling but also motionless, still. The other three words you can rule out because you would never use them to describe a stone, with (E) meaning timid; (C) meaning pure, unblemished; and (B) meaning hesitant to speak out.

Exercise 2

1. D	4. C	7. B	10. C	13. B
2. B	5. B	8. B	11. B	14. C
3. D	6. B	9. B	12. B	15. D

1. **The correct answer is (D).** The second clause suggests that the missing word has to do with returning to jail. Choice (A) is syntactically incorrect; there might be *fewer criminals. Recidivism,* meaning a tendency to relapse into criminal habits, is the exact term called for. Choice (E) is exaggerated patriotism.

2. **The correct answer is (B).** Of the five words offered, all mean renewal in some sense. Only (B) has a negative connotation: it means a revival of something undesirable or ill advised, like disease or civil war, after a dormant or inactive period. Choices (A) and (C) denote a revival of intellectual activity, like the Harlem Renaissance or the Irish Literary Renaissance. Choice (D) denotes a restoration to a former and better condition, and (E) means any renewal of life or consciousness.

3. **The correct answer is (D).** You can answer this by a process of elimination: (A) is a person who indulges in sexual promiscuity; (B) is a retiree getting a pension; (C) is a peeping Tom; and (E) is someone who derives pleasure from inflicting pain on others. *Reprobate* denotes a morally unprincipled person.

4. **The correct answer is (C).** The only word here related to wet eyes is *lachrymose,* meaning "tearful." (E) is cane sugar; (B) is related to fat; (D) means afflicted with coma; and (A) means warlike.

5. **The correct answer is (B).** Which word catches the essence of the second clause? Choice (E), meaning spoken with pompous authority does not fit; nor does (D), meaning set forth; nor does (C), meaning producing abundant works or results; nor does (A), meaning limited. But *prolix,* meaning wordy, verbose fits perfectly.

6. **The correct answer is (B).** Neither side has suffered a complete failure, (C), nor an overwhelming defeat, (D), nor a sudden collapse,

(E); yet neither side has won. When opposing forces are deadlocked, it's a *stalemate*. A battle cannot become a *truce,* (A).

7. **The correct answer is (B).** The missing word must include prediction, secrecy, mystery. Three of the five choices have nothing at all to do with fortune-telling: *bovine,* (E), means cowlike; *asinine,* (D), unconsciously foolish; and *aquiline,* (C), like an eagle. *Illicit,* (A), means secretive with a connotation of illegality, but *sibylline* means mysterious and prophetic.

8. **The correct answer is (B).** *Disbandment,* (E), can be ruled out at once: you cannot direct a program that no longer exists. Choice (A) would be the program's actual functioning, as distinct from (B), the point at which it was conceived; (C), its high point or climax; and (D), its completion. Presumably she has seen the program from (B) through (A), and (C) and (D) have not yet occurred.

9. **The correct answer is (B).** The only trait that we hear about ("forever arguing") fits the only word offered that means quarrelsome: *contentious.* Such a person might also be *restless,* (D), incapable of resting, or even *restive,* (C), restless and resistant to control; but we have evidence only for (B).

10. **The correct answer is (C).** The word "not" indicates a shift in a meaning between the two parts of the sentence: If peace can be maintained only by the brave, the desire for peace cannot be equated with *cowardice.*

11. **The correct answer is (B).** Secret meetings for romantic purposes are called *trysts.*

12. **The correct answer is (B).** If he is corruptible, or open to bribery, then he is *venal.* He might also have to be (E), that is, pretending to be moral when he isn't, and to the people making the bribes he may be (A), that is, compliant, submissive, maybe even slavish, (C). In the miscarriages of justice attendant upon his venality, he probably engages in *vilifying,* (D), those who haven't paid him. But (B) is the central meaning of the missing word.

13. **The correct answer is (B).** *Promiscuous..orgy,* (A), seems unlikely because it is possible to extricate oneself from that situation. Choice (C) is ruled out because *counterfeit* is not used as a noun in this way; (D) is ruled out because it's not idiomatic: we don't talk about being caught in a prison; and (E) is ruled out because *anathema* is a denunciation or excommunication, and this is not an idiomatic use of the word. Choice (B) makes sense: Getting involved with cheap, shoddy, *sleazy* politicians can get you trapped in a bog, or *quagmire,* from which, by definition, it's impossible to escape.

14. **The correct answer is (C).** The missing word must fit the explanation given in the second clause. This rules out (E) and (A), because Algebra I cannot be taken instead of Algebra II or simultaneously. Choice (D) is irrelevant, meaning a job that pays well with little work. Choice (B) is correct in the sense that Algebra I occurs before Algebra II, but (C) is stronger because it makes Algebra I a requirement as well.

15. **The correct answer is (D).** The easiest word to fit in means "a least bit" and is normally used in the negative: "not a *whit* wiser." *Omega,* (E), is the last letter of the Greek alphabet, and (B) is a unit of distance in astronomy. Choice (C) is not used to measure intelligence. Choice (A) might do, suggesting that wisdom can be weighed, but in the presence of (D), it is inferior.

Exercise 3

1. B	4. B	7. D	10. B	13. D
2. D	5. C	8. E	11. E	14. E
3. C	6. A	9. D	12. A	15. B

1. **The correct answer is (B).** If both parties can live with the solution, it can be considered *tenable*.

2. **The correct answer is (D).** *Postprandial* means after a meal, especially a dinner. Choice (A) shifts the meaning. Other choices are irrelevant: (B) is a grammatical term; (C) has a variety of meanings in travel, military life, and communications; and (E) is a term for the buttocks.

3. **The correct answer is (C).** There is nothing to suggest that he uses this experience as either (D) or (E), or that he has withdrawn from the world for these studies, which is what *eremite,* (B), would imply, or that he bases his opinions on varied sources, which is what *eclectic,* (A), would imply. However, he is without doubt an *authority* on this particular subject.

4. **The correct answer is (B).** The word you choose should link their esteem with his statesmanship. That rules out (D), in chronic bad health; (A), having to do with sexual intercourse; and (C), easily forgiven. There is no hint of a farewell, which is what (E) is about. But (B) fits because he is revered, *venerated*.

5. **The correct answer is (C).** There is no way of measuring a *threat,* (A), a *fantasy,* (E), or a *circumstance,* (B). We would not say that a

graph, (D), has been reduced. But *incidence* makes sense, denoting extent or frequency.

6. **The correct answer is (A).** To escape pursuit, the film star would seek *refuge* (shelter) in her palatial home.

7. **The correct answer is (D).** *Thank .. trouble,* (B), can be ruled out: it seems unlikely that anyone would thank a teacher for this; we do like to be thanked for our trouble in doing something, but "my trouble to do so" is not idiomatic. Choice (C) is ruled out because it also sounds unlikely that a teacher would be fired for this or declare it a pleasure; and (E) is ruled out because it is not idiomatic: it might be "a matter of honor to do so," but not "my honor." Choices (A) and (D), both referring to a right, seem close. But *privilege* would connote some benefit or advantage to the teacher, while *prerogative* means simply an exclusive right.

8. **The correct answer is (E).** The first clause implies that his lying is beyond his control; it is caused by illness or disease: he is *pathological.* Choice (C) would be redundant; *prevaricating* means lying.

9. **The correct answer is (D).** The second clause explains what the missing word means. Only (D) suffices: *hegira* means "a flight from danger." Choices (A) and (B) connote some pleasant excitement. Choice (C) refers to a dispersion, a scattering of people.

10. **The correct answer is (B).** The word "but" signifies a change in meaning between the two parts of the sentence. Snakebites may sometimes cause death, but they are not *inevitably,* or necessarily, fatal.

11. **The correct answer is (E).** *Blade,* (C), would do if the palm were grass, but a palm leaf is called a *frond.*

12. **The correct answer is (A).** You need an adjective that tells the kind of job. Choice (B), meaning concise but comprehensive, is incongruous here. Choice (E) means pretentious, boastfully showy. Choice (C) is potentially untrue: his day can include traffic management and delivering babies as well as guarding payrolls. However, the frequency of the last kind of activity denies (D). Choice (A), meaning chief, main, or first, is correct by both logic and process of elimination.

13. **The correct answer is (D).** If quick recognition fails you, then a simple elimination of unlikely first words would leave you the most likely one. A rocking motion is not likely to make one feel *oily, bionic,* or *callow.* It might make one feel *languid* (listless), but that would not be followed by an attack of *panic.* The only possible choice is (D).

14. **The correct answer is (E).** Soup is best served in a deep, broad, covered dish called a *tureen*.

15. **The correct answer is (B).** A tower on a mosque is, by definition, a *minaret. Gibbets,* (A), are gallows. A *jihad,* (C), is a holy war. *Staffs,* (D), may project upward, but not on a building. A weapon that combines an axelike blade with a pointed spear is a *halberd,* (E).

Exercise 4

1. B	4. A	7. C	10. B	13. B
2. D	5. B	8. D	11. A	14. C
3. B	6. A	9. C	12. D	15. B

1. **The correct answer is (B).** By definition, a *staccato* rhythm is a "choppy beat."

2. **The correct answer is (D).** The second clause indicated she reacted with swiftness, a synonym for *celerity.* That means she did not hold back, did not display any *reserve,* (C). Choices (A) and (B)—the latter meaning vitality, liveliness—would not be alarming; and she would hardly say yes to a proposal with sharpness, or *acerbity,* (E).

3. **The correct answer is (B).** It sounds not only dull but insipid, weak, insubstantial—*jejune.* There is nothing about being (A), meaning concerned with current events; (C), meaning concerned with past events; (D), meaning intellectual and spiritual to the exclusion of the sensuous and physical; or (E), meaning self-admiring, that would necessarily make a novel dull.

4. **The correct answer is (A).** The sentence would make no sense if the judge were *determined,* (D), or if he *vowed,* (C), to stick to the truth, and certainly he would not use coaxing or flattery, which is what (E) would involve. On the other hand, he would make an earnest, solemn appeal, which is what (A) means. Choice (B) is irrelevant in this context, meaning the act or result of a judge's hearing and settling a case.

5. **The correct answer is (B).** The bottled water was necessary because the well water was tainted with chemicals and no longer *potable* (safe to drink).

6. **The correct answer is (A).** Choice (B) is illogical. Choice (D) is begging the question: how much weight does the envelope or container add? Choice (E) means that anything of any weight *except*

70 pounds could be mailed. Choices (A) and (C) express the idea of setting a realistic limit, but (C) is awkward and unidiomatic.

7. **The correct answer is (C).** The crucial words are "government" and "company." A large grant of money given to a private enterprise by a government, usually in support of a project regarded as in the public interest, is a *subsidy*. Choice (B) is irrelevant because it's a brief summary of a larger composition, and (D) is irrelevant because *memoranda* are used for internal, not external, communication. Choice (E) is fixed compensation, paid at regular intervals to an industrial employee for work done. Choice (A) is money given for some special service, usually to a finder who is unknown at the time the *reward* is posted.

8. **The correct answer is (D).** Answer (C) is ruled out because such proof would require service in the job, not just previous experience. Choice (E) is eliminated because this word, reserved for laws, doctrines, policies, means "announced to the public," usually by a government. Choices (A) and (B) are unidiomatic and meaningless in this context. Choice (D) is the only choice that makes sense.

9. **The correct answer is (C).** As breeding places for disease and crime, slums have an extremely negative effect on their inhabitants and on society. The only answer choice with a negative meaning is *undermine*.

10. **The correct answer is (B).** The word "but" alerts you to a change to an opposite condition; another key word, "estuary," means that wide part of a river where it blends with the sea. There, the sweet water becomes salty, briny, that is, *brackish*. There it no longer is drinkable, or *potable* (E). There is no indication that (A), (C), or (D) would be true.

11. **The correct answer is (A).** The second clause describes the kind of societies that by definition are democratic. Choice (E) is the next nearest, as it refers to the lower classes. Choice (C) means agricultural, and (B) and (D) refer to governments that have a single ruler with absolute power.

12. **The correct answer is (D).** If you did not know that *minatory* means menacing, threatening, you could arrive at the right answer by eliminating (A) and (B) because there is no indication of anything sexual in the communication, (C) because there is no mention of laser photography, and (E) because it is redundant and not as specific as (D); it is already clear, because he is "charged with" something, that it is *proscribed,* that is, forbidden, whereas (D) assumes that and gives the charge a name.

13. **The correct answer is (B).** In order to pick his teacher's brain, the pupil must have the right to approach it, and the means of doing so; that is, by definition, he must have *access* to it. Choice (A), (C), (D), and (E) do not fit the idiom of the first clause.

14. **The correct answer is (C).** A person who has drawn up his will in legal fashion is a *testator.* The *deceased* testator, (E), would no longer have the chance to make changes. Being a *witness,* (A), that is, a *testifier,* (D), or even an embezzler, swindler, or *peculator,* (B), would have no bearing on a person's right to testate.

15. **The correct answer is (B).** The only word listed that has to do with snoring is *stertorous,* meaning sounding like a snore. One trap here is (A), which means relating to the sternum—*all* breathing might be described this way. Another trap is (C) because it is related to sleep: it means sleep-inducing. Choice (E) may sound like snoring, but it refers to the student who ranks second in his graduation class and so qualifies to deliver the salutatory, the speech of welcome. Choice (D) is not an adjective but a verb meaning to channel some unacceptable form of expression into some acceptable form of expression.

Exercise 5

1. B	4. B	7. D	10. B	13. B
2. D	5. C	8. D	11. E	14. C
3. D	6. E	9. B	12. D	15. C

1. **The correct answer is (B).** Even if you never heard of Buck Rogers, you get the idea that he was the original, the model for all the space cadets who followed. This makes him more than just a *pioneer,* (D), it makes him a *prototype.*

2. **The correct answer is (D).** If her novels were so widely read, her admirers must have been *legion* (numerous).

3. **The correct answer is (D).** The word "but" indicates that the two clauses have opposite meanings. The other crew members panicked, but she remained very calm, or *imperturbable.*

4. **The correct answer is (B).** You get the main idea from the phrase "explicit love scenes," even if you miss the sexual implication of the title (*The Art of Love,* a work by Ovid). You get another clue from the parallel structure: "the authorities thought it too ----; [the authorities thought] its more explicit love scenes, ----." Choices (A) and (C) are ruled out then because they might "want" those scenes *deleted* or *eliminated,* but they can't "think" them so; (D) is ruled out

because there's nothing scandalous about being *pastoral* or *rustic;* and (E) is ruled out because *depicted* is a meaningless word here. But (B) works because *erotic* ties in with "explicit love scenes," and the authorities can think of it as *taboo.*

5. **The correct answer is (C).** The second clause gives you the clue to the two missing words in the first clause. The first word must correspond with "how to" (implying instruction), and the second word must correspond with "fire and brimstone" (implying strong language that makes readers fear hellfire). Choice (A) gives these, but in the wrong order; (B) makes both of them instructional. Choices (D) and (E) don't come near our requirement. But (C) does: *didactic* corresponds with "how to," and *inspirational* corresponds with "fire and brimstone."

6. **The correct answer is (E).** You need no knowledge of the play, only the ability to decipher the text. If the person she dismissed had prevented Juliet from being alone with her lover, then that person might have been a chaperone. The person dismissed is unlikely to be a shipworker, (A). A 14-year-old would rarely have *students,* (B), and a *confidante,* (C), would not stand in the way of love. Choice (D) would have been another lover—highly unlikely. Choice (E) refers to a servant who acts as a chaperone.

7. **The correct answer is (D).** This can be a fast decision if you see that *termagant* is the only word that applies exclusively to a woman: it means a scolding, quarrelsome woman, a shrew. Choice (A), hater of women, is most likely to refer to a man. Choice (B) is also ruled out because she is not described as morally unprincipled, which is what *sinner* implies. Choice (C) is eliminated because she is not a male villain, a *knave.* Even if she does talk like one, she isn't really (E), an affectionate word for sailor (short for *tarpaulin*).

8. **The correct answer is (D).** You can rule out (C) because *corespondent* relates to adultery, not money. *Domicile,* (E), is a word for home, or legal residence. Choice (D) is defined as someone who stands in special relation of trust, confidence, or responsibility, one who holds something in trust for you, a *trustee.*

9. **The correct answer is (B).** His net worth could not be weighed or assessed, so by definition, it was *imponderable.* True as the other choices may be, none so exactly states the situation as (B).

10. **The correct answer is (B).** Your main clues are the words "freedom" and "revenge," suggesting that he has just been released from captivity and intends to retaliate against those who put him into *incarceration.* Choices (C) and (A) are contradictions of the second clause, meaning, respectively, a feeling of remorse for one's sins and an act performed to show contrition.

11. **The correct answer is (E).** "On the other hand" implies a contrast, in this case between workers and some opposing group. Only (E) provides the appropriate relationship.

12. **The correct answer is (D).** People who think the province they live in is all the world are *provincial,* that is, narrow in their interests and curiosity. The word is used here ironically, because it is the word city people use to describe country people out in the provinces beyond the metropolis. Choice (A), meaning internationally sophisticated, is belied by the second clause in the sentence. Choice (B), meaning cautious, and (C), meaning prepared for the future, are traps: they are words close enough to (D) to distract the hasty test-taker.

13. **The correct answer is (B).** The word to describe "voice" must be related to "loudness" as the second missing word is related to "honest heart." Of the five words describing voices, only *sonorous*—meaning full in sound—is paired with a word related to "honest heart," that is, *candor.* A *silky* voice, (D), surely is smooth, but it is paired with *shenanigans,* which are hardly in demand.

14. **The correct answer is (C).** Choice (E) is a pointless repetition of *unconsciously* in the main clause, while (A) and (B) contradict the word. Choice (D) makes no sense in context. Either by a process of elimination or through insight, you choose (C), meaning through another person's experience, through a substitute who takes the risks for us.

15. **The correct answer is (C).** The main clue is "hostile." While hostility can be expressed physically, it is unlikely that he would feel (A); it is more likely that he would sense an attitude. A hostile crowd would not have *sympathy,* (B). The only word describing a negative attitude is *animus,* (C), a synonym for hatred. Choice (D) is debris; (E) is an evil spirit who rapes women in their sleep.

EXERCISES: LEVEL D SENTENCE COMPLETIONS

EXERCISE 1

Select the word or pair of words that best completes each sentence. Mark the letter that appears before your answer.

1. Beverly Sills, the opera singer, was given the ---- "Bubbles" because of her sparkling personality.

   (A) honorific
   (B) soubrette
   (C) sobriquet
   (D) briquette
   (E) role

2. We usually buy flowers for ---- reasons; there is really nothing of the ---- in the purchase.

   (A) morganatic .. utilitarian
   (B) ulterior .. impractical
   (C) aesthetic .. practical
   (D) lugubrious .. elation
   (E) festive .. funereal

3. Despite the flawless ---- I was unable to read the letter; it was written in Hungarian.

   (A) grammar
   (B) spelling
   (C) rhetoric
   (D) meter
   (E) calligraphy

4. The beggar smiled ---- as he threw back the nickel, saying, "Here! You must need it more than I do."

   (A) sweetly
   (B) blindly
   (C) intermittently
   (D) sardonically
   (E) infinitely

5. Most people eat to live; a(n) ---- lives to eat.

   (A) aesthete
   (B) spartan
   (C) trencherman
   (D) gourd
   (E) nutritionist

6. Get those ---- out of my sight; I won't tolerate a bunch of tattered beggars in front of my restaurant!

   (A) muffins
   (B) ragamuffins
   (C) felons
   (D) miscreants
   (E) poltroons

7. The governor changed her mind at the last minute and granted a pardon; had she remained ----, an innocent person would have died.

   (A) committed
   (B) uncommitted
   (C) governor
   (D) exacerbated
   (E) adamant

8. Augmentation of the deficit caused much ---- for the general manager from the board of directors.

   (A) adulation
   (B) commendation
   (C) approbation
   (D) reprobation
   (E) felicitation

9. Everyone knew that the press secretary had more ---- than his predecessor; he could never be pinned down to a substantive answer.

   (A) lubricity
   (B) complicity
   (C) duplicity
   (D) lucidity
   (E) temerity

10. The shark's ---- hold on life is unrivaled; it can remain viable even after half a day out of water.

    (A) constant
    (B) tenacious
    (C) relative
    (D) tenuous
    (E) transient

11. His ---- smile indicated to me that he was guilty as sin, but I would be absolutely unable to prove it in court.

    (A) sardonic
    (B) sympathetic
    (C) affable
    (D) schizophrenic
    (E) paranoiac

12. Fountains are ---- in Rome; you can hardly turn a corner without spotting one.

    (A) vicarious
    (B) ubiquitous
    (C) meticulous
    (D) vacuous
    (E) insidious

13. I will grant them ---- when they can govern themselves.

    (A) federation
    (B) release
    (C) autonomy
    (D) autocracy
    (E) hegemony

14. There was a three-year ---- in her education; she missed second, third, and fourth grades because of illness.

    (A) vacation
    (B) surplus
    (C) deficiency
    (D) hiatus
    (E) relapse

15. Beneath the thin ---- of civilization lies the ---- in humans, feral and vicious.

    (A) layer .. psyche
    (B) history .. superego
    (C) veneer .. beast
    (D) protection .. subconscious
    (E) frosting .. id

EXERCISE 2

Select the word or pair of words that best completes each sentence. Mark the letter that appears before your answer.

1. You cannot be present in fifth-century Britain, but you can experience it ---- by reading Joy Chant's *The High Kings*.

   (A) directly
   (B) reminiscently
   (C) vicariously
   (D) subliminally
   (E) infinitely

2. If my house were to ---- yours, you'd be complaining constantly about my stereo.

   (A) face
   (B) approach
   (C) affront
   (D) abut
   (E) equal

3. Catherine, a passionate woman, agreed to marry a rich, ---- neighbor even though she loved a(n) ----, uneducated orphan.

   (A) sophisticated .. orphaned
   (B) indigent .. impoverished
   (C) opulent .. unschooled
   (D) affluent .. untutored
   (E) educated .. poor

4. An erstwhile friendly argument degenerated into a(n) ---- that led to blows.

   (A) debacle
   (B) altercation
   (C) litigation
   (D) fisticuffs
   (E) rhubarb

5. Don't deal with that ----; he's no more a doctor than Satan is a saint!

   (A) devil
   (B) cherub
   (C) seraph
   (D) quack
   (E) sage

6. Those were ---- days; we didn't have a worry in the world!

   (A) fraternal
   (B) prewar
   (C) early
   (D) halcyon
   (E) spartan

7. Physics was Einstein's ----; he did not claim to be a great mathematician.

   (A) bugaboo
   (B) forte
   (C) hobby
   (D) avocation
   (E) Waterloo

8. There should be no ---- between them; neither has done anything to make the other bitter.

   (A) matrimony
   (B) acrimony
   (C) alimony
   (D) testimony
   (E) litigation

9. As much as we tried to throw him off balance, he remained ----.

   (A) equilibrated
   (B) offset
   (C) immaculate
   (D) imperturbable
   (E) disproportionate

10. I wish they wouldn't go around attempting to ---- my people, who are happy with the religion they have.

    (A) persecute
    (B) orient
    (C) proselytize
    (D) baptize
    (E) secularize

11. Art was merely his ----; although he could paint and did, he remained best known for his political prowess.

    (A) profession
    (B) calling
    (C) weakness
    (D) preference
    (E) avocation

12. The villagers had nothing but ---- for their lord; he protected them from bandits and shared his land with them.

    (A) mitigation
    (B) adulation
    (C) tribulation
    (D) trepidation
    (E) consternation

13. Even a trip to the ---- would not take him far enough away from me; the world is not big enough for both of us!

    (A) continent
    (B) pole
    (C) antipode
    (D) tropics
    (E) arctic

14. There had been no ----; the cards were honestly dealt, and I lost the hand.

    (A) diamonds
    (B) chicanery
    (C) knaves
    (D) elation
    (E) contusion

15. There was a(n) ---- in the party; one group decided to back Smith and the other, Garcia.

    (A) hiatus
    (B) concordat
    (C) entente
    (D) ambiguity
    (E) schism

EXERCISE 3

Select the word or pair of words that best completes each sentence. Mark the letter that appears before your answer.

1. Dreyfus was ---- after Zola presented proof of his innocence.

   (A) indicted
   (B) proliferated
   (C) exonerated
   (D) exasperated
   (E) prolific

2. You would not be so ---- if you worked out at the gym; you have loose fat all over!

   (A) flaccid
   (B) placid
   (C) pliant
   (D) complacent
   (E) gaunt

3. She was known for her ----; no one was more ---- than she.

   (A) communism .. conservative
   (B) economy .. profligate
   (C) virtue .. wanton
   (D) conservatism .. leftist
   (E) altruism .. selfless

4. Being a stickler for punctuality is just one of my ----; you'll have to accept this little fault as part of me.

   (A) aversions
   (B) peccadillos
   (C) armadillos
   (D) perversions
   (E) weaknesses

5. A few ---- lectures would be greatly appreciated; any change from your usual long-windedness would be welcome.

   (A) prolix
   (B) pithy
   (C) abrogated
   (D) protracted
   (E) verbose

6. Ancient Greek authors believed that literature should contain a perfect balance between the social and the personal, objectivity and ----, ---- and emotion.

   (A) selectivity .. passion
   (B) subjectivity .. reason
   (C) subjection .. rationality
   (D) passion .. socialism
   (E) personality .. sociability

7. I think this is gobbledygook. Can you ---- it?

   (A) smell
   (B) taste
   (C) touch
   (D) sense
   (E) understand

8. The IRS is doing its best to make a ---- of me; it takes every cent I have!

   (A) millionaire
   (B) mendicant
   (C) mentor
   (D) manager
   (E) manatee

9. Fiedler always conducted with great ----; his brilliance was unrivaled for over fifty years.

   (A) eclat
   (B) elan
   (C) elite
   (D) eclair
   (E) encomium

10. Whenever I got home late, I was greeted with a ---- from both parents on the dangers of the night; it would last for hours.

    (A) monologue
    (B) screed
    (C) chat
    (D) brevet
    (E) premonition

11. The ancient tomb was a shambles, all dug up and pillaged; some ---- had got there before us.

    (A) relatives
    (B) undertakers
    (C) ghouls
    (D) morticians
    (E) bureaucrats

12. Your ---- is inopportune; I am not in the mood for riddles at this time.

    (A) opposition
    (B) leniency
    (C) conundrum
    (D) lemma
    (E) equation

13. He took such a(n) ---- position that nothing could change it.

    (A) tenable
    (B) inalienable
    (C) entrenched
    (D) fractious
    (E) refectory

14. The ---- committed by the invading troops was complete; not a single house or a blade of grass remained standing.

    (A) defoliation
    (B) spoliation
    (C) depravity
    (D) postmortem
    (E) asceticism

15. His troubles were not ----; they were more of the spirit.

    (A) illusory
    (B) clerical
    (C) lay
    (D) personal
    (E) somatic

EXERCISE 4

Select the word or pair of words that best completes each sentence. Mark the letter that appears before your answer.

1. If you act ---- at their party, you won't be asked back; they don't want spiteful and irritating people at their affairs.

   (A) contrite
   (B) passionate
   (C) frenetic
   (D) frantic
   (E) splenetic

2. The ---- from the factory stack was ----; the thick, black smoke was evil-smelling and noxious.

   (A) outflow .. aromatic
   (B) overflow .. salubrious
   (C) view .. provoking
   (D) effluvium .. noisome
   (E) effluent .. redolent

3. The ---- of a Stradivarius violin is unique; no known technology can duplicate its tone.

   (A) string
   (B) pitch
   (C) timbre
   (D) wood
   (E) bridge

4. The candidate's ---- was carefully planned; she traveled to six cities and spoke at nine rallies.

   (A) pogrom
   (B) itinerary
   (C) adjournment
   (D) apparition
   (E) diet

5. The cavern was so ---- that the children huddled together in terror around the feeble torches.

   (A) stalactitic
   (B) ferocious
   (C) tenebrous
   (D) cold
   (E) located

6. Their ---- abated as the causes of the bitterness began to disappear, one by one.

    (A) storm
    (B) banter
    (C) forensics
    (D) apathy
    (E) acerbity

7. The professor's oldest colleague was selected to give the ---- at the
funeral.

    (A) eulogy
    (B) elegy
    (C) epigraph
    (D) eponymy
    (E) epitaph

8. The novel was advertised as a ---- romance of unbridled passion
and burning desire.

    (A) gossamer
    (B) torrid
    (C) dulcet
    (D) gelid
    (E) pristine

9. Her fortune was now secured; nobody could ---- it from her.

    (A) preempt
    (B) litigate
    (C) wrest
    (D) coax
    (E) embezzle

10. The sails, touched by the westerly ----, slowly drew the ship
landward.

    (A) storm
    (B) nimbuses
    (C) sirocco
    (D) zephyrs
    (E) gales

11. The old ---- had a bad word for everyone in her company; she was
the consummate shrew.

    (A) virago
    (B) imago
    (C) bear
    (D) senator
    (E) codger

12. If he continues to ---- liquor at this rate, he will end up as an alcoholic.

    (A) buy
    (B) imbibe
    (C) secrete
    (D) accumulate
    (E) cache

13. The professor was in high ----; someone had put glue on his seat, and now he couldn't rise!

    (A) mass
    (B) gear
    (C) anxiety
    (D) dudgeon
    (E) humor

14. The soldiers ---- their spears; the enemy troops, feeling the threat, backed away.

    (A) threw
    (B) showed
    (C) sharpened
    (D) burnished
    (E) brandished

15. Let's keep away from the populated part of the ----; the smaller islands are more attractive and unspoiled.

    (A) commonwealth
    (B) sound
    (C) archipelago
    (D) bay
    (E) peninsula

EXERCISE 5

Select the word or pair of words that best completes each sentence. Mark the letter that appears before your answer.

1. The farce was so ---- I couldn't stop laughing.
   - (A) dispirited
   - (B) obscure
   - (C) pitiful
   - (D) titillating
   - (E) mirthless

2. His writing was replete with ---- like "miserably wretched" or "an original prototype."
   - (A) hyperboles
   - (B) apologies
   - (C) tautologies
   - (D) metonymies
   - (E) synecdoches

3. In the face of an uncooperative Congress, the President may find himself ---- to accomplish the political program to which he is committed.
   - (A) impotent
   - (B) equipped
   - (C) neutral
   - (D) contingent
   - (E) potent

4. The treaty cannot go into effect until it has been ---- by the Senate.
   - (A) considered
   - (B) debated
   - (C) ratified
   - (D) tabled
   - (E) voted on

5. The financially strapped city managed to get a ---- on repaying the principal of its municipal bonds; the grace time saved it from bankruptcy.
   - (A) lien
   - (B) foreclosure
   - (C) moratorium
   - (D) crematorium
   - (E) cancelation

6. The living room was a ---- of furniture ranging from eighteenth century to glass-and-steel modern.

   (A) museum
   (B) potpourri
   (C) plethora
   (D) prolix
   (E) diaspora

7. His behavior was strictly ----; he was acting like a child.

   (A) kittenish
   (B) playful
   (C) puerile
   (D) febrile
   (E) senile

8. Out of sheer ---- she kept putting money into a business that had proven a lost cause.

   (A) wealth
   (B) adversity
   (C) valiance
   (D) perversity
   (E) pragmatism

9. After the quarrel, he sent flowers as a ---- gesture.

   (A) rueful
   (B) conciliatory
   (C) sartorial
   (D) stringent
   (E) benevolent

10. Getting a 90 on the history test ---- him with confidence.

    (A) titillated
    (B) reviled
    (C) inflated
    (D) imbued
    (E) reimbursed

11. It would be ---- to ask for a raise now; the boss is in no mood to grant us a boon.

    (A) propitious
    (B) improper
    (C) impetuous
    (D) impolitic
    (E) fortuitous

12. Do not undertake a daily program of ---- exercise such as jogging without first having a physical checkup.

   (A) light
   (B) spurious
   (C) hazardous
   (D) strenuous
   (E) token

13. The police received a(n) ---- call giving them valuable information that led to an arrest. The caller refused to give his name out of fear of reprisals.

   (A) anonymous
   (B) asinine
   (C) private
   (D) candid
   (E) obscene

14. It is not the function of a newspaper to reflect on ---- but simply to record ----, leaving ethical judgments to the individual reader.

   (A) causes .. opinions
   (B) morality .. events
   (C) deeds .. values
   (D) accuracy .. stories
   (E) validity .. hearsay

15. Your teacher can't control everything; she's not ----.

   (A) omnipresent
   (B) germane
   (C) ambivalent
   (D) redundant
   (E) omnipotent

ANSWER KEY AND EXPLANATIONS

LEVEL D

Exercise 1

1. C	4. D	7. E	10. B	13. C
2. C	5. C	8. D	11. A	14. D
3. E	6. B	9. A	12. B	15. C

1. **The correct answer is (C).** It couldn't be (E) because *role* would need the word "of" to link with "Bubbles"—"role of Bubbles." Choice (A) would make sense if "Bubbles" were a title of respect. Choice (C) is much more appropriate, for a *sobriquet* is an affectionate, humorous nickname. Choice (B) is a coquettish maiden in an operetta. Choice (D), a block of fuel, and (B) both have slight similarities in spelling and sound to (C) in an effort to trick you.

2. **The correct answer is (C).** Which of the five choices for the first blank seems like a common, "usual" reason? *Festive,* (E), seems appropriate until you realize that *aesthetic,* (C), is even more so, because an aesthetic arrangement can both strike the desired mood (*festive* or *funereal*) and be beautiful. *Practical* follows through with the expected opposite meaning. *Lugubrious,* meaning sad, hardly seems suitable, especially when paired with *elation,* (D), which is not idiomatic in this structure anyhow. Choice (B) sounds possible, but not likely on a regular basis. Used to describe a marriage between a member of royalty and a commoner, *morganatic,* (A), is way off.

3. **The correct answer is (E).** If you were "unable to read" it, you wouldn't know how "flawless" the *grammar,* (A), *spelling,* (B), or *rhetoric,* (C) was, or even if it had *meter,* (D). But you could judge the penmanship, handwriting, or *calligraphy,* (E).

4. **The correct answer is (D).** From context and the use of the word "threw," you can plainly pick choice (D), meaning scornfully, mockingly, cynically.

5. **The correct answer is (C).** If you didn't know that (C) is by definition a hearty eater, you could arrive at it by eliminating (A), because an *aesthete* wouldn't do anything so piggish; (B), because a *spartan* lives a life of restraint and austerity; (D), because *gourds* are not people but hollowed-out shells of certain fruits; and (E), because being a specialist in nutrition says nothing about one's eating habits.

6. **The correct answer is (B).** The only word here related to "tattered beggars" is *ragamuffins.* There is nothing about their being beggars in rags that would necessarily mean that they are criminals or *felons,* (C); villains or *miscreants;* (D), or base cowards, *poltroons,* (E). Choice (A) is the reliable trap for the hasty reader.

7. **The correct answer is (E).** If the governor had not changed her mind, she would have been, by definition, *adamant,* or hard as a diamond. You might hesitate over (A) and (B)—but committed or uncommitted to what?—you can eliminate (D) because there's no hint she was aggravated or *exacerbated,* you can eliminate (C) because she must have remained as *governor* if she granted the pardon.

8. **The correct answer is (D).** "Augmentation" means increase—that is, they were now losing even more money—so the directors must have expressed negative feelings to the manager. And there's only one negative word in the choices listed: *reprobation,* meaning disapproval. The deficit would hardly call forth flattery, or *adulation,* (A); praise, or *commendation,* (B); approval, or *approbation,* (C); or congratulation, or *felicitation,* (E).

9. **The correct answer is (A).** You need only pick up the clue in the words "he could never be pinned down." In other words, he was tricky, shifty, slippery; he had *lubricity.* There are no signs that he was an accomplice in anything, which (B) implies, or was engaged in double-dealing, or *duplicity,* (C). And there were no indications that he had clarity, that is, *lucidity* (D), or boldness, *temerity* (E).

10. **The correct answer is (B).** The word missing in the first clause must relate meaningfully to the second clause. Choice (B), meaning stubborn or persistent, is the only choice that makes sense.

11. **The correct answer is (A).** The guilty one seems likely to escape scot-free, so his smile is very likely to be *sardonic* (mocking).

12. **The correct answer is (B).** If there are fountains at every corner, they may be considered *ubiquitous* (existing everywhere).

13. **The correct answer is (C).** One cannot "grant" *federation,* (A). On the other hand, *autonomy* means self-government, and a kingly "I" could grant it. He could also grant (D), rule by one person, but that would not allow "them" to "govern themselves." Choice (E), meaning control of one country by another, seems to be what the "I" is considering giving up. Choice (B) would do if (C) were not a more specific word for freedom and self-government.

14. **The correct answer is (D).** Either you spot *hiatus* immediately because you know it means a gap, an interruption, or you reason it out by eliminating (A) because such a long illness could not be

called a *vacation;* (B) because it would hardly create an excess, a *surplus* of schooling; and (E) because this word suits "illness" more than it does education. Choice (C) would do if (D) were not far more specific.

15. **The correct answer is (C).** The main clues are "beneath," "civilization," and "feral," the last meaning characteristic of a wild, savage beast. Choice (C) springs into place at once then because *veneer* is a thin finishing or surface layer, and *beast* matches "feral." The four pairs containing Freudian terms are all traps because the *psyche,* (A), contains much more than just the *feral*—it includes humans' civilized mental powers; (B), the *superego,* or conscience, is the opposite of feral; and (D) and (E), the *subconscious* and the *id,* both include much that is not feral but creative.

Exercise 2

1. C	4. B	7. B	10. C	13. C
2. D	5. D	8. B	11. E	14. B
3. E	6. D	9. D	12. B	15. E

1. **The correct answer is (C).** To experience it *directly,* (A), you would have to be present then; *infinitely,* (E), is equally impossible because no human experience can be endless; *reminiscently,* (B), would require your being there in actuality before you could think back on it; and *subliminally,* (D), would be only a partial experience even of the reading, which includes a lot of conscious as well as subconscious impressions. So the right word is *vicariously,* that is, through imaginative participation in the experiences of others.

2. **The correct answer is (D).** Since (C) and (E) do not indicate distance, they have no meaning in this context. Choice (B) is impossible with stationary buildings. Choice (A) is not close enough. Choice (D) means that our houses actually touched.

3. **The correct answer is (E).** The words "rich," "even though," and "uneducated" suggest the two men are being contrasted in terms of their relative wealth and education. Choice (A) plausibly completes the neighbor's description, but creates repetition in the word "orphan." Choice (B) creates a contradiction in the neighbor, impossibly making him both poor (*indigent*) and rich at the same time. Choice (C) creates redundancy in both descriptions: rich and *opulent* are synonyms, and so are *unschooled* and uneducated. Choice (D) does likewise—*affluent* means rich, and *untutored* means uneducated. Choice (E) creates the full contrast intended: one is rich and *educated,* the other *poor* and uneducated.

4. **The correct answer is (B).** The sentence describes three stages in the growth of a disagreement. The missing word then might be halfway between "friendly argument" and "blows." That rules out (A), which denotes a disastrous collapse or defeat; (C), meaning legal action, which should not lead to blows; and (D), a brawl, which would already have involved blows. Choice (E), meaning a heated argument, would do except that, used in this sense, *rhubarb* is slang, and this sentence is formal English. Choice (B), which also means a heated quarrel, is formal enough to fit.

5. **The correct answer is (D).** Satan is not a saint, so the "he" is not really a doctor. The only word here that describes a person who does not have the medical skills he pretends to have is *quack,* a particular kind of impostor. Choice (A), a synonym for Satan, adds nothing to the description, while (B) and (C), denoting different ranks of angels, contradicts the second clause. Choice (E), a wise man, also contradicts the meaning of the second clause.

6. **The correct answer is (D).** Choice (E) can be ruled out because *spartan* means austere, rigorous. Choices (A), (B), and (C) are all pleasant to recollect, but there is a better word that includes all their meanings and more. Choice (D) means calm, golden, prosperous, carefree.

7. **The correct answer is (B).** If Einstein claimed no greatness in mathematics, then physics must have been his field of eminence. So (A) is incorrect, because it means an object of dread and concern. Choice (E) is incorrect because it means a disastrous defeat. Choices (C) and (D) are pastimes, not one's most serious activity. That leaves *forte,* meaning area of expertise.

8. **The correct answer is (B).** The correct word must describe the situation between them if they had embittered each other. Marriage, *matrimony,* (A), or statements under oath, *testimony,* (D) do not fit here. Choice (C) is ruled out because *alimony* cannot be shared. It could possibly be legal action, *litigation,* (E). But (B) is definite: it means bitterness, animosity.

9. **The correct answer is (D).** You need the word closest in meaning to "in balance" probably in a psychological, not a literal, sense. That rules out (E), meaning out of proportion; (C), spotless, unpolluted; and (A) and (B), which deal with balance in a physical, material sense. Choice (D) means unshakably calm, undisturbed—the closest of the five.

10. **The correct answer is (C).** You infer that "they" are trying to convert "my people" from one religion to another, in other words, by definition, to *proselytize* them. This does not always mean they

have to punish them for their present beliefs, (A), or change any of their religious activities into worldly ones—for example, change religious into civil marriage, that is, *secularize* marriage, (E). "They" can't *baptize*, (D), "my people" until "they" have converted them. "They" may *orient*, (B), "my people," but this is not what "they" are "attempting" to do.

11. **The correct answer is (E).** The word "merely" indicates that "art" was the lesser of his two pursuits, about which nothing is said except that "he could paint." In politics, on the other hand, he achieved superiority in skill and strength ("prowess"), indicating it was his main activity, his vocation. Art, then, was his hobby, his *avocation*, an activity engaged in aside from his regular profession.

12. **The correct answer is (B).** The word chosen must name a suitable response to his nobility and generosity, and it must fit into the syntactical frame "had … for." Only *adulation* (warm praise) indicates a positive response, and only adulation uses "for." The last three choices all denote negative responses: (C) means great distress; (D) means dread or alarm; and (E) means sudden amazement or frustration. Choice (A), meaning an act of moderating in force or intensity, is irrelevant here.

13. **The correct answer is (C).** No matter how far away (A), (B), (D), and (E) may be, they are all outdistanced by (C), which means, by definition, "a place exactly on the opposite side of the globe."

14. **The correct answer is (B).** The stress on honest dealing tells us that dishonesty is what is being denied. Only (B), meaning deception or trickery, fits. Choice (C) would be men who trick and deceive, not the act itself. Choice (D), meaning joy, liveliness, and (E), a bruise, are irrelevant. While related to card-playing, (A) creates a nonsensical statement.

15. **The correct answer is (E).** Choices (B) and (C) can be ruled out because they denote formal agreements, whereas the party is suffering from disagreement. This produces not a gap, (A), but a division, a *schism* into two contradictory parts or opinions. Choice (D) denotes having two or more meanings.

Exercise 3

1. C	4. B	7. E	10. B	13. C
2. A	5. B	8. B	11. C	14. B
3. E	6. B	9. A	12. C	15. E

1. **The correct answer is (C).** You don't need to know anything about the famous Dreyfus case to find the correct answer in the context itself. The sentence could just as well read "Smith was ---- when Rodriguez...." By definition, if a man is proven innocent, he is declared blameless, *exonerated.* Being proven innocent does not lead to being formally charged, or *indicted,* (A), but to just the opposite: being cleared. Dreyfus would have to be cloned to be *proliferated,* (B), meaning multiplied rapidly, and he certainly was not *exasperated,* (D), that is, angered, irked, or annoyed. Choice (E) means fruitful and is irrelevant.

2. **The correct answer is (A).** The main clue is "loose fat," which indicates that the person spoken to is flabby, or *flaccid.*

3. **The correct answer is (E).** The sentence structure requires two compatible words. Only (E) offers this: *altruism,* meaning concern for others, makes sense when linked with *selfless.* A person known for *communism* would not be dubbed *conservative* but radical, (A); someone known for *economy* is not *profligate* (wasteful, uneconomical) but prudent in management, (B); a person known for *virtue* is not *wanton* (immoral, lewd) but moral, chaste, (C); and someone known for *conservatism* is not *leftist* but rightist, (D).

4. **The correct answer is (B).** Choice (E) serves as a word for "little faults," but (B) is better because *peccadillos* are, literally, "small faults." (C) is a trap for readers who vaguely remember a word ending in *-adillos* used in this connection. Choice (D) is too strong, meaning "practices considered deviant," and (A) is contradictory to what is needed.

5. **The correct answer is (B).** You need an adjective meaning the opposite of "long-winded." That rules out (A) and (E), both of which mean wordy, and (D), which means drawn-out. Choice (C) is the nonsense choice, meaning abolished, nullified. Choice (B) means concise, terse, brief, and to the point.

6. **The correct answer is (B).** The phrase "perfect balance" and the first example, "the social and the personal," indicate you must supply opposites for "objectivity" and for "emotion," in that order. Objectivity is that state of mind that views outer reality factually,

without reference to personal feelings, in a way that all people could agree on. Opposite is the state of mind that views outer reality in terms of personal emotions and individual need: *subjectivity*. In this context, the opposite of emotion is *reason*. Hence, (B) is correct.

7. **The correct answer is (E).** Context supplies the answer, in this case "gobbledygook," a word describing unclear, verbose language full of bureaucratic or technical jargon. The word was coined from the sound a turkey makes plus *gook*, meaning sticky, slimy stuff. So, while *gook* suggests you can *smell*, (A), *taste*, (B), *touch*, (C), or, generally speaking, *sense*, (D) it, the full word means, in effect, that you can't *understand*, (E), it.

8. **The correct answer is (B).** You need not know that IRS stands for Internal Revenue Service; you need know only that someone says that X takes all his money and thus makes him a ----. Choice (B) makes sense, because a *mendicant* is a penniless person, a beggar.

9. **The correct answer is (A).** Don't worry about who Fiedler was. Context tells you all you need know: he performed as a conductor with "brilliance." And that is the definition of *eclat*. Choice (B), meaning style, flair, would do if (A) were not listed. Choice (E) is a formal tribute or eulogy; (C) means the best or most skilled people of a given group; and (D) is a French pastry.

10. **The correct answer is (B).** A *monologue*, (A), is a dramatic soliloquy, and only one person does the speaking; (B) is perfect, for it denotes a long, monotonous harangue, while (C) is much too general and weak. The others are far-fetched: (E) means an intuition of some future event, and (D) is a commission promoting an officer to higher rank without higher pay.

11. **The correct answer is (C).** Grave robbers are properly called *ghouls* (from the Arabic). Choice (B), as they used to be called, and (D), as they prefer to be called now, usually bury corpses rather than dig them up. There is nothing to indicate that these ghouls are (A) or (E).

12. **The correct answer is (C).** The best approach is to start with the word most closely related to "riddles." That's (C), a riddle in which a fanciful question is answered with a pun. For example, "What does a cat get when it crosses the desert?" "Sandy claws." There is no indication that the person being addressed is either antagonistic, (A), or tolerant, (B).

13. **The correct answer is (C).** Choice (E) can be ruled out at once: it's a room where meals are served; (D) means cranky, irritable, troublemaking. Choice (B), denoting a possession that cannot be transferred to another person (e.g., *inalienable* rights), does not fit

well. Choice (A) sounds right—it means defensible, logical—but the last four words describe something not amenable to logic. He is dug in, ready for a last-ditch battle.

14. **The correct answer is (B).** You can arrive at the answer by a process of elimination: (A) is ruled out because houses were destroyed too, and *defoliation* refers only to plant life; (C) can be ruled out because there is no evidence of moral corruption or *depravity,* only of a policy of leaving nothing for an enemy to thrive on; (D) can be eliminated because such destruction could not take place after death; and (E) can be ruled out because *asceticism,* or self-denial, involves an act of will.

15. **The correct answer is (E).** It makes sense to assume that the missing word denotes something in contrast to "spirit." *Illusory,* (A), is not a good contrast to spiritual; (E), meaning related to the body, is a sharper contrast. Choice (D) is wrong because troubles of the spirit would have to be *personal*—it's his spirit. Choices (B) and (C) are traps for the hasty reader who free-associates from "spirit" to clergy and laity.

Exercise 4

1. E	4. B	7. A	10. D	13. D
2. D	5. C	8. B	11. A	14. E
3. C	6. E	9. C	12. B	15. C

1. **The correct answer is (E).** The word selected must include spiteful, irritable as part of its meaning. Choice (A) is way off: it means repentant. Choice (D), meaning emotionally upset from fear, pain, or worry, and (C), meaning frantic to the point of frenzy, do not connote the malice of spitefulness. Choice (B) is too general: it means, simply, emotional. Choice (E) is closest: *splenetic* means irritable, peevish, ill-tempered.

2. **The correct answer is (D).** The first missing word must be related to "thick, black smoke," and the second missing word must be related to "evil-smelling and noxious." Only (D) offers such a pair. *Effluvium* means an outflow of vapor or fumes; *noisome* means offensive, disgusting, filthy.

3. **The correct answer is (C).** You need know nothing about a Stradivarius violin in order to answer this question. From context, the crucial fact about a Stradivarius seems to be its "tone." Of the five choices offered, the word most closely related to tone is *timbre.* When used in reference to a musical instrument or a voice, timbre refers

to its distinctive tone. Choice (B) is ruled out because nothing has a unique *pitch;* pitch is simply an indication of how high or low a sound is in the register of sounds. Many instruments and many voices can duplicate any given pitch (including that of a Stradivarius). Choices (A), (D), and (E) are components of a string instrument; but none of them can produce the instrument's characteristic tone by itself.

4. **The correct answer is (B).** Ask yourself: Which of the five choices pertains to travel and can be "carefully planned"? Choices (A) and (E) both need to be well organized, but a *pogrom* is a massacre of a minority group, and a *diet* is a regulated selection of foods. An *adjournment,* (C), is undertaken by a group, not a single person: it involves a suspension of that group's proceedings until a later time. True, a candidate makes appearances, but they are not "carefully planned" to be ghostly, as the word *apparition,* (D), implies. Choice (B) is the appropriate word, denoting a route or a proposed route for a journey.

5. **The correct answer is (C).** Eliminate (A) because there is nothing about *stalactites* (deposits of minerals pointing downward from a cave ceiling) that would in themselves terrify children; eliminate (B) because we describe as *ferocious* (savage, fierce) something alive or at least moving, like a lion or a storm; and eliminate (D) and (E) because neither *coldness* nor *location* would themselves so affect children. Choice (C) makes sense: *tenebrous* means dark and gloomy, explaining both the terror and the need for children to get close to whatever light is available.

6. **The correct answer is (E).** Whatever it is that "abated" (diminished, lessened), it is characterized by "bitter" feelings. This rules out (A), not normally connected with bitterness; (B), which is good-natured teasing or joshing; (C), which is the art and science of debate; and (D), which is indifference. Choice (E) denotes acrimony, animosity, sharpness—in short, bitterness itself.

7. **The correct answer is (A).** What is the name of the kind of talk that is delivered at a funeral? *Eulogy.* If you know this, the answer pops out at you. If you did not know it, consider each of the choices in their turn. *Epigraph* is a quote at the beginning of a piece of writing. *Eponymy* is something with the same name as something else. *Epitaph* is what is written on a gravestone. That leaves (A) and (B). *Elegy* is a poem written in memory. You don't give a poem. That leaves (A), the correct answer.

8. **The correct answer is (B).** Any romance that is filled with unbridled passion is surely *torrid* (scorching).

9. **The correct answer is (C).** The choices offered all pose different threats to her financial security. Such an overall, practically absolute

statement about security requires a verb that covers all possibilities. Choices (A), (B), (D), and (E) are thus ruled out because each represents a limited and specific threat: (A) means to gain possession by proving prior right; (B), by taking legal action; (D), by persuading and pleading; and (E), by violating her trust. But (C) covers all these and more: it means to usurp; obtain by pulling violently with twisting motions; extract by guile, extortion, or persistent effort.

10. **The correct answer is (D).** The force drawing the ship landward must have been a gentle one, because it just "touched" the sails and moved the ship "slowly." These requirements rule out a *storm,* (A), and *gales,* (E), which act more forcefully; *sirocco,* (C), which is a Mediterranean wind; and *nimbuses,* (B), which are rain clouds. But *zephyrs* are gentle breezes, usually from the west.

11. **The correct answer is (A).** You rule out (E) because a *codger* is a man. Choice (C), denoting an ill-mannered person, would do if (A) were not offered. A *virago* is a noisy, domineering woman, a scold; the word is a synonym for shrew.

12. **The correct answer is (B).** He will never become alcoholic if he just *buys,* (A), *accumulates,* (D), or stores liquor in a hiding place, which is what both (C) and (E) mean. He must drink it, too, which means he *imbibes* it.

13. **The correct answer is (D).** Choice (A) and (B) are tempting because either would complete a common phrase, but neither makes sense joined with the rest of the sentence. Choice (E) sounds unlikely unless he were a masochist, and (C) is rather extreme for such a temporary discomfort, and both (E) and (C) sound unidiomatic. But (D) does make sense and does complete another common phrase meaning "in a sullen, angry, indignant mood or humor."

14. **The correct answer is (E).** Choice (C) and (D) are unlikely: this was hardly the time for the soldiers to undertake such a long process as *sharpening* or polishing (*burnishing*) their spears. Choice (A) seems extreme, while (B) seems too temperate. They waved, flourished, or *brandished* their spears in a menacing manner that could be seen by the enemy troops and had the described effect.

15. **The correct answer is (C).** "Smaller" suggests that these "islands" are being compared with larger islands. Certainly they would not be called "smaller islands" if they were being compared with a *commonwealth,* (A), or a *peninsula,* (E); and what they are being compared with is "populated," so it can't be a body of water, (B) and (D). It makes sense that the larger islands would be the more populated ones, the smaller islands unpopulated or "unspoiled." Such a chain or series of islands is called an *archipelago.*

Exercise 5

1. D	4. C	7. C	10. D	13. A
2. C	5. C	8. D	11. D	14. B
3. A	6. B	9. B	12. D	15. E

1. **The correct answer is (D).** You rule out (E), because it means without humor; (C), because it means arousing pity; (B), because it means vague; and (A), because it means disheartened. Choice (D) is perfect—it means agreeably exciting.

2. **The correct answer is (C).** From the characteristics of the two examples you must decide: Which type of figure of speech do they belong to? Being "wretched" is the same as being "miserable." A "prototype" is the same as an "original." "Miserably" and "original" add nothing to the words they seemingly modify. His writing, then, is replete with redundancies, needless use of the same sense in different words—that is, *tautologies.* You can arrive at the answer by a process of elimination. The two quoted phrases are not *apologies,* (B), in any sense of the word. They are not exaggerations, (A), nor are they certain figures of speech (D) and (E).

3. **The correct answer is (A).** The President can't be *neutral,* (C), because the word means "uncommitted to either side." His success may be dependent, or *contingent,* (D), on Congress's help, but he can't be contingent. Choices (B) and (E) are exactly the opposite of the situation described: the President is ill-*equipped,* not *potent* enough to achieve his goals, which leaves you with (A): *impotent.*

4. **The correct answer is (C).** The context makes it clear that some (unnamed) action by the Senate is required before a treaty becomes valid, legal, binding. Which choice denotes a definite result, a conclusion of a process of treaty-making? Choice (D) means that the process is indefinitely suspended. Choices (A) and (B) describe inconclusive stages of the process. Not even (E) can be said to put the treaty "into effect," because the voting could go either way, for approval or rejection. You are left with (C), the result of a favorable vote.

5. **The correct answer is (C).** Your main clue is the phrase "the grace time," meaning that the city won temporary immunity from the penalties that could have been exacted for missing its deadline, or the "due date" of payment. Such a temporary suspension is called a *moratorium.* The city would not have wanted to get a *lien,* (A), or *foreclosure,* (B), which would have brought on the penalties in full. Choice (E) would have been an impossible dream for the city,

an impossible nightmare for the bondholders. Choice (D) is a place where bodies are cremated.

6. **The correct answer is (B).** A *potpourri* is a combination of various incongruous elements, like a Louis XIV escritoire and a stereo system.

7. **The correct answer is (C).** If you don't spot *puerile* at once as the best word—it means boyish, juvenile, immature—you can arrive at it by a process of elimination. The word "strictly" makes other choices incompatible with "like a child." Strictly *senile,* (E), behavior means acting feebly aged. Strictly *febrile,* (D), behavior means consistently feverish. Strictly *kittenish,* (A), behavior does not refer to a man. Strictly *playful,* (B), behavior does not sound idiomatic. To cover all aspects of childlike behavior, you need the broad, general word *puerile.*

8. **The correct answer is (D).** *Perversity* is behavior that can be described as obstinate persistence in an error. Choice (A) sounds likely in meaning, but it's not idiomatic. Choice (B) is impossible— she couldn't do this out of hardship, which is what *adversity* means; it's a choice intended to trap the student who has a vague idea of the sound of the right word. Choice (C) would be considered a plausible explanation—some bravery is needed to maintain such a foolish course—if the broader psychological term were not offered. Choice (E) is a contradiction: A *pragmatist* is one who especially looks for the meaning of a course of action in its results.

9. **The correct answer is (B).** To make up for a quarrel, a person would send flowers as a *conciliatory* gesture (one intended to regain good will).

10. **The correct answer is (D).** Choice (B) is irrelevant: it means scolded abusively. Choice (C) has bad connotations, meaning his confidence was blown up excessively. Choice (A), meaning pleasantly excited, sounds too slight and temporary to describe such a profound reaction as new "confidence." Choice (E) is absurd, meaning "paid [him] back." So the test results must have inspired, permeated, that is, *imbued* him with self-assurance.

11. **The correct answer is (D).** Rule out (A) right away: it would mean the circumstances are favorable. It couldn't be (C), meaning impulsive or sudden, or (E), meaning accidental or unplanned, because this very sentence shows it is premeditated. Choice (B) would be too strong: there would be nothing irregular, abnormal, or incorrect about asking; it would just be (the only remaining choice) unwise or inexpedient, that is, not good politics, *impolitic,* (D), right now.

12. **The correct answer is (D).** Jogging is not an exercise to be called *light,* (A); nor is it symbolic of the real thing, that is, *token* exercise, (E), or false, counterfeit, or *spurious,* (B). At the other extreme, it's not dangerous, not *hazardous,* (C). But because it does require great effort and exertion, it can be called so *strenuous* as to require a doctor's okay.

13. **The correct answer is (A).** The call could not have been *asinine,* (B), or foolish, if it yielded "valuable information." It wasn't *private,* (C), if it pertained to public business. To have such an effect, it would obviously have to be open, frank, fair, truthful, that is, *candid,* (D)—so why would that be mentioned? In this context, it seems unlikely that the call was *obscene,* (E). But if a person communicating something in writing or in speech "refused to give his name," the communication is called *anonymous.*

14. **The correct answer is (B).** If the newspaper leaves ethical judgments to the reader, it makes no attempt to reflect on *morality.* It is doing no more than recording *events.*

15. **The correct answer is (E).** A person who controls everything is by definition *omnipotent.*

CHECK OUT

Before you go on to the next chapter, can you
- Describe different ways to approach sentence completion questions?
- Identify your strengths and weaknesses in answering sentence completion questions?

Passage-Based Reading

4

Your goals for this chapter are to:
- Identify the three different types of passage-based reading questions.
- Learn strategies for answering the three different types of passage-based reading questions.
- Test your ability to answer passage-based reading questions.

WHAT IS PASSAGE-BASED READING?

The passage-based reading questions on the SAT assess your ability to understand what you read. In the past, the SAT contained only long passages on the arts and literature. On the current SAT, the passages range from 100 to 850 words long and are taken from a variety of fields, including not only the humanities but also social sciences, such as psychology and economics, and natural sciences, such as biology and chemistry. The passages can be presented individually or in pairs. The paired passages require you to compare and contrast information.

TYPES OF PASSAGE-BASED READING QUESTIONS

There are three types of SAT passage-based reading questions.

1. *Vocabulary-in-context* questions ask you to define a specific word in the passage.

2. *Literal comprehension* questions require you to identify information directly stated in the passage.

3. *Extended reasoning* questions ask you to analyze, evaluate, and pull together information from the passage(s). These questions involve finding causes/effects, making inferences, analyzing, and using logical reasoning. Most of the passage-based reading questions involve extended reasoning.

Examples:

Questions 1–3 are based on the following passage.

In the vast majority of cases, a person will be happier if he has no rigid and arbitrary notions, for gardens are moody, particularly with the novice rather than the expert. If plants grow and thrive, he should be happy; and if the plants that thrive chance
(5) not to be the ones that he planted, they are plants nevertheless, and nature is satisfied with them.

Vocabulary-in-context question

1. The word *novice* in the first sentence means
   (A) adept.
   (B) mature.
   (C) beginner.
   (D) impatient.
   (E) austere.

Literal comprehension question

2. According to the author of this passage, an intelligent person should approach the task of gardening
   (A) with an easygoing, relaxed attitude.
   (B) with specific ideas about crops to plant and ways to make them flourish.
   (C) only after having completed extensive training.
   (D) determined to master nature.
   (E) as a career rather than a hobby, because gardening brings great rewards.

Extended reasoning question

3. This passage was most likely written by
   (A) someone whose garden failed miserably.
   (B) a gardener with specific ideas about plants, soil, and climate conditions.
   (C) a plant salesperson.
   (D) someone who breeds rare plants such as orchids.
   (E) an expert gardener seeking to reassure an amateur gardener.

Answers

1. **The correct answer is (C).** Use the context clue "novice <u>rather than the expert</u>."

2. **The correct answer is (A).** The answer is in the second sentence.

3. **The correct answer is (E).** You can infer this from the speaker's knowledgeable, self-assured tone.

ANSWERING VOCABULARY-IN-CONTEXT QUESTIONS

Some of these questions ask you to define difficult and unfamiliar words. Other questions test your ability to define familiar words that are used in uncommon ways. In either instance, use context clues and word parts (prefixes, roots, suffixes) to help you define the words. Follow these three steps:

1. Skim the passage and find the word that you need to define.

2. Use context clues and/or word parts to define the word. Restate the meaning in your own words.

3. Look for the answer choice that best matches your definition.

Example:

Read the following passage and answer the sample SAT questions that follow.

> Think "bank robbery" and you think "stick 'em up." But that's for amateurs, desperadoes, and the pages of history. This is, after all, the twenty-first century. In October 2001, the Kaiping Sub-branch of the Bank of China in Guangdong province, People's
> *(5)* Republic of China, discovered that a local organized crime group had embezzled, stolen, and laundered at least $500 million from its vaults through accounts in Hong Kong, Macau, Canada, and the United States.

1. As used in line 2, the word *desperadoes* most nearly means
   (A) juvenile delinquents.
   (B) sophisticated, polished bank robbers.
   (C) youthful crooks.
   (D) historical lawbreakers.
   (E) bold, reckless criminals.

2. Which words best captures the meaning of *embezzled* in line 6?
   (A) Misappropriated
   (B) Destroyed
   (C) Hid
   (D) Depleted
   (E) Turned into smaller currency

3. In line 6, *laundered* is used to mean
   (A) got caught with the money.
   (B) marked the money with indelible dye.
   (C) disguised the source of the money.
   (D) spent all the money.
   (E) gave away all the money.

Answers

1. **The correct answer is (E).** Use the context clues "bank robbery" and "stick 'em up."

2. **The correct answer is (A).** Use the context clue "stolen."

3. **The correct answer is (C).** Infer the slang meaning from the everyday meaning of *laundered*, "to wash."

ANSWERING LITERAL COMPREHENSION QUESTIONS

These questions require you to find information that is directly stated in the passage. Follow these three steps:

1. Skim the question stems—not the answers. Then read the passage all the way through.

2. Read the questions and answer choices.

3. Choose your answer. Return to the passage to find the relevant detail that confirms your choice.

Example:

Read the following passage and answer the sample SAT questions that follow.

> For the past fifty years, whatever has been done for the cause of progress and good against absolute governments and heredity aristocracies has been done in the name of the Rights of Man; in the name of liberty as the means, and of well-being as the
> (5) object of existence. All the acts of the French Revolution and the revolutions which followed and imitated it were consequences of the Declaration of the Rights of Man. All the revolutionary schools preached that man is born for happiness, that he has the

right to seek it by all the means in his power, that no one has
(10)   the right to impede him in this search, and that he has the right
of overthrowing all the obstacles which he may encounter on his
path. When all barriers are torn down, man will be free.

And nevertheless, in these past fifty years, the sources of
social wealth and the sum of material blessings have steadily
(15)   increased. Production has doubled. Commerce and continual
crisis, inevitable in the utter lack of organization, have acquired
a greater force of activity and a wider sphere for its operations.
Communication has almost everywhere been made secure and
rapid, and the price of commodities has fallen in consequence of
(20)   the diminished cost of transport.

1. As stated in this passage, the Declaration of the Rights of Man
   had success in
   (A)   establishing absolute governments.
   (B)   prompting the French Revolution.
   (C)   stopping all revolutions after the French Revolution.
   (D)   building up heredity aristocracies.
   (E)   preventing the cause of progress and good against absolute
         governments.

2. According to the information in this passage, when people
   have achieved the right to seek happiness and to overthrow all
   obstacles in their path to happiness,
   (A)   poverty has been abolished.
   (B)   a utopia has been achieved.
   (C)   the aristocracy has been overthrown.
   (D)   liberty has been achieved.
   (E)   liberty, equality, and fraternity reign.

3. According to this passage, decreases in the cost of merchandise
   resulted from
   (A)   increases in the amount of available labor.
   (B)   equal division in the consumption of material goods.
   (C)   decreases in costs of movement of goods.
   (D)   more laborers becoming merchants.
   (E)   better rapport between capital and labor.

Answers

1. **The correct answer is (B).** The answer is directly stated in the first paragraph: "All the acts of the French Revolution and the revolutions which followed and imitated it were consequences of the Declaration of the Rights of Man."

2. **The correct answer is (D).** The answer is directly stated in the first paragraph: "When all barriers are torn down, man will be free."

3. **The correct answer is (C).** The answer is directly stated in the second paragraph: "...the price of commodities has fallen in consequence of the diminished cost of transport."

ANSWERING EXTENDED REASONING QUESTIONS

These questions require you to find information that is not directly stated in the passage. As a result, you will have to make inferences— "read between the lines"—and analyze what you read. To make an inference, combine story clues with what you already know to find unstated information. These questions may also ask you to compare and contrast information in two passages. Follow these three steps:

1. Read the passage(s) all the way through. As you read, restate the information in your own words. Think about the author's attitude toward the material, the tone of the passage, and the author's purpose or reason for writing. Ask yourself, "What is the author trying to express?"

2. Read the questions and answer choices. Choose your answer.

3. Use the process of elimination. Guess if you can eliminate even one choice.

Example:

Read the following passage and answer the sample SAT questions that follow.

It is remarkable, the character of the pleasure we derive from the best books. They impress us with the conviction that one nature wrote and the same reads. But for the evidence thence afforded to the philosophical doctrine of the identity of all minds,
(5)   we should suppose some preestablished harmony, some foresight of souls that were to be, and some preparation of stores for their future wants, like the fact observed in insects, who lay up food before death for the young grub they shall never see.

I would not be hurried by any love of system, by any exag-
(10)   geration of insects, to underrate the Book. We all know the

human mind can be fed by any knowledge. And great and heroic men have existed who had almost no other information than by the printed page. I would only say that it needs a strong head to bear that diet. One must be an inventor to read well. As the

(15) proverb says, "He that would bring home the wealth of the Indies, must carry out the wealth of the Indies." There is then creative reading as well as creative writing. When the mind is braced by labor and invention, the page of whatever book we read becomes luminous with manifold allusion.

1. The author uses the images of insects (line 7) to parallel his discussion of
   (A) past writers storing knowledge for future readers.
   (B) authors working in grubby surroundings.
   (C) selfless parents toiling blindly for unknowing children.
   (D) the act of creating art.
   (E) the food chain.

2. The proverb that the author cites in lines 15–16 is used to support his theory that
   (A) the rich need more education than the poor.
   (B) a person must apply knowledge to extract knowledge.
   (C) all the wealth in the world will not make a person a genius.
   (D) books are expensive, but they are worth the money.
   (E) only a writer can be a good reader.

3. A good title for this passage might be
   (A) "Creative Thought."
   (B) "Rating Books."
   (C) "The Wealth of the Past."
   (D) "Visions of the Future."
   (E) "Creative Reading."

Answers

1. **The correct answer is (A).** Just as insects store food for the young they may never see, so do writers store knowledge for readers they may never know.

2. **The correct answer is (B).** The author believes that reading requires a certain amount of application if it is to be fruitful.

3. **The correct answer is (E).** All the details describe the creative reader.

CHECK IN

Directions: Answer each question based on what is directly stated or suggested in each passage. Mark the letter that appears before your answer.

Questions 1–2 are based on the following passage.

It was 1934, and the nation was reeling from the Great Depression: unemployment stood at 24.9% and the Dow Jones average was sputtering from a low of 50 to a high of 108. Since the ascent of Adolph Hitler to the position of Chancellor in
(5)   Germany in January 1933, groups in America supporting his fascist ideology and Nazi vision had become more and more vocal, claiming fascism could be the answer to American woes.

President Roosevelt was deeply concerned. It was already clear in Germany that the Nazis, after coming to power, were
(10)   removing democratic safeguards there, abrogating certain international treaties, and making noise about needing more "living space," which soon translated into capturing neighboring lands.

1. As used in line 10, *abrogating* means
   (A) validating.
   (B) enforcing.
   (C) setting aside.
   (D) endorsing.
   (E) legalizing.

2. The mood of this passage is best described as
   (A) reassuring.
   (B) fiery.
   (C) eerie.
   (D) foreboding.
   (E) blithe.

Questions 3–5 are based on the following passage.

Phrenology is the name given by Thomas Ignatius Forster to the empirical system of psychology formulated by F. J. Gall, and developed by his followers. The principles upon which it is based are five: (1) the brain is the organ of the mind; (2) the mental
(5)   powers of man can be analyzed into a definite number of independent faculties; (3) these faculties are innate, and each has its seat in a definite region of the surface of the brain; (4) the size of each such region is the measure of the degree to which the

(10) faculty seated in it forms a constituent element in the character of the individual; (5) the correspondence between the outer surface of the skull and the contour of the brain-surface beneath is sufficiently close to enable the observer to recognize the relative sizes of these several organs by the examination of the outer surface of the head. It professes primarily to be a system

(15) of psychology, but its second and more popular claim is that it affords a method whereby the disposition and character of the subject may be ascertained.

3. The writer uses the word *organ* in line 4 to mean
   (A) musical instrument.
   (B) pipe.
   (C) organism.
   (D) creature.
   (E) vital part.

4. You can infer from the information in this passage that *phrenology* is
   (A) the oldest and most respectable subcategory of psychology.
   (B) a type of intelligence.
   (C) a pseudo-science based on "reading" the bumps on your head.
   (D) a system of thought endorsed by many followers all over the world.
   (E) a way to determine if someone is lying or telling the truth.

5. This article most likely appeared in
   (A) an encyclopedia.
   (B) a popular magazine.
   (C) a standard medical textbook.
   (D) a commercial web page.
   (E) an advertisement for a self-help movement.

Questions 6–12 are based on the following passage.

Sugar pine cones are cylindrical, slightly tapered at the end and rounded at the base. Found one today nearly twenty-four inches long and six in diameter, the scales being open. The average length of full-grown cones on trees favorably situated is nearly

(5) eighteen inches. The noble pine tree is an inexhaustible study and source of pleasure. I never weary of gazing at its grand tassel cones, the fine purplish color of its bark, and its magnificent outsweeping, down-curving feathery arms forming a crown always bold and striking and exhilarating. In habit and general

(10) port it looks somewhat like a palm, but no palm that I have yet seen displays such majesty of form and behavior either when

poised silent and thoughtful in sunshine, or wide-awake waving
in storm winds with every needle quivering. When young it is
very straight and regular in form like most other conifers; but
(15)   at the age of 50 to 100 years it begins to acquire individuality,
so that no two are alike in their prime or old age. Every tree
calls for special admiration. The diameter of the largest near
the ground is about ten feet, though I've heard of some twelve
feet thick or even fifteen. The diameter is held to a great height,
(20)   the taper being almost imperceptibly gradual. Its companion,
the yellow pine, is almost as large. The long silvery foliage of
the younger specimens forms magnificent cylindrical brushes
on the top shoots and the ends of the upturned branches, and
when the wind sways the needles all one way at a certain angle,
(25)   every tree becomes a tower of white quivering sunfire. Well may
this shining species be called the silver pine. The needles are
sometimes more than a foot long, almost as long as those of the
long-leaf pine of Florida.

6. In this passage, the word *scales* (line 3) is used to mean
   - (A)   measures.
   - (B)   weights.
   - (C)   scrapings.
   - (D)   husks.
   - (E)   balance.

7. By "favorably situated" (line 4), the author probably means
   - (A)   in an approved site.
   - (B)   positioned pleasantly.
   - (C)   newly planted.
   - (D)   far from the sea.
   - (E)   having sufficient sun and water.

8. By "general port" (lines 9–10), the author refers to
   - (A)   a place where ships dock.
   - (B)   the manner in which a person carries himself or herself.
   - (C)   placement on the left.
   - (D)   an opening for intake.
   - (E)   a hole for firing weapons.

9. In comparing the pine to a palm tree, the author
   - (A)   finds neither tree especially impressive.
   - (B)   finds the pine less majestic.
   - (C)   thinks that he is more like a pine tree than a palm tree.
   - (D)   finds both trees equally majestic.
   - (E)   finds the palm less majestic and assigns the pine human
     characteristics.

10. In his description of the sugar pine, the author includes
    (A)   height and thickness.
    (B)   various uses.
    (C)   planting time.
    (D)   height, thickness, and coloration.
    (E)   taste.

11. Which of the following would be the best title for this passage?
    (A)   "Sugar from the Pine"
    (B)   "A Noble Tree"
    (C)   "The Tree of the Sierras"
    (D)   "Comparing Pines and Firs"
    (E)   "The Yellow Pine"

12. You can infer that the author's attitude toward the pine tree is
    (A)   deferential.
    (B)   daunted.
    (C)   imperious.
    (D)   contrite.
    (E)   charitable.

Questions 13–14 are based on the following passage.

     Economic considerations in Afghanistan have played second
fiddle to political and military upheavals during more than two
decades of war, including the nearly 10-year Soviet military
occupation (which ended February 15, 1989). During that con-
(5) flict, one third of the population fled the country, with Pakistan
and Iran sheltering a combined peak of 4 to 6 million refugees.
Gross domestic product has fallen substantially over the past
20 years because of the loss of labor and capital and the disruption of trade and transport; severe drought added to the
(10) nation's difficulties in 1998–2002. International efforts to rebuild
Afghanistan were addressed at the Tokyo Donors Conference for
Afghan Reconstruction in January 2002, when $4.5 billion was
pledged, $1.7 billion for 2002. Priority areas for reconstruction
include upgrading education, health, and sanitation facilities;
(15) providing income-generating opportunities; enhancing adminis-
trative and security arrangements, especially in regional areas;
developing the agricultural sector; rebuilding transportation,
energy, and telecommunication infrastructures; and reabsorbing
2 million returning refugees.

13. The author includes a summary of Afghanistan's recent history in order to
    (A) create sympathy for the nations that are helping Afghanistan.
    (B) compare and contrast Afghanistan to other nations of similar population and gross national product.
    (C) drum up additional support for Afghanistan.
    (D) set the rebuilding effort in context.
    (E) relieve the burden that other nations are carrying.

14. Which of the following statements would the author of this passage most likely endorse?
    (A) Afghanistan can be rebuilt quickly with outside aide because it has a strong infrastructure.
    (B) It will take many years and a great deal of assistance to rebuild Afghanistan.
    (C) Afghanistan can never be restored to its former glory.
    (D) America must help rebuild Afghanistan because we need a strong, sympathetic ally in the region.
    (E) The Tokyo Donors Conference was a dismal failure.

ANSWER KEY AND EXPLANATIONS

1. C	4. C	7. E	10. D	13. D
2. D	5. A	8. B	11. B	14. B
3. E	6. D	9. E	12. A	

1. **The correct answer is (C).** As used in line 10, *abrogating* means "setting aside." You can infer this from the statement that the Nazis "were removing democratic safeguards" and would soon be capturing neighboring lands. They are disregarding the rules they had followed earlier.

2. **The correct answer is (D).** The mood of this passage is best described as *foreboding,* an apprehension of misfortune to come. You can infer this from sentences such as "President Roosevelt was deeply concerned."

3. **The correct answer is (E).** The writer uses *organ* to mean "vital part." You can infer this from the statement "the brain is the organ of the mind" and its placement first on the list.

4. **The correct answer is (C).** By paraphrasing the last two lines, you can infer that *phrenology* is a fake or quack science based on reading the bumps on your head.

5. **The correct answer is (A).** The factual tone, straightforward organization, and ample examples suggest that this article likely appeared in an encyclopedia.

6. **The correct answer is (D).** The author is referring to the plates on a pine cone. Choice (D), *husks,* is the closest synonym.

7. **The correct answer is (E).** By "favorably situated," the author probably means having sufficient sun and water. This allows the pine cones to grow to their maximum size.

8. **The correct answer is (B).** A person's posture is the only meaning that works in context.

9. **The correct answer is (E).** The first part of the answer is in these lines: "but no palm that I have yet seen displays such majesty of form and behavior either when poised silent and thoughtful in sunshine, or wide-awake waving in storm winds with every needle quivering." The second part of the answer can be inferred from the words "behavior" and "wide-awake," which show human qualities.

10. **The correct answer is (D).** Thickness is found in lines 17–18: "The diameter of the largest near the ground is about ten feet, though I've heard of some twelve feet thick or even fifteen."

Height is found in lines 19–20: "The diameter is held to a great height…" and coloration is found in line 7: "the fine purplish color of its bark."

11. **The correct answer is (B).** "A Noble Tree" is the best title because it best reflects the subject.

12. **The correct answer is (A).** You can infer that the author's attitude toward the pine tree is deferential or respectful of the tree's majesty.

13. **The correct answer is (D).** The summary sets the rebuilding effort in context. Without this brief history, readers cannot grasp the enormity of the task that lies ahead in the country.

14. **The correct answer is (B).** The author most likely endorses the idea that it will take many years and a great deal of assistance to rebuild Afghanistan. The details in the passage contradict choices (A), (C), and (E). Choice (D) is not supported by information in the passage.

EXERCISES: LEVEL A PASSAGE-BASED READING

Directions: Each passage below is followed by a series of questions that require you to analyze, interpret, or evaluate the written work. Answer these questions on the basis of what each passage states or implies. Mark the letter that appears before your answer.

EXERCISE 1

Katherine Prescott Wormeley was born in England and moved with her family to the United States in the late 1840s. When the Civil War broke out, she joined the United States Sanitary Commission, a private organization designed to supplement the United States Army's medical division. She was in a place called Harrison's Landing when Abraham Lincoln came to meet General McClellan and discuss the fight for control of Richmond.

For the last two hours I have been watching President Lincoln and General McClellan as they sat together in earnest conversation on the deck of a steamer close to us. I am thankful, I am *happy,* that the President has come—has sprung across that

(5)   dreadful intervening Washington, and come to see and hear and judge for his own wise and noble self.

While we were at dinner someone said, chancing to look through a window: "Why, there's the President!" and he proved to be just arriving on the *Ariel,* at the end of the wharf close

(10)   to which we are anchored. I stationed myself at once to watch for the coming of McClellan. The President stood on deck with a glass, with which, after a time, he inspected our boat, waving his handkerchief to us. My eyes and soul were in the direction of general headquarters, over where the great balloon was slowly

(15)   descending. Presently a line of horsemen came over the brow of the hill through the trees, and first emerged a firm-set figure on a brown horse, and after him the staff and bodyguard. As soon as the General reached the head of the wharf he sprang from his horse, and in an instant every man was afoot and

(20)   motionless. McClellan walked quickly along the thousand-foot pier, a major general beside him, and six officers following. He was the shortest man, of course, by which I distinguished him as the little group stepped onto the pier. When he reached the *Ariel* he ran quickly up to the afterdeck, where the President

(25)   met him and grasped his hand. I could not distinguish the play of his features, though my eyes still ache with the effort to do so.

He is stouter than I expected.... He wore the ordinary blue coat and shoulder straps; the coat, fastened only at the throat, and blowing back as he walked, gave to sight a gray flannel shirt and
(30)   a—suspender!

They sat down together, apparently with a map between them, to which McClellan pointed from time to time with the end of his cigar. We watched the earnest conversation which went on, and which lasted until 6 P.M.; then they rose and
(35)   walked side by side ashore—the President in a shiny black coat and stovepipe hat, a whole head and shoulders taller, as it seemed to me, than the General. Mr. Lincoln mounted a led horse of the General's, and together they rode off, the staff fol-lowing, the dragoons presenting arms and then wheeling round
(40)   to follow, their sabres gleaming in the sunlight. And so they have passed over the brow of the hill, and I have come to tell you about it. The cannon are firing salutes—a sound of strange peacefulness to us, after the angry, irregular boomings and the sharp scream of the shells to which we are accustomed....

1. What does the author mean by "that dreadful intervening Washington" (lines 4–5)?
   (A) Politics are always interfering with the war.
   (B) Lincoln's office stands in the way of his leadership.
   (C) Lincoln has crossed Washington to come to Harrison's Landing.
   (D) The fame of a previous President keeps Lincoln in the shadows.
   (E) Washington is mediating between North and South.

2. How does the author feel toward Lincoln?
   (A) She trusts his judgment.
   (B) She suspects his motives.
   (C) She regrets his arrival.
   (D) She finds him undistinguished.
   (E) She has no opinion.

3. The word "glass" is used in line 12 to refer to
   (A) a goblet.
   (B) a mirror.
   (C) a window.
   (D) a telescope.
   (E) bifocals.

4. The "great balloon. . . slowly descending" (lines 14–15) is apparently
   - (A) the sun setting.
   - (B) remnants of a firestorm over the Potomac.
   - (C) the moon over the river.
   - (D) a mirage.
   - (E) McClellan's transport arriving.

5. Why do the author's eyes ache?
   - (A) She has been sobbing for hours.
   - (B) She struggled to see Lincoln's expression.
   - (C) The wind has blown smoke from the battle.
   - (D) She is writing in darkness.
   - (E) There was glare over the water.

6. The phrase "by which I distinguished him" (line 22) might be rewritten
   - (A) "which made him seem elegant."
   - (B) "in that way I understood his speech."
   - (C) "it was easy to see."
   - (D) "I was more refined than he."
   - (E) "which is how I picked him out."

7. A synonym for "dragoons" (line 39) might be
   - (A) wagons.
   - (B) troops.
   - (C) horses.
   - (D) haulers.
   - (E) demons.

8. Why does Wormeley refer to the cannon salutes as peaceful?
   - (A) They are far quieter than the scream of shells.
   - (B) A truce has been declared.
   - (C) She is contrasting them to the cannonfire of war.
   - (D) Both A and B
   - (E) Both B and C

EXERCISE 2

Thomas Bulfinch (1796–1867) translated and popularized myths of the ancient Greeks, Romans, and other cultures. Here, he describes the legends surrounding Orion, the hunter for whom a constellation is named.

Orion was the son of Neptune. He was a handsome giant and a mighty hunter. His father gave him the power of wading through the depths of the sea, or, as others say, of walking on its surface.

(5)   Orion loved Merope, the daughter of Œnopion, king of Chios, and sought her in marriage. He cleared the island of wild beasts, and brought the spoils of the chase as presents to his beloved; but as Œnopion constantly deferred his consent, Orion attempted to gain possession of the maiden by violence.

(10)   Her father, incensed at this conduct, having made Orion drunk, deprived him of his sight and cast him out on the seashore. The blinded hero followed the sound of a Cyclops' hammer till he reached Lemnos, and came to the forge of Vulcan, who, taking pity on him, gave him Kedalion, one of his men, to be his guide

(15)   to the abode of the sun. Placing Kedalion on his shoulders, Orion proceeded to the east, and there meeting the sun-god, was restored to sight by his beam.

After this he dwelt as a hunter with Diana, with whom he was a favourite, and it is even said she was about to marry him.

(20)   Her brother was highly displeased and often chid her, but to no purpose. One day, observing Orion wading through the sea with his head just above the water, Apollo pointed it out to his sister and maintained that she could not hit that black thing on the sea. The archer-goddess discharged a shaft with fatal aim. The

(25)   waves rolled the dead body of Orion to the land, and bewailing her fatal error with many tears, Diana placed him among the stars, where he appears as a giant, with a girdle, sword, lion's skin, and club. Sirius, his dog, follows him, and the Pleiads fly before him.

(30)   The Pleiads were daughters of Atlas, and nymphs of Diana's train. One day Orion saw them and became enamoured and pursued them. In their distress they prayed to the gods to change their form, and Jupiter in pity turned them into pigeons, and then made them a constellation in the sky. Though their

(35)   number was seven, only six stars are visible, for Electra, one of them, it is said left her place that she might not behold the ruin of Troy, for that city was founded by her son Dardanus. The sight had such an effect on her sisters that they have looked pale ever since.

1. When Bulfinch says "as others say" in line 3, he probably is referring to
   - (A) the meaning of "wade" in other languages.
   - (B) Orion's powers as described by the gods themselves.
   - (C) other translations or interpretations of the myth.
   - (D) a Christian explanation of the myth.
   - (E) the fact that Orion could perform both feats.

2. The word "spoils" (line 7) means
   - (A) leftovers.
   - (B) stains.
   - (C) joys.
   - (D) damage.
   - (E) booty.

3. The word "chid" (line 20) means
   - (A) remarked.
   - (B) lost.
   - (C) embraced.
   - (D) irked.
   - (E) scolded.

4. The "black thing on the sea" (lines 23–24) is
   - (A) a seal.
   - (B) a boat containing Diana's beloved.
   - (C) Orion's head.
   - (D) Diana's reflection.
   - (E) impossible to determine from the information given.

5. The word "discharged" (line 24) is used to mean
   - (A) performed.
   - (B) shot.
   - (C) executed.
   - (D) emptied.
   - (E) dismissed.

6. The word "train" (line 31) is used to mean
   - (A) locomotive.
   - (B) gown.
   - (C) veil.
   - (D) series.
   - (E) entourage.

7. Unlike the first three paragraphs, the last
   - (A) deals with a constellation other than Orion.
   - (B) explains Orion's death.
   - (C) connects myth to the world of nature.
   - (D) Both A and B
   - (E) Both B and C

8. The purpose of this myth is to
   - (A) teach a lesson about responsibility.
   - (B) review the powers of the Greek gods.
   - (C) explain certain astronomical phenomena.
   - (D) Both A and B
   - (E) Both B and C

Exercise 3

Sigmund Freud lived most of his life in Vienna, Austria. He trained in medicine and established The International Psychoanalytic Association in 1910. This excerpt is from a translation of a 1923 work, The Ego and the Id.

There are certain people who behave in a quite peculiar fashion during the work of analysis. When one speaks hopefully to them or expresses satisfaction with the progress of the treatment, they show signs of discontent and their condition invariably

(5)   becomes worse. One begins by regarding this as defiance and as an attempt to prove their superiority to the physician, but later one comes to take a deeper and juster view. One becomes convinced, not only that such people cannot endure any praise or appreciation, but that they react inversely to the progress of

(10)   the treatment. Every partial solution that ought to result, and in other people does result, in an improvement or a temporary suspension of symptoms produces in them for the time being an exacerbation of their illness; they get worse during the treatment instead of getting better. They exhibit what is known as a

(15)   'negative therapeutic reaction.'

There is no doubt that there is something in these people that sets itself against their recovery, and its approach is dreaded as though it were a danger. We are accustomed to say that the need for illness has got the upper hand in them

(20)   over the desire for recovery. If we analyse this resistance in the usual way—then, even after allowance has been made for an attitude of defiance towards the physician and for fixation to the various forms of gain from illness, the greater part of it is still left over; and this reveals itself as the most powerful of all

(25)   obstacles to recovery, more powerful than the familiar ones of narcissistic inaccessibility, a negative attitude towards the physician and clinging to the gain from illness.

In the end we come to see that we are dealing with what may be called a 'moral' factor, a sense of guilt, which is finding

(30)   satisfaction in the illness and refusing to give up the punishment of suffering. We shall be right in regarding this disheartening explanation as final. But as far as the patient is concerned this sense of guilt is dumb; it does not tell him he is guilty; he does not feel guilty, he feels ill. This sense of

(35)   guilt expresses itself only as a resistance to recovery which is extremely difficult to overcome. It is also particularly difficult to convince the patient that this motive lies behind his continuing to be ill; he holds fast to the more obvious explanation that treatment by analysis is not the right remedy for his case.

1. How does Freud feel about the syndrome he describes?
   - (A) He feels it is curious.
   - (B) He feels it is routine.
   - (C) He feels it is unmanageable.
   - (D) He feels it is predictable.
   - (E) He feels it is ridiculous.

2. The word "defiance" (line 5) is used to mean
   - (A) boldness.
   - (B) respect.
   - (C) scorn.
   - (D) recalcitrance.
   - (E) contempt.

3. The word "juster" (line 7) means
   - (A) more honest.
   - (B) more lawful.
   - (C) fairer.
   - (D) clearer.
   - (E) more precise.

4. By "reacting inversely" (line 9), Freud means that these patients
   - (A) act contrary to a physician's expectations.
   - (B) get worse when they should get better.
   - (C) get better when they should get worse.
   - (D) Both A and B
   - (E) Both B and C

5. The word "exacerbation" (line 13) means
   - (A) intensification.
   - (B) discharge.
   - (C) enforcement.
   - (D) hatred.
   - (E) inference.

6. The approaching danger Freud refers to in lines 17–18 is
   - (A) the need to feel sick.
   - (B) negative attitudes.
   - (C) despair.
   - (D) recovery from illness.
   - (E) a sense of guilt.

7. Freud's study of this syndrome leads him to think that
   (A)   most patients respond badly to praise.
   (B)   patients' guilt may keep them from getting well.
   (C)   patients need to trust their physicians.
   (D)   Both A and B
   (E)   Both B and C

8. The word "dumb" (line 33) is used to mean
   (A)   slow.
   (B)   dull.
   (C)   dense.
   (D)   stupid.
   (E)   silent.

9. Does Freud feel that analysis is not right for the patients he describes?
   (A)   Yes, he feels they are in love with their illnesses.
   (B)   Yes, he feels that they are too ill to recover.
   (C)   Yes, he senses that they need another remedy.
   (D)   No, but the patients often feel that way.
   (E)   No, but analysis may harm such patients.

10. A good title for this passage might be
   (A)   "Doctors and Patients."
   (B)   "Guilt and Suffering."
   (C)   "An Inverse Reaction to Progress."
   (D)   "The Need for Analysis."
   (E)   "Narcissism."

EXERCISE 4

*Edwin Markham was primarily a poet. He was associated with the
"muckraking movement" of the early twentieth century. Muckrakers
were a loosely allied set of novelists, essayists, and magazine editors
whose goal was the raising of society's consciousness and the exposure
of social ills. This excerpt is from a 1906 essay Markham wrote for the
muckraking magazine* Cosmopolitan.

In the North..., for every one thousand workers over sixteen
years of age there are eighty-three workers under sixteen...;
while in the South, for every one thousand workers in the mills
over sixteen years of age there are three hundred and fifty-three

(5)   under sixteen. Some of these are eight and nine years old, and
some are only five and six. For a day or a night at a stretch these
little children do some one monotonous thing—abusing their eyes
in watching the rushing threads; dwarfing their muscles in an
eternity of petty movements; befouling their lungs by breathing

(10) flecks of flying cotton; bestowing ceaseless, anxious attention for
hours, where science says that "a twenty-minute strain is long
enough for a growing mind." And these are not the children of
recent immigrants, hardened by the effete conditions of foreign
servitude. Nor are they Negro children who have shifted their

(15) shackles from field to mill. They are white children of old and
pure colonial stock. Think of it! Here is a people that has outlived the bondage of England, that has seen the rise and fall of
slavery—a people that must now fling their children into the
clutches of capital, into the maw of the blind machine...

(20)   Fifty thousand children, mostly girls, are in the textile mills
of the South. Six times as many children are working now as
were working twenty years ago. Unless the conscience of the
nation can be awakened, it will not be long before one hundred
thousand children will be hobbling in hopeless lock-step to these

(25) Bastilles of labor....
Think of the deadly drudgery in these cotton mills.
Children rise at half-past four, commanded by the ogre scream
of the factory whistle; they hurry, ill fed, unkempt, unwashed,
half dressed, to the walls which shut out the day and which

(30) confine them amid the din and dust and merciless maze of
the machines. Here, penned in little narrow lanes, they look
and leap and reach and tie among acres and acres of looms.
Always the snow of lint in their faces, always the thunder of
the machines in their ears. A scant half hour at noon breaks

(35) the twelve-hour vigil, for it is nightfall when the long hours end
and the children may return to the barracks they call "home,"

often too tried to wait for the cheerless meal which the mother, also working in the factory, must cook, after her factory day is over. Frequently at noon and at night they fall asleep with the

(40) food unswallowed in the mouth. Frequently they snatch only a bite and curl up undressed on the bed, to gather strength for the same dull round tomorrow, and tomorrow, and tomorrow.

1. The words "abusing," "dwarfing," and "befouling" (lines 7–9) are used by Markham to show
   (A) the health hazards for children who work in the mills.
   (B) the quality of the workers in the mills.
   (C) how little respect for life millworkers have.
   (D) how adults fare no better than children.
   (E) the varying jobs available for children.

2. Markham quotes "science" (lines 11–12) to support his point that
   (A) young muscles are built by hard labor.
   (B) mill work is dangerous.
   (C) children should not work long hours.
   (D) Both A and B
   (E) Both B and C

3. The word "effete" (line 13) means
   (A) decent.
   (B) flourishing.
   (C) childless.
   (D) barren.
   (E) unwholesome.

4. By "shifted their shackles from field to mill" (lines 14–15), Markham means
   (A) mill owners have taken their slaves from country to city.
   (B) the workers have changed from field slaves to slaves of the mills.
   (C) slave owners have moved their money indoors.
   (D) the workers have slipped the bonds of slavery to work in the mills.
   (E) the workers have left a life of servitude for a better life.

5. By "the maw of the blind machine" (line 19), Markham compares mill labor to a
   (A) senseless device.
   (B) matriarchal society.
   (C) cruel, unfeeling mother.
   (D) Cyclops-like ogre.
   (E) tool that blinds workers.

6. What does Markham mean by "Bastilles of labor" (line 25)?
   (A) America needs a revolution.
   (B) The mills are prisons.
   (C) Children work for freedom.
   (D) Work is the drug of the masses.
   (E) We are no better than Europeans.

7. Paragraph 3 continues Markham's metaphor of
   (A) prisons.
   (B) monsters.
   (C) flight.
   (D) Both A and B
   (E) Both B and C

8. The word "penned" (line 31) is used to compare the children to
   (A) writers.
   (B) animals.
   (C) wrestlers.
   (D) pigs.
   (E) ranch hands.

9. The word "barracks" (line 36) is used to refer to the fact that the children's homes are
   (A) in a camp.
   (B) manned by armed guards.
   (C) dreary and uniform.
   (D) militarily clean.
   (E) old and run-down.

10. Markham repeats the word "tomorrow" (line 42) to
   (A) remind us that the future is here.
   (B) imply endless repetitiveness.
   (C) suggest that it is not too late to change.
   (D) arouse us to the fact that these children will grow up.
   (E) contrast the past with the present.

EXERCISE 5

Ralph Waldo Emerson is one of America's best-known essayists. In 1837, he was called on to give the Phi Beta Kappa address to Harvard students and their guests. He spoke on The American Scholar.

It is remarkable, the character of the pleasure we derive from the best books. They impress us with the conviction that one nature wrote and the same reads. We read the verses of one of the great English poets, of Chaucer, of Marvell, of Dryden, with

(5)   the most modern joy,—with a pleasure, I mean, which is in great part caused by the abstraction of all *time* from their verses. There is some awe mixed with the joy of our surprise, when this poet, who lived in some past world, two or three hundred years ago, says that which lies close to my own soul, that which I also

(10)   had well-nigh thought and said. But for the evidence thence afforded to the philosophical doctrine of the identity of all minds, we should suppose some preestablished harmony, some foresight of souls that were to be, and some preparation of stores for their future wants, like the fact observed in insects, who lay

(15)   up food before death for the young grub they shall never see.

I would not be hurried by any love of system, by any exaggeration of instincts, to underrate the Book. We all know, that as the human body can be nourished on any food, though it were boiled grass and the broth of shoes, so the human mind can be

(20)   fed by any knowledge. And great and heroic men have existed who had almost no other information than by the printed page. I would only say that it needs a strong head to bear that diet. One must be an inventor to read well. As the proverb says, "He that would bring home the wealth of the Indies, must carry

(25)   out the wealth of the Indies." There is then creative reading as well as creative writing. When the mind is braced by labor and invention, the page of whatever book we read becomes luminous with manifold allusion. Every sentence is doubly significant, and the sense of our author is as broad as the world. We then see,

(30)   what is always true, that as the seer's hour of vision is short and rare among heavy days and months, so is its record, perchance, the least part of his volume. The discerning will read, in his Plato or Shakespeare, only that least part,—only the authentic utterances of the oracle;—all the rest he rejects, were it never so

(35)   many times Plato's and Shakespeare's.

Of course there is a portion of reading quite indispensable to a wise man. History and exact science he must learn by laborious reading. Colleges, in like manner, have their indispensable office,—to teach elements. But they can only

(40)   highly serve us when they aim not to drill, but to create; when
they gather from far every ray of various genius to their hospi-
table halls, and by the concentrated fires, set the hearts of their
youth on flame.

1. By "one nature wrote and the same reads" (lines 2–3), Emerson
   means that
   (A) the author is rereading his own work.
   (B) nature writing is read by the same people.
   (C) author and reader live in the same era.
   (D) author and reader are in accord.
   (E) the reader does not remember his own writing.

2. The word "abstraction" (line 6) is used to mean
   (A) conception.
   (B) notion.
   (C) preoccupation.
   (D) elimination.
   (E) inattention.

3. Emerson uses the image of insects (lines 14–15) to parallel his
   discussion of
   (A) past writers storing knowledge for future readers.
   (B) authors working in grubby surroundings.
   (C) soulless parents toiling blindly for unknowing children.
   (D) the act of creating art.
   (E) the food chain.

4. A good title for paragraph 2 might be
   (A) "Creative Writing."
   (B) "Creative Reading."
   (C) "Rating Books."
   (D) "The Wealth of the Indies."
   (E) "Visions of the Past."

5. The proverb Emerson cites (lines 24–25) is used to support his
   theory that
   (A) one must apply knowledge to extract knowledge.
   (B) the rich need more education than the poor.
   (C) all the wealth in the world will not make a man a genius.
   (D) the wealth of the present is found in the past.
   (E) only a writer can be a good reader.

6. The word "braced" (line 26) is used to mean
   - (A)   upset.
   - (B)   beamed.
   - (C)   paired.
   - (D)   clamped.
   - (E)   bolstered.

7. By "manifold allusion" (line 28), Emerson means
   - (A)   diverse references.
   - (B)   numerous mentions.
   - (C)   mechanical fantasies.
   - (D)   multiple delusions.
   - (E)   many-sided remarks.

8. The word "oracle" (line 34) means
   - (A)   wonder.
   - (B)   seer.
   - (C)   composer.
   - (D)   naturalist.
   - (E)   reader.

9. The word "office" (line 39) is used to mean
   - (A)   site.
   - (B)   employment.
   - (C)   department.
   - (D)   duty.
   - (E)   study.

10. Emerson calls for an educational system that
   - (A)   includes works of the masters.
   - (B)   teaches students to write brilliantly.
   - (C)   inspires creativity in scholars.
   - (D)   Both A and B
   - (E)   Both B and C

ANSWER KEY AND EXPLANATIONS

LEVEL A

Exercise 1

1. C	3. D	5. B	7. B
2. A	4. E	6. E	8. C

1. **The correct answer is (C).** This passage is quite literal. Lincoln has crossed Washington, which lay between his starting point and his destination.

2. **The correct answer is (A).** Lincoln has come to "judge for his own wise and noble self" (line 6), for which the author is thankful.

3. **The correct answer is (D).** Any of these choices could be a synonym for glass, but only one fits the context.

4. **The correct answer is (E).** Again, the line is quite literal. McClellan is arriving by hot-air balloon.

5. **The correct answer is (B).** The author specifically explains this in lines 25–26.

6. **The correct answer is (E).** Plugging the choices into the context of the sentence proves that only (E) is an exact translation.

7. **The correct answer is (B).** The context gives this away, even if you have never seen the word before.

8. **The correct answer is (C).** The last sentence of the excerpt contrasts these strangely peaceful cannon salutes to the terrible sounds "to which we are accustomed."

Exercise 2

1. C	3. E	5. B	7. A
2. E	4. C	6. E	8. C

1. **The correct answer is (C).** Bulfinch assigns Orion two potential powers—wading through the depths and walking on the water. He appears to prefer the former, but acknowledges that some say the latter—presumably other translators.

2. **The correct answer is (E).** *Booty,* or loot, makes sense in context.

3. **The correct answer is (E).** "Chid" is an archaic word, but none of the other choices expresses the annoyance that Diana's brother apparently feels.

4. **The correct answer is (C).** If you do not understand this, you might be guilty of making the same mistake Diana made.

5. **The correct answer is (B).** To "discharge a shaft" is to shoot an arrow.

6. **The correct answer is (E).** Each choice is either a synonym for train or something of which a train might be a part, but only *entourage* names something of which the sisters could logically be a constituent.

7. **The correct answer is (A).** The first three paragraphs deal with the life of Orion and his death and resurrection in constellation form. The last tells about the formation of the Pleiads.

8. **The correct answer is (C).** Most myths explain natural phenomena, and this one is no exception. It does not teach a lesson, (A), and it mentions only a few Greek gods, (B).

Exercise 3

1. A	3. C	5. A	7. B	9. D
2. D	4. D	6. D	8. E	10. C

1. **The correct answer is (A).** He does not say exactly this, but he does say it is peculiar (line 1), an exact synonym.

2. **The correct answer is (D).** The patients do not seem to exhibit the outright rudeness implied by (C) or (E); they are simply ornery. (D) comes closest to this shade of meaning.

3. **The correct answer is (C).** Only (C) works in context.

4. **The correct answer is (D).** Be sure to read all the choices. The patients certainly behave in a way contrary to a doctor's expectations, (A), but they also get worse just when they seem to be getting better, (B). The answer, therefore, is (D).

5. **The correct answer is (A).** The illness is getting worse; it is intensifying.

6. **The correct answer is (D).** Rereading the entire sentence reveals the antecedent for its approach: "recovery."

7. **The correct answer is (B).** If (A) were true, the syndrome would not be "peculiar." Freud may believe (C), but he never says so. (B) is supported by lines 28–31.

8. **The correct answer is (E).** The patient's sense of guilt tells him nothing; it is silent, or dumb.

9. **The correct answer is (D).** Beware of choices that are not entirely correct. Freud may believe that patients are in love with their ill-nesses, (A), but that does not mean they should skip analysis. Only (D) is supported by the text.

10. **The correct answer is (C).** Look for the best and most specific title. (A) is too broad, as are (B) and (D). (E) is too narrow.

Exercise 4

| 1. A | 3. E | 5. D | 7. D | 9. C |
| 2. C | 4. B | 6. B | 8. B | 10. B |

1. **The correct answer is (A).** The words appear in a list of children's tasks, and they clearly describe the harm those tasks do.

2. **The correct answer is (C).** Rereading the quotation itself proves that the topic is the length of time growing minds should spend on a task.

3. **The correct answer is (E).** This is an unusual word used unusually. If (A) or (B) were true, the children would not be "hardened." Choices (C) and (D) make little sense. Children might be "hardened" by "unwholesome conditions."

4. **The correct answer is (B).** Do not read more into this than is there. Markham merely speaks of a simple shift in "shackles" or servitude, not an improvement in status.

5. **The correct answer is (D).** Maw means "jaws," particularly of a meat-eating animal. Even if you do not know this, the underlying monster theme in the passage gives you a clue.

6. **The correct answer is (B).** The Bastille is a French prison. Using the context of the sentence, you can determine that children "hobbling in lock-step" are likely to be headed for prison.

7. **The correct answer is (D).** Both of these metaphors exist throughout the passage.

8. **The correct answer is (B).** Having compared the children to human prisoners, Markham now compares them to animals "penned in narrow little lanes."

9. **The correct answer is (C).** Nothing in the passage leads you to believe (B) or (D), and there is no evidence to support (E). Choice (A) may be true in a way, but (C) is the better answer.

10. **The correct answer is (B).** Drudgery is Markham's focus. Realizing that helps you understand the use of this repetition to parallel the repetition of the children's dreary days.

Exercise 5

| 1. D | 3. A | 5. A | 7. A | 9. D |
| 2. D | 4. B | 6. E | 8. B | 10. C |

1. **The correct answer is (D).** Emerson is marveling at the writer's and reader's sympathetic natures—they might be the same person (but they clearly are not).

2. **The correct answer is (D).** Of the many synonyms for abstraction, only the meaning that relates to removal works here.

3. **The correct answer is (A).** Rereading the passage makes the connection clear: Just as insects store food for young they may never see, so do writers store knowledge for readers they may never know.

4. **The correct answer is (B).** Most of the paragraph deals with the work involved in being a creative reader.

5. **The correct answer is (A).** Emerson believes that reading requires a certain amount of application if it is to be fruitful. In other words, one must bring something to a reading passage in order to extract something from it.

6. **The correct answer is (E).** The meaning that parallels "supported" is the best choice here.

7. **The correct answer is (A).** This is a tricky passage and may require the rereading of the entire paragraph. Emerson says that creative reading allows a reader to bring to a passage all the references of his or her own background knowledge.

8. **The correct answer is (B).** If you have any doubt, the use of the word *seer* in line 30 should clarify your thinking.

9. **The correct answer is (D).** Even if you do not know this connotation for *office,* you should be able to tell that no other choice makes sense.

10. **The correct answer is (C).** He may well believe (A) and (B), but
    only (C) is supported by the text (in lines 38–43).

EXERCISES: LEVEL B PASSAGE-BASED READING

Each passage below is followed by a series of questions that require you to analyze, interpret, or evaluate the written work. Answer these questions on the basis of what each passage states or implies. Mark the letter that appears before your answer.

EXERCISE 1

Jean Toomer was one of the most interesting writers of the Harlem Renaissance of the 1920s. He wrote experimental plays, poetry, and the novel Cane, *from which this excerpt is taken.*

For a long while she was nothing more to me than one of those skirted beings whom boys at a certain age disdain to play with. Just how I came to love her, timidly, and with secret blushes, I do not know. But that I did was brought home to me one night, the

(5)   first night that Ned wore his long pants. Us fellers were seated on the curb before an apartment house where she had gone in. The young trees had not outgrown their boxes then. V Street was lined with them. When our legs grew cramped and stiff from the cold of the stone, we'd stand around a box and whittle it. I

(10)   like to think now that there was a hidden purpose in the way we hacked them with our knives. I like to feel that something deep in me responded to the trees, the young trees that whinnied like colts impatient to be let free… On the particular night I have in mind, we were waiting for the top-floor to go out. We wanted

(15)   to see Avey leave the flat. This night she stayed longer than usual and gave us a chance to complete our plans of how we were going to stone and beat that feller on the top floor out of town. Ned especially had it in for him. He was about to throw a brick up at the window when at last the room went dark. Some

(20)   minutes passed. Then Avey, as unconcerned as if she had been paying an old-maid aunt a visit, came out.… I just stood there like the others, and something like a fuse burned up inside of me. She never noticed us, but swung along lazy and easy as any-thing.… Some one said she'd marry that feller on the top floor.

(25)   Ned called that a lie because Avey was going to marry nobody but him. We had our doubts about that, but we did agree that she'd soon leave school and marry some one. The gang broke up, and I went home, picturing myself as married.

Nothing I did seemed able to change Avey's indifference

(30)   to me. I played basketball, and when I'd make a long clean shot

she'd clap with the others, louder than they, I thought. I'd meet
her on the street, and there'd be no difference in the way she
said hello. She never took the trouble to call me by my name....
It was on a summer excursion down to Riverview that she first
(35)   seemed to take me into account. The day had been spent riding
merry-go-rounds, scenic-railways, and shoot-the-chutes. We had
been in swimming, and we had danced. I was a crack swimmer
then. She didn't know how. I held her up and showed her how to
kick her legs and draw her arms. Of course she didn't learn in
(40)   one day, but she thanked me for bothering with her. I was also
somewhat of a dancer. And I had already noticed that love can
start on a dance floor. We danced. But though I held her tightly
in my arms, she was way away. That college feller who lived on
the top floor was somewhere making money for the next year.
(45)   I imagined that she was thinking, wishing for him. Ned was
along. He treated her until his money gave out. She went with
another feller. Ned got sore. One by one the boys' money gave
out. She left them. And they got sore. Every one of them but me
got sore....

1. The word "disdain" (line 2) means
   (A)   dislike.
   (B)   contend.
   (C)   regard.
   (D)   offend.
   (E)   unnerve.

2. "The first night that Ned wore his long pants" (lines 4–5) is used
   to reveal
   (A)   that the events took place long ago.
   (B)   that the boys involved were fairly young.
   (C)   that Ned was younger than the narrator.
   (D)   Both A and B
   (E)   Both B and C

3. The word "whittle" (line 9) means
   (A)   cut.
   (B)   signal.
   (C)   knock.
   (D)   dull.
   (E)   play.

4. Toomer's narrator compares himself to a tree in terms of his
   - (A) sturdiness.
   - (B) youth.
   - (C) desire to break free.
   - (D) Both A and B
   - (E) Both B and C

5. The word "flat" (line 15) is used to refer to a
   - (A) remark.
   - (B) soda.
   - (C) joke.
   - (D) lodging.
   - (E) tire.

6. By "take me into account" (line 35), the narrator means
   - (A) "employ me."
   - (B) "forgive me."
   - (C) "notice me."
   - (D) "interest me."
   - (E) "chastise me."

7. The word "sore" (line 47) is used to mean
   - (A) pained.
   - (B) angry.
   - (C) tender.
   - (D) bruised.
   - (E) wounded.

8. The passage tells a tale of
   - (A) wounded pride.
   - (B) envy and regret.
   - (C) unrequited love.
   - (D) sorrow and guilt.
   - (E) unfounded fears.

Exercise 2

Best known as the author of Robinson Crusoe, *Daniel Defoe was a prolific writer. His* Journal of the Plague Year, *published in 1722, is the convincing "journal" of a man identified only as "H.F." It tells of a real plague that decimated the Continent the year Defoe was five.*

It was now the beginning of August, and the plague grew very violent and terrible in the place where I lived, and Dr. Heath coming to visit me, and finding that I ventured so often out in the streets, earnestly persuaded me to lock myself up, and my
(5)   family, and not to suffer any of us to go out of doors; to keep all our windows fast, shutters and curtains close, and never to open them; but first, to make a very strong smoke in the room where the window or door was to be opened, with rosin and pitch, brimstone or gunpowder, and the like; and we did this for
(10)   some time; but as I had not laid in a store of provision for such a retreat, it was impossible that we could keep within doors entirely. However, I attempted, though it was so very late, to do something towards it; and first, as I had convenience both for brewing and baking, I went and bought two sacks of meal, and
(15)   for several weeks, having an oven, we baked all our own bread; also I bought malt, and brewed as much beer as all the casks I had would hold, and which seemed enough to serve my house for five or six weeks; also I laid in a quantity of salt butter and Cheshire cheese; but I had no flesh meat, and the plague raged
(20)   so violently among the butchers and slaughterhouses on the other side of our street, where they are known to dwell in great numbers, that it was not advisable so much as to go over the street among them.

And here I must observe again that this necessity of going
(25)   out of our houses to buy provisions was in a great measure the ruin of the whole City, for the people caught the distemper on these occasions one of another, and even the provisions themselves were often tainted; at least I have great reason to believe so; and therefore I cannot say with satisfaction what I know is
(30)   repeated with great assurance, that the market people and such as brought provisions to town were never infected. I am certain the butchers of Whitechapel, where the greatest part of the flesh meat was killed, were dreadfully visited, and that at last to such a degree that few of their shops were kept open, and those that
(35)   remained of them killed their meat at Mile End and that way, and brought it to market upon horses.

However, the poor people could not lay up provisions, and there was a necessity that they must go to market to buy, and others to send servants or their children; and as this was a

(40)   necessity which renewed itself daily, it brought abundance of
unsound people to the markets, and a great many that went
thither sound brought death home with them.

It is true people used all possible precaution; when anyone
bought a joint of meat in the market they would not take it off

(45)   the butcher's hand, but took it off the hooks themselves. On the
other hand, the butcher would not touch the money, but have it
put into a pot full of vinegar, which he kept for that purpose. The
buyer carried always small money to make up any odd sum, that
they might take no change. They carried bottles of scents and

(50)   perfumes in their hands, and all the means that could be used
were used, but then the poor could not do even these things; and
they went at all hazards.

1. When the doctor says "not to suffer any of us to go out of doors"
   (line 5), he means
   (A) going outdoors will cause suffering.
   (B) the narrator should not allow his family to go out.
   (C) they should go outdoors to avoid the suffering inside.
   (D) going outdoors will prevent suffering.
   (E) the narrator should not prevent his family from going out.

2. The word "fast" (line 6) is used to mean
   (A) fleet.
   (B) steadfast.
   (C) swift.
   (D) fastened.
   (E) permanent.

3. By "laid in a store of provision" (line 10), the narrator refers to
   (A) putting up a supply of food.
   (B) telling a story of salvation.
   (C) preserving the past.
   (D) lying in a bed of flour sacks.
   (E) sleeping in his place of business.

4. The word "retreat" (line 11) is used to mean
   (A) departure.
   (B) evacuation.
   (C) flight.
   (D) escape.
   (E) refuge.

5. The "distemper" (line 26) refers to
   (A) the plague.
   (B) bad feelings.
   (C) anger.
   (D) fear.
   (E) a disease common to dogs.

6. How does the narrator feel about the meat available in the city?
   (A) Only flesh meat is available.
   (B) It comes from within the city.
   (C) It is inedible.
   (D) It seems it is never infected.
   (E) It is tainted.

7. The word "sound" (line 42) is used to mean
   (A) severe.
   (B) solid.
   (C) clamorous.
   (D) drifting.
   (E) healthy.

8. The last paragraph mainly discusses
   (A) the inability of the poor to protect themselves.
   (B) the effects of the plague on business.
   (C) symptoms of the plague.
   (D) safeguards against getting the plague.
   (E) doctors' advice and warnings.

9. In general, the narrator believes that the plague was worsened by the people's need to
   (A) socialize.
   (B) self-medicate.
   (C) shop.
   (D) travel abroad.
   (E) fight.

10. The narrator implies that the people worst hit were
    (A) city-dwellers.
    (B) doctors.
    (C) children.
    (D) servants.
    (E) the poor.

EXERCISE 3

*Sarah Orne Jewett was born in Maine in 1849. At the age of twenty,
she published her first story, and she went on to write stories and
novels about the Mainers she knew. This excerpt is from* The Hiltons'
Holiday, *first published in 1896.*

An hour later the best wagon was ready, and the great expedition set forth. The little dog sat apart, and barked as if it fell
entirely upon him to voice the general excitement. Both seats
were in the wagon, but the empty place testified to Mrs. Hilton's

(5) unyielding disposition. She had wondered why one broad seat
would not do, but John Hilton meekly suggested that the wagon
looked better with both. The little girls sat on the back seat
dressed alike in their Sunday hats of straw with blue ribbons,
and their little plaid shawls pinned neatly about their small

(10) shoulders. They wore gray thread gloves, and sat very straight.
Susan Ellen was half a head the taller, but otherwise, from
behind, they looked much alike. As for their father, he was in
his Sunday best—a plain black coat, and a winter hat of felt,
which was heavy and rusty-looking for that warm early summer

(15) day. He had it in mind to buy a new straw hat at Topham, so
that this with the turnip seed and the hoe made three important
reasons for going.

"Remember an' lay off your shawls when you get there, an'
carry them over your arms," said the mother, clucking like an

(20) excited hen to her chickens. "They'll do to keep the dust off your
new dresses goin' an' comin'. An' when you eat your dinners
don't get spots on you, an' don't point at folks as you ride by, an'
stare, or they'll know you come from the country. An' John, you
call into Cousin Ad'line Marlow's an' see how they all be, an'

(25) tell her I expect her over certain to stop awhile before hayin'. It
always eases her phthisic to git up here on the highland, an' I've
got a new notion about doin' over her best-room carpet sense I
see her that'll save rippin' one breadth. An' don't come home all
wore out; an', John, don't you go an' buy me no kick-shaws to

(30) fetch home. I ain't a child, an' you ain't got no money to waste.
I expect you'll go, like's not, an' buy you some kind of a foolish
boy's hat; do look an' see if it's reasonable good straw, an' won't
splinter all off round the edge. An' you mind, John"—

"Yes, yes, hold on!" cried John impatiently; then he cast a

(35) last affectionate, reassuring look at her face, flushed with the
hurry and responsibility of starting them off in proper shape.
"I wish you was goin' too," he said, smiling. "I do so!" Then the
old horse started, and they went out at the bars, and began the

(40) careful long descent of the hill. The young dog, tethered to the
lilac bush, was frantic with piteous appeals; the little girls
piped their eager goodbys again and again, and their father
turned many times to look back and wave his hand. As for their
mother, she stood alone and watched them out of sight.

(45) There was one place far out on the high-road where she
could catch a last glimpse of the wagon, and she waited what
seemed a very long time until it appeared and then was lost
to sight again behind a low hill. "They're nothin' but a pack o'
child'n together," she said aloud; and then felt lonelier than she
expected. She even stooped and patted the unresigned little dog

(50) as she passed him, going into the house.

1. The words "great expedition" (lines 1–2) are used by the author
   (A) literally.
   (B) ironically.
   (C) snidely.
   (D) cruelly.
   (E) matter-of-factly.

2. The word "voice" (line 3) is used to mean
   (A) sing.
   (B) vote.
   (C) desire.
   (D) call.
   (E) express.

3. The author's description of John's apparel
   (A) reveals his relative poverty.
   (B) shows his stylishness.
   (C) explains his behavior.
   (D) contrasts his appearance with his character.
   (E) is mean-spirited.

4. The mother is compared to a hen in terms of her
   (A) brooding nature.
   (B) coloration.
   (C) eating habits.
   (D) lazy, good temper.
   (E) concern over her children.

5. The mother is worried that her children might
   (A) misbehave in their cousin's home.
   (B) eat more than they should.
   (C) be considered unsophisticated.
   (D) Both A and B
   (E) Both B and C

6. The word "kick-shaws" (line 29) apparently refers to
   - (A) money.
   - (B) something to eat.
   - (C) a kind of hat.
   - (D) odds and ends.
   - (E) parasols.

7. The author's feeling toward her characters can be summed up as
   - (A) unyielding.
   - (B) affectionate.
   - (C) uncaring.
   - (D) troubled.
   - (E) mystified.

8. The tone of the final paragraph emphasizes
   - (A) gratitude.
   - (B) remorse.
   - (C) dreariness.
   - (D) impulsiveness.
   - (E) isolation.

Exercise 4

Patrice Lumumba (1925–1961) was president of the Congolese National Movement and the first Prime Minister of the Congo after it achieved independence from Belgium. Amidst the unrest that followed independence, he was deposed and assassinated. This speech was given by Lumumba in 1959 to an audience in Brussels, Belgium.

We have capable men who are just waiting for a chance to get to work. I visited Guinea recently: there are eleven ministers in the government, and seven state secretaries who have min-isterial status. Only three of these eighteen ministers have

(5) studied at a university; the others have finished high school, held jobs, and acquired a certain amount of experience, and the government of Guinea has brought in French technicians to help it in the field of law, economics, agronomy, and every other area of activity. So I think it is possible today to set up a

(10) Congolese government.

We have chosen January 1961 as our deadline. We thus have two years in which to prepare ourselves, and we are convinced that two years from now we will be in a position to take over the responsibilities of running our country, with

(15) the Belgians working side by side with us to help us and guide our footsteps. If Belgium understands us, if Belgium takes this fervent desire—the desire of the Congolese people—into consid-eration, she will be entitled to our friendship. The people will see for themselves that when the proper moment came and we

(20) decided we were capable of self-rule, the Belgians did not stand in our way. On the contrary: they will have helped and guided us. The question of future relations between Belgium and the Congo will resolve itself automatically. There will be no difficulty whatsoever. We are the ones to say: look, we still need Belgium

(25) in this field of endeavor, we still need European technicians. But if the Belgian people, the Belgian government, refuse to take our demands into consideration, what will happen as a result? The government perpetuates bitterness and fosters a climate of continual discontent, and whatever the Belgians may say,

(30) whatever their wishes in the matter may be, we are going to gain our independence, come what may. In the end the Congolese people are liable to say: "Belgium has always been opposed to our emancipation. We've had enough of that now; we're going our own separate way…." And that is precisely the problem.

(35) Everyone—the financiers, the colonialists—keeps asking for guarantees. But such guarantees depend entirely on them, because winning our independence does not mean that we are

(40) going to seize property belonging to Belgians; we are not thieves, we respect other people's property. It is a matter of a gentleman's agreement with the status of an international right; when any citizen finds himself in another country, his property and his person must be protected. This is the problem as we see it.

(45) So today we want our country to be independent. We want to run our country now so that we may draw up agreements between an independent Congo and an independent Belgium on an equal footing, and thus foster friendship between these two peoples. I am very happy to meet young Belgians here who share our ideas, progressive young Belgians who agree with us, who will help press for Congolese independence tomorrow and

(50) are joining forces with us. This is encouraging. It proves that they are dissatisfied, that they disapprove of the attitude of certain Belgians in the Congo today. I do not want to make any sort of sweeping general statement: there are Belgians in the Congo—certain civil servants, certain colonists, certain doctors,

(55) certain missionaries—who have always treated Africans in a dignified way. But they are no more than a minority. Why are the majority opposed? Belgians in the Congo believe that when the blacks get their independence tomorrow, they are going to seize everything Belgians own. This is still the usual reaction

(60) among typical Europeans, even after the new policy, even after the declaration on January 13. They keep saying, "These are the blacks who are going to take our places tomorrow, and where will that put *us?* Where will we go?"

1. Lumumba brings in the example of Guinea to demonstrate that
   (A) colonial power can hold a country together.
   (B) those who would govern need a background in law.
   (C) liberation from the French is possible.
   (D) ministers need not be educated.
   (E) an independent African government can exist.

2. The word "fervent" (line 17) means
   (A) impassioned.
   (B) maniacal.
   (C) hotheaded.
   (D) dispassionate.
   (E) torpid.

3. How does Lumumba feel about friendship with Belgium?
   (A) It is unlikely to come about for many years.
   (B) It is possible if Belgium helps the Congo.
   (C) It is not possible if Belgium opposes the Congolese.
   (D) Both A and B
   (E) Both B and C

4. Paragraph 2 moves back and forth between
   (A) humor and bitterness.
   (B) pleasantries and deference.
   (C) warnings and recommendations.
   (D) raillery and lightheartedness.
   (E) profanity and charity.

5. The words "gentleman's agreement" (lines 39–40) refer to
   (A) a deal without benefit for either side.
   (B) a bargain sealed in blood.
   (C) a written contract.
   (D) an unspoken understanding.
   (E) an oath of allegiance.

6. Paragraph 3 is primarily
   (A) about young Belgians.
   (B) used to contrast with paragraph 2.
   (C) a specious argument.
   (D) an analysis of Belgian resistance.
   (E) a summation of Lumumba's main points.

7. The word "press" (line 49) is used to mean
   (A) publish.
   (B) constrict.
   (C) push.
   (D) crush.
   (E) iron.

8. According to Lumumba, why are Belgians afraid?
   (A) They are racist.
   (B) They think a Congolese government will imprison them.
   (C) They think the Congolese will take what they have.
   (D) Both A and B
   (E) Both B and C

EXERCISE 5

In 1865, the naturalist Louis Agassiz, accompanied by his wife and a
party of scientists and volunteers, embarked on a journey to Brazil to
record information about fish and other wildlife in the rivers of that
nation. Aboard ship, Agassiz talked to his assistants about the proper
study of nature. As usual, his discussion was recorded by his wife.

When less was known of animals and plants the discovery of
new species was the great object. This has been carried too
far, and is now almost the lowest kind of scientific work. The
discovery of a new species as such does not change a feature in
(5)   the science of natural history, any more than the discovery of a
new asteroid changes the character of the problems to be investigated by astronomers. It is merely adding to the enumeration of
objects.

     We should look rather for the fundamental relations among
(10) animals; the number of species we may find is of importance
only so far as they explain the distribution and limitation of
different genera and families, their relations to each other and
to the physical conditions under which they live. Out of such
investigations there looms up a deeper question for scientific
(15) men, the solution of which is to be the most important result of
their work in coming generations. The origin of life is the great
question of the day. How did the organic world come to be as
it is? It must be our aim to throw some light on this subject by
our present journey. How did Brazil come to be inhabited by the
(20) animals and plants now living there? Who were its inhabitants
in past times? What reason is there to believe that the present
condition of things in this country is in any sense derived from
the past? The first step in this investigation must be to ascertain
the geographical distribution of the present animals and plants.
(25) Suppose we first examine the Rio San Francisco. The basin
of this river is entirely isolated. Are its inhabitants, like its
waters, completely distinct from those of other basins? Are its
species peculiar to itself, and not repeated in any other river
of the continent? Extraordinary as this result would seem, I
(30) nevertheless expect to find it so. The next water-basin we shall
have to examine will be that of the Amazons, which connects
through the Rio Negro with the Orinoco. It has been frequently
repeated that the same species of fish exist in the waters of the
San Francisco and in those of Guiana and of the Amazons. At
(35) all events, our works on fishes constantly indicate Brazil and
Guiana as the common home of many species; but this observation has never been made with sufficient accuracy to merit

(40) confidence. Fifty years ago the exact locality from which any animal came seemed an unimportant fact in its scientific history, for the bearing of this question on that of origin was not then perceived. To say that any specimen came from South America was quite enough; to specify that it came from Brazil, from the Amazons, the San Francisco, or the La Plata, seemed a marvellous accuracy in the observers. In the museum at Paris,

(45) for instance, there are many specimens entered as coming from New York or from Pará; but all that is absolutely known about them is that they were shipped from those sea-ports. Nobody knows exactly where they were collected. So there are specimens entered as coming from the Rio San Francisco, but it is by no

(50) means sure that they came exclusively from that water-basin. All this kind of investigation is far too loose for our present object. Our work must be done with much more precision; it must tell something positive of the geographical distribution of animals in Brazil.

(55) Therefore, my young friends who come with me on this expedition, let us be careful that every specimen has a label, recording locality and date, so secured that it will reach Cambridge safely. It would be still better to attach two labels to each specimen, so that, if any mischance happens to one, our

(60) record may not be lost. We must try not to mix the fishes of different rivers, even though they flow into each other, but to keep our collections perfectly distinct. You will easily see the vast importance of thus ascertaining the limitation of species, and the bearing of the result on the great question of origin.

1. How does Agassiz feel about the discovery of new species?
   (A) It is taking place less and less.
   (B) All species have now been cataloged.
   (C) It cannot take the place of true science.
   (D) It is the great goal of science.
   (E) It is no longer particularly important.

2. Agassiz wants to focus upon
   (A) the enumeration of animals and plants.
   (B) the interrelationships of species.
   (C) a scientific study of man.
   (D) Both A and B
   (E) Both B and C

3. The word "genera" (line 12) refers to
   - (A) classifications.
   - (B) brain power.
   - (C) plants.
   - (D) habits.
   - (E) people.

4. Agassiz sees his future work as answering the question
   - (A) "Can we learn from history?"
   - (B) "Is there a God?"
   - (C) "How many species are there?"
   - (D) "Where did man come from?"
   - (E) "How did life originate?"

5. The word "distribution" (line 24) is used to mean
   - (A) shipping.
   - (B) dispersion.
   - (C) donation.
   - (D) offering.
   - (E) quality.

6. How might you paraphrase the sentence "Are its inhabitants … from those of other basins" (lines 26–27)?
   - (A) Do the animals here resemble the water?
   - (B) Do the inhabitants of this basin ever visit other basins?
   - (C) Can we distinguish the animals of these waters from each other?
   - (D) Since these waters differ from others, are the animals found here different as well?
   - (E) Can we tell the difference between this basin and another?

7. The word "common" (line 36) is used to mean
   - (A) familiar.
   - (B) collective.
   - (C) provincial.
   - (D) typical.
   - (E) unremarkable.

8. Agassiz uses the phrase "a marvellous accuracy" (lines 43–44) to
   - (A) show how unlikely it was for observers to be so specific.
   - (B) give his opinion about the current generation of scientists.
   - (C) make a heartfelt plea for understanding.
   - (D) Both A and B
   - (E) Both B and C

9. Agassiz urges his young colleagues to be
   (A) prudent.
   (B) daring.
   (C) meticulous.
   (D) curious.
   (E) adventurous.

10. By "perfectly distinct" (line 62) Agassiz means that the collections should be
    (A) wholly dissimilar.
    (B) flawlessly obvious.
    (C) completely lucid.
    (D) absolutely separate.
    (E) quite clear.

Answer Key and Explanations

LEVEL B

Exercise 1

1. A	3. A	5. D	7. B
2. D	4. E	6. C	8. C

1. **The correct answer is (A).** Only one choice really fits the context of the sentence.

2. **The correct answer is (D).** Wearing long pants is not a big deal today, but at the time Toomer describes, a young man's graduation to long pants was a rite of passage. Clearly, then, the events took place long ago, (A), and the boys were young, (B). There is no evidence to support (C).

3. **The correct answer is (A).** To *whittle* is to cut or carve. Rereading the paragraph clarifies what the boys are doing.

4. **The correct answer is (E).** He feels that "something deep in me responded to the trees, the young trees that whinnied like colts impatient to be let free..." (lines 11–13).

5. **The correct answer is (D).** *Flat* has many meanings, but only its relation to lodging makes sense in this context.

6. **The correct answer is (C).** You can choose the correct answer by plugging the choices into the sentence in question. The narrator is desperate for Avey to notice him.

7. **The correct answer is (B).** The boys might have felt wounded or pained, but more than this, they felt angry. Only the narrator did not, and he feels this proves his love.

8. **The correct answer is (C).** *Unrequited* means "unanswered." The narrator's love for Avey appears to be entirely one-sided.

Exercise 2

1. B	3. A	5. A	7. E	9. C
2. D	4. E	6. E	8. D	10. E

1. **The correct answer is (B).** To understand this archaic construction, it may be necessary to go back and reread the paragraph in which it is found. Clearly, the doctor does *not* want the narrator to go out, although he never threatens them as in (A).

2. **The correct answer is (D).** *Fast* is another multiple-meaning word. All of the choices are potential synonyms, but only one applies to windows.

3. **The correct answer is (A).** Again, it is easiest to decipher an archaic construction when you use the context surrounding it. The narrator is telling about his inability to keep indoors entirely due to his family's need for provisions.

4. **The correct answer is (E).** Remembering that the family was urged to remain indoors, try these synonyms in place of the specified word, and it becomes clear that the narrator refers to the refuge that is his house.

5. **The correct answer is (A).** Rereading the context reveals that *distemper* is just one of the narrator's euphemisms for the plague.

6. **The correct answer is (E).** Although other people repeat "with great assurance" that the provisions are not infected, the narrator has "great reason to believe" that they are (lines 28–29).

7. **The correct answer is (E).** The word *sound* is contrasted with *unsound;* the healthy people meet the unhealthy, plague-ridden people at the markets and come home sick.

8. **The correct answer is (D).** The first line of the last paragraph gives the paragraph's main idea; you need not read further. If you do, however, you will see that the narrator discusses several means of protecting oneself against disease. He mentions the poor only in the final sentence, so (A) cannot be considered the main point of discussion.

9. **The correct answer is (C).** This is really the main point of the passage—that despite people's desire to protect themselves, their need to buy food led them into danger.

10. **The correct answer is (E).** He talks about people who live in the city, (A), but the narrator never states that those people are worse off than those in the country. He does, however, in

paragraphs 3 and 4, mention the fact that poor people could not protect themselves from disease.

Exercise 3

1. B	3. A	5. C	7. B
2. E	4. E	6. D	8. E

1. **The correct answer is (B).** It is not a "great expedition"; it is only a small family going to market, but it is a big event for them. Jewett uses the words ironically; she means to point out the contradiction between the actual event and the excitement surrounding it.

2. **The correct answer is (E).** Substitute the choices into the sentence if you have any question. (D) is close, but (E) is better.

3. **The correct answer is (A).** John's "Sunday best" is unseasonal and plain, demonstrating that he is not a man of means.

4. **The correct answer is (E).** Find the point in the story where this comparison takes place (lines 19–20). At that point, the mother is clucking over her children.

5. **The correct answer is (C).** She never mentions (A) or (B) in her litany of advice, but the mother does tell her children not to point or stare at folks, "or they'll know you come from the country" (line 23) and may be considered unsophisticated.

6. **The correct answer is (D).** The word refers to something John might buy, but there is no evidence to support (B), (C), or (E).

7. **The correct answer is (B).** She understands them well, so (E) is incorrect. She seems sympathetic, so neither (A) nor (C) fits. The mood is fairly humorous and upbeat, so (D) is out. Generally, the author's attitude is affectionate; she laughs at the characters, but kindly.

8. **The correct answer is (E).** *Far out, very long time, lost to sight,* and *lonelier* are all clues to the emphasis on isolation.

Exercise 4

1. E	3. E	5. D	7. C
2. A	4. C	6. E	8. C

1. **The correct answer is (E).** Lumumba mentions (D), but that is certainly not his main point. The example of Guinea is a positive example of a liberated African country running its own affairs.

2. **The correct answer is (A).** Lumumba would never imply that his people were (B) or (C). Their desire is strong, it is *impassioned*.

3. **The correct answer is (E).** This is the main idea of paragraph 2. If Belgium understands the Congolese, "she will be entitled to our friendship" (line 18). If not, "the Congolese people are liable to say…'we're going our own separate way'" (lines 31–34). Both (B) and (C) are correct, so the answer must be (E).

4. **The correct answer is (C).** The threat is barely under the surface of paragraph 2. The Congo is "going to gain our independence, come what may" (lines 30–31). It will do this with or without Belgian support, but Lumumba makes clear the ways in which Belgian support would be the best solution.

5. **The correct answer is (D).** The "gentleman's agreement" to which Lumumba refers is the unspoken understanding that a citizen will be protected under the laws of whatever country he finds himself in.

6. **The correct answer is (E).** Paragraph 3 is brief and to the point. It is a synopsis of Lumumba's purpose in addressing the crowd.

7. **The correct answer is (C).** This multiple-meaning word has only one connotation that fits the sentence.

8. **The correct answer is (C).** There is no support for (A) or (B) in the text of this speech. Lumumba addresses the concerns of financiers and colonialists who fear losing their property in the takeover.

Exercise 5

| 1. E | 3. A | 5. B | 7. B | 9. C |
| 2. B | 4. E | 6. D | 8. A | 10. D |

1. **The correct answer is (E).** The discovery of species, Agassiz says, is "now almost the lowest kind of scientific work" (line 3). Other things are more important.

2. **The correct answer is (B).** He reveals his focus in the first line of paragraph 2—the number of species is not as important as the way in which species relate to one another.

3. **The correct answer is (A).** Reread the entire sentence to understand this unfamiliar word. Choices (C) and (E) cannot be correct; Agassiz is talking about animals.

4. **The correct answer is (E).** He calls the origin of life "the great question of the day" (lines 16–17). If that is not clue enough, Agassiz's list of questions that follow (lines 17–23) support this choice.

5. **The correct answer is (B).** Even if you do not know the word *dispersion,* the process of elimination should invalidate the remaining choices.

6. **The correct answer is (D).** Read all the choices before deciding. Only (D) corresponds to the whole meaning of the excerpted sentence.

7. **The correct answer is (B).** *Common* has many meanings. In this case, Agassiz means a home that species have in *common.*

8. **The correct answer is (A).** Agassiz is contrasting the haphazard accuracy of previous scientists with his desired accuracy. He notes that when some scientists *were* accurate, this was considered "marvellous" or remarkable.

9. **The correct answer is (C).** The only urging Agassiz gives his aides is to be accurate in recording their specimens. He wants precision, careful labeling, and meticulous recordkeeping.

10. **The correct answer is (D).** Reread the sentence if you have a question here. Agassiz wants the fishes of different rivers kept "perfectly distinct"—absolutely separate.

EXERCISES: LEVEL C PASSAGE-BASED READING

Directions: Each pair of passages below is followed by a series of questions that require you to analyze, interpret, evaluate, compare, and contrast the written works. Answer these questions on the basis of what each passage states or implies. Mark the letter that appears before your answer.

EXERCISE 1

The emancipation of African-Americans and the emancipation of women were two entwined issues of the mid-nineteenth century. These excerpts from an autobiographical letter by a former slave and from a speech by a leader in the fight for women's rights show that they shared a common foe.

Passage A—James L. Bradley, former slave (1835)

I will begin as far back as I can remember. I think I was between two and three years old when the soul-destroyers tore me from my mother's arms, somewhere in Africa, far back from the sea. They carried me a long distance to a ship;
(5) all the way I looked back, and cried. The ship was full of men and women loaded with chains; but I was so small, they let me run about on deck.

After many long days, they brought us into Charleston, South Carolina. A slaveholder bought me, and took me up into
(10) Pendleton County. I suppose that I staid with him about six months. He sold me to a Mr. Bradley, by whose name I have ever since been called. This man was considered a wonderfully kind master; and it is true that I was treated better than most of the slaves I knew. I never suffered for food, and never was
(15) flogged with the whip; but oh, my soul! I was tormented with kicks and knocks more than I can tell. My master often knocked me down, when I was young. Once, when I was a boy, about nine years old, he struck me so hard that I fell down and lost my senses. I remained thus some time, and when I came to myself,
(20) he told me he thought he had killed me. At another time, he struck me with a currycomb, and sunk the knob into my head....

I used to work very hard. I was always obliged to be in the field by sunrise, and I labored till dark, stopping only at noon long enough to eat dinner. When I was about fifteen years old,
(25) I took what was called the cold plague, in consequence of being over-worked, and I was sick a long time. My master came to me

one day, and hearing me groan with pain, he said, "This fellow will never be of any more use to me—I would as soon knock him in the head, as if he were an opossum." … My master had kept
(30)   me ignorant of everything he could. I was never told anything about God, or my own soul. Yet from the time I was fourteen years old, I used to think a great deal about freedom. It was my heart's desire; I could not keep it out of my mind. Many a sleepless night I have spent in tears, because I was a slave. I
(35)   looked back on all I had suffered—and when I looked ahead, all was dark and hopeless bondage. My heart ached to feel within me the life of liberty.

Passage B—Elizabeth Cady Stanton, from *Address to the Legislature of New York on Women's Rights* (1854)

Look at the position of woman as mother. There is no human love so strong and steadfast as that of the mother for her child;
(40)   yet behold how ruthless are your laws touching this most sacred relation. Nature has clearly made the mother the guardian of the child; but man, in his inordinate love of power, does continually set nature and nature's laws at open defiance. The father may apprentice his child, bind him out to a trade, without the
(45)   mother's consent—yea, in direct opposition to her most earnest entreaties, prayers and tears.…

Again, as the condition of the child always follows that of the mother, and as by the sanction of your laws the father may beat the mother, so may he the child. What mother can not bear me
(50)   witness to untold sufferings which cruel, vindictive fathers have visited upon their helpless children? Who ever saw a human being that would not abuse unlimited power? Base and ignoble must that man be who, let the provocation be what it may, would strike a woman; but he who would lacerate a trembling
(55)   child is unworthy the name of man. A mother's love can be no protection to a child; she can not appeal to you to save it from a father's cruelty, for the laws take no cognizance of the mother's most grievous wrongs. Neither at home nor abroad can a mother protect her son. Look at the temptations that surround the paths
(60)   of our youth at every step; look at the gambling and drinking saloons, the clubrooms, the dens of infamy and abomination that infest all our villages and cities—slowly but surely sapping the very foundations of all virtue and strength.

By your laws, all these abominable resorts are permitted.
(65)   It is folly to talk of a mother moulding the character of her son, when all mankind, backed up by law and public sentiment,

conspire to destroy her influence. But when women's moral power shall speak through the ballot-box, then shall her influence be seen and felt....

1. By "soul-destroyers" (Passage A, line 2), Bradley apparently refers to
   (A) religious zealots.
   (B) white women.
   (C) slaves.
   (D) Africans.
   (E) slave traders.

2. How does Bradley feel about his master, Mr. Bradley?
   (A) He was a wonderfully kind master.
   (B) He treated Bradley well.
   (C) He was not as kind as people thought.
   (D) He was no better than a slave.
   (E) He got along with him well.

3. Why did Bradley's "heart ache" (Passage A, line 36)?
   (A) He was homesick.
   (B) He wanted a friend.
   (C) He was dreadfully ill.
   (D) He was treated badly.
   (E) He longed for freedom.

4. In Passage B, what does "steadfast" mean (line 39)?
   (A) Rapid
   (B) True
   (C) Habitual
   (D) Frequent
   (E) Vacillating

5. The word "sanction" (Passage B, line 48) means
   (A) permission.
   (B) devoutness.
   (C) lucidity.
   (D) rank.
   (E) eloquence.

6. Stanton uses the word "infest" (Passage B, line 62) to imply that
   (A) our country is overrun with domineering men.
   (B) power is slowly changing hands.
   (C) drinking causes disease.
   (D) immorality is a kind of creeping plague.
   (E) the atmosphere of cities is festive.

7. Bradley would probably agree with Stanton that
   - (A) a man who strikes a child is unworthy.
   - (B) gambling and drinking sap one's strength.
   - (C) moral power can speak through the ballot-box.
   - (D) Both A and B
   - (E) Both B and C

8. Stanton's main point is that
   - (A) laws pit mother against child.
   - (B) sons will always follow their fathers' paths.
   - (C) laws remove a mother's right to protect her child.
   - (D) a mother's influence on her sons is unimportant.
   - (E) few can argue with laws that protect children.

9. A quotation from Passage B that might apply to Passage A is
   - (A) "Who ever saw a human being that would not abuse unlimited power?"
   - (B) "Neither at home nor abroad can a mother protect her son."
   - (C) "Look at the temptations that surround the paths of our youth at every step…."
   - (D) Both A and B
   - (E) Both B and C

10. As Bradley's master kept him ignorant of God, so
    - (A) might a father apprentice his child to a master.
    - (B) does a mother remain ignorant of her child's welfare.
    - (C) does a mother bear witness to sufferings of her child.
    - (D) can parents keep their children home from school.
    - (E) can a father keep his son ignorant of morality.

Exercise 2

All cultures teach an element of respect for the elderly and sick, and nearly all cultures present moralistic tales to stress this lesson. Here are two very different tales, one from the Indians of the Northeast and one from the Hispanic Southwest.

Passage A—*An Unwelcome Visitor,* a legend of the Iroquois

When the frosts were unlocked from the hillsides there came into one of the villages of the red men a mild and quiet old man whom none of them had ever seen before. He stood beside the field where the young men played at their games, and when
(5)   some of the fathers approached to bid him welcome to their village and wigwams they saw that his body was covered with sores, and they made excuses to turn aside that they might not meet him. When none went to him and called him brother, he turned to the village and walked slowly from door to door of the
(10)   wigwams. The women saw him and as he approached their doors they covered their children's faces that they might not see his features, and wished in their hearts that he would not enter. When the little man read their thoughts, with saddened eyes and heavy steps he would turn away and seek another habi-
(15)   tation, where he would again see that he was not welcome and turn his weary footsteps from the door. When he had visited all the wigwams in the village without finding a welcome in any, he went suddenly to the forest and they saw him no more....

Finally there remained but two more villages to visit and he
(20)   feared that he should find none who would bid him enter their homes that they might minister to his wants. At last, however, as he approached a humble cabin his eyes brightened, for he read in the heart of the woman who saw him coming that she had taken pity on his forlorn condition and that her hospitality
(25)   would overcome the dread his appearance caused. Said the woman: "Thou art welcome, my brother, for thou art a stranger."

Then said the strange man: ... "Listen, my sister: Thou of all thy race hast had in thy heart pity and love for a suffering and friendless creature that have led thee to give him shelter in thy
(30)   house. Know then, my sister, that thy name shall henceforth be great. Many wonders shall be taught thee, and thy sons will be made chiefs and thy daughters princesses. I am Quarara, and bear messages from the Great Spirit." Then Quarara described to the woman a plant which she went forth into the forest
(35)   and procured. She returned to the hut and prepared it as he

bade her, and when it was administered to him he recovered from his sickness and the sores left him. Quarara remained at the woman's wigwam many moons and brought upon himself all manner of fevers, plagues and diseases, and for each one

(40)   he described the medicine root or herb that would perform its cure....

      Then said the strange man, Quarara, to her: "Thou, Oh! sister, knowest now what the Great Spirit would have thee teach his children freely. Thou hast been patient and kind

(45)   and thy heart is filled with gentleness. Thy family shall be called Sagawahs, the healers, and thou and thy family shall be remembered throughout all generations."

Passage B—*The Boy and His Grandfather,* a tale of the Southwest

      In the old days it was not unusual to find several generations living together in one home. Usually, everyone lived in peace

(50)   and harmony, but this situation caused problems for one man whose household included, besides his wife and small son, his elderly father.

      It so happened that the daughter-in-law took a dislike to the old man. He was always in the way, she said, and she insisted he

(55)   be removed to a small room apart from the house.

      Because the old man was out of sight, he was often neglected. Sometimes he even went hungry. They took poor care of him, and in winter the old man often suffered from the cold. One day the little grandson visited his grandfather.

(60)   "My little one," the grandfather said, "go and find a blanket and cover me. It is cold and I am freezing."

      The small boy ran to the barn to look for a blanket, and there he found a rug.

      "Father, please cut this rug in half," he asked his father.

(65)   "Why? What are you going to do with it?"

      "I'm going to take it to my grandfather because he is cold."

      "Well, take the entire rug," replied his father.

      "No," his son answered, "I cannot take it all. I want you to cut it in half so I can save the other half for you when you are as

(70)   old as my grandfather. Then I will have it for you so you will not be cold."

      His son's response was enough to make the man realize how poorly he had treated his own father. The man then brought his father back into his home and ordered that a warm room be pre-

(75)   pared. From that time on he took care of his father's needs and visited him frequently every day.

1. What is it that keeps the villagers from greeting the old man in Passage A?
   - (A) He is a stranger.
   - (B) He is old.
   - (C) He is covered with sores.
   - (D) They are unfriendly.
   - (E) They fear attack.

2. The word "minister" (Passage A, line 21) is used to mean
   - (A) mind.
   - (B) tend.
   - (C) assemble.
   - (D) preach.
   - (E) negotiate.

3. The word "great" (Passage A, line 31) is used to mean
   - (A) excellent.
   - (B) prodigious.
   - (C) weighty.
   - (D) exalted.
   - (E) spacious.

4. The word "procured" (Passage A, line 35) means
   - (A) obtained.
   - (B) captured.
   - (C) dried.
   - (D) restored.
   - (E) healed.

5. The words "many moons" (Passage A, line 38) refer to
   - (A) people's faces.
   - (B) the name of a place.
   - (C) a measure of size.
   - (D) a length of time.
   - (E) a strange natural occurrence.

6. The last paragraph of Passage A could be called a(n)
   - (A) repetition.
   - (B) fantasy.
   - (C) oath.
   - (D) summary.
   - (E) blessing.

7. Quarara turns the woman and her children into
   (A) toads.
   (B) chiefs.
   (C) a new race.
   (D) medicine men and women.
   (E) ministers.

8. By "several generations" (Passage B, line 48), the author means
   (A) many years.
   (B) separate lifetimes.
   (C) children, parents, and grandparents.
   (D) several breeding periods.
   (E) more than one beginning.

9. One difference between Passage A and Passage B is that
   (A) Passage A takes place in the past.
   (B) people in Passage B ignore an old man.
   (C) people in Passage A ignore an old man.
   (D) Passage A deals with illness as well as age.
   (E) Passage B has no moral.

10. The woman in Passage A and the man in Passage B learn that
    (A) illness is not a crime.
    (B) respecting one's elders can be beneficial.
    (C) children may understand more than adults.
    (D) Both A and B
    (E) Both B and C

ANSWER KEY AND EXPLANATIONS

LEVEL C

Exercise 1

1. E	3. E	5. A	7. A	9. D
2. C	4. B	6. D	8. C	10. E

1. **The correct answer is (E).** Whoever the "soul-destroyers" are, we know that they tore Bradley from his mother's arms and carried him to a ship. The best answer is (E).

2. **The correct answer is (C).** He was "considered" wonderfully kind, (A), and Bradley was treated "better than most," (B), but Bradley was also kicked and knocked about by his master.

3. **The correct answer is (E).** The last sentence makes this cause-and-effect evident.

4. **The correct answer is (B).** Stanton means that a mother's love for her child is the strongest and truest love there is.

5. **The correct answer is (A).** Do not confuse the root of this word with that of sanctity, (B). Plugging the choices into the sentence proves that only (A) fits.

6. **The correct answer is (D).** The word *infest* is deliberately chosen to remind us of disease and corruption. Although Stanton discusses drink, (C) is not supported by the text, so (D) must be the answer.

7. **The correct answer is (A).** Of (A), (B), and (C), only a man striking a child echoes Bradley's experience. Because he deplored his treatment at the hands of his master, he would probably agree with Stanton.

8. **The correct answer is (C).** She certainly does not believe (D) and seems to contradict (B). Neither (A) nor (E) is supported by the text, although Stanton might agree with them. Her main thesis is that a mother's desire and right to protect her child (especially from that child's father) are countermanded by the nation's laws.

9. **The correct answer is (D).** Be sure to read all the choices. Abuse of power, (A), is clearly a theme in both passages. Bradley saw that his own mother was unable to protect him, (B). Because (A) and (B) are correct, the answer is (D).

10. **The correct answer is (E).** Look for the phrase that produces a parallelism to arrive at the correct answer. Choices (A) and (C)

are true, according to Stanton, but they are not parallel. Choices (B) and (D) are unsupported by the text. Only (E) provides a supported parallelism.

Exercise 2

1. C	3. D	5. D	7. D	9. D
2. B	4. A	6. E	8. C	10. B

1. **The correct answer is (C).** In fact, the villagers go forth to greet the man, old and unknown as he is, until they see his sores.

2. **The correct answer is (B).** *Minister* has many meanings. Here it is used as a verb that means "tend."

3. **The correct answer is (D).** A name cannot be any of these choices except exalted, or glorified.

4. **The correct answer is (A).** If you do not know this word, try out the choices in context to find the correct answer. Choices (C), (D), and (E) are synonyms for *cured,* not *procured.*

5. **The correct answer is (D).** Again, context gives you the clue you need to determine the meaning of this possibly unfamiliar phrase.

6. **The correct answer is (E).** In the last paragraph, Quarara makes a prediction that is more of a benediction, or blessing. He tells the woman that her kindness has led to her family's being favored.

7. **The correct answer is (D).** The sons will be chiefs (line 32), but the family as a whole will be "healers," or medicine men and women (line 46).

8. **The correct answer is (C).** Only (C) makes sense in the context of many generations living under one roof.

9. **The correct answer is (D).** The question asks you to find a difference between the passages—something that is true for one but not for the other. On the contrary, (A), (B), and (C) are true for both, and (E) is true for neither—both take place in the past, feature people ignoring an old man, and teach a moral. Only the issue of illness is in Passage A but not in Passage B.

10. **The correct answer is (B).** Both the introduction to the passages and the passages themselves confirm this moral. In Passage A, the woman and her family are rewarded for her kindness. In Passage B, the man sees that his kindness now will be rewarded when he himself is old.

EXERCISES: LEVEL D PASSAGE-BASED READING

Directions: Each passage or pair of passages below is followed by a series of questions that require you to analyze, interpret, evaluate, compare, and contrast the written works. Answer these questions on the basis of what each passage states or implies. Mark the letter that appears before your answer.

EXERCISE 1

This passage is about Aaron Copland, one of the most celebrated American composers.

Copland's music of the late 1920s culminates in two key works, both uncompromising in their modernism: the *Symphonic Ode* of 1929 and the *Piano Variations* of 1930. The fate of these compositions contrasts sharply. While the *Piano*
(5) *Variations* is not often performed in concert, it is well known to pianists because, although it does contain virtuoso passages, even those of very modest ability can "play at" the work in private. It represents the twentieth-century continuation of the great tradition of keyboard variations—the tradition
(10) that produced such works as the Bach *Goldberg Variations*, and Beethoven's *Diabelli Variations*. Copland's *Symphonic Ode*, on the other hand, remains almost unknown: An intense symphonic movement, it was considered unperformable by the conductor Serge Koussevitzky, otherwise the most potent
(15) American champion of Copland's work during the first half of the century. Koussevitzky did perform a revised version in 1932; but even with a second, more extensive revision in 1955, the *Ode* is seldom played. It is Copland's single longest orchestral movement. Perhaps as a reaction to the performance problems
(20) of the *Symphonic Ode*, Copland's next two orchestral works deal in shorter units of time: the *Short Symphony* of 1933 requires fifteen minutes for three movements and the six *Statements* for orchestra of 1935 last only nineteen minutes. Yet, in fact, these works were more complex than the *Ode* ; in particular, the wiry,
(25) agile rhythms of the opening movement of the *Short Symphony* proved too much for both the conductors Serge Koussevitzky and Leopold Stokowski. In the end it was Carlos Chávez and the Orquesta Sinfónica de México who gave the *Short Symphony* its premiere.

(30)   It may have been partly Copland's friendship with Carlos Chávez that drew him to Mexico. Copland first visited Mexico in 1932 and returned frequently in later years. His initial delight in the country is related in his letter of January 13, 1933, to Mary Lescaze, in which he glowingly describes the Mexican

(35) people and the Mexican landscape. His interest in Mexico is also reflected in his music, including *El Salón México* (1936) and the *Three Latin American Sketches* (1972).

      Mexico was not Copland's only Latin American interest. A 1941 trip to Havana suggested his *Danzón Cubano*. By the early

(40) 1940s he was friends with South American composers such as Jacobo Ficher, and in 1947 he toured South America for the State Department. (Some of the folk music he heard in Rio de Janeiro on this trip appears in his later works.) Copland in fact envisioned "American music" as being music of the Americas

(45) as a whole. His own use of Mexican material in the mid-1930s helped make his style more accessible to listeners not willing to accept the challenges of modern symphonic music.

1. What is the author's tone toward Copland's music?
   - (A) Strident skepticism
   - (B) Clinical objectivity
   - (C) Respectful description
   - (D) Qualified enthusiasm
   - (E) Unqualified praise

2. The word "virtuoso" in line 6 could best be replaced with
   - (A) ostentatious.
   - (B) intricate.
   - (C) raucous.
   - (D) abstruse.
   - (E) publicized.

3. In the first paragraph, the author states that *Symphonic Ode* and *Piano Variations* had different fates in that
   - (A) one was largely ignored while the other was almost universally praised.
   - (B) one, a simpler piece, won popular acclaim, while the other, a more complex piece, won critical acclaim.
   - (C) one, a simpler piece, became widely known by pianists, but the other, a more complex piece, remained largely unknown.
   - (D) one, featuring Mexican influences, was popular in Latin America, and the other, a modernist piece, was popular in the United States.
   - (E) both were initially acclaimed but only one became part of Copland's corpus of beloved works.

4. Koussevitzky is mentioned as an example of a(n)
   - (A) American conductor who admired Copland's work, but nonetheless found some pieces too difficult to perform.
   - (B) friend of Copland's who agreed to perform his less popular works.
   - (C) European composer who took issue with the difficulty of Copland's early work.
   - (D) musician who appreciated Copland's work but was unable to play it.
   - (E) European conductor who performed Copland's work.

5. The author of the passage believes that Copland's works immediately subsequent to the *Symphonic Ode* were possibly written
   - (A) for Copland's new relationship with Carlos Chávez and the Orquesta Sinfónica de México.
   - (B) to be simpler than the *Symphonic Ode*, on account of its difficulty in being performed.
   - (C) to be shorter than the *Symphonic Ode*, because the *Ode* was not being performed.
   - (D) to demand even more of conductors and musicians attempting to play Copland's music.
   - (E) to reflect Copland's new interest in Latin America.

6. In the sentence beginning "Yet, in fact, these works..." in lines 23–27, the author suggests that
   - (A) parts of the *Short Symphony* simply weren't melodic enough to engage audiences.
   - (B) the *Statements* were too brief to warrant a formal performance.
   - (C) even those who admired Copland's work lost patience with the *Short Symphony* and *Statements*.
   - (D) the *Statements* and *Short Symphony* determined which performers were truly excellent and which were mediocre.
   - (E) the *Short Symphony* had melodies that were too quick to be played even by famous musicians.

7. The author suggests that Copland believed Latin American music
   - (A) was unfamiliar enough to a North American audience that he needed to introduce them to it.
   - (B) was different enough from North American music that incorporating aspects of it would make his music unique and exciting.
   - (C) influenced and was influenced by North American music.
   - (D) primarily originated in Mexico and Cuba.
   - (E) embodied the polar opposite of modernist aesthetics.

8. The sentence beginning "His own use of Mexican material..." in lines 45–47 suggests that the modernist music which also influenced Copland's compositions was
   (A)   superior in quality to his Latin American influences.
   (B)   dry and passionless.
   (C)   technically more challenging to perform.
   (D)   inaccessible but rewarding.
   (E)   outmoded by the 1930s.

EXERCISE 2

In many cultures, the wealthy hired servants or kept slaves to take care of their children. These two narratives, one the true story of an ex-slave and one a work of fiction by a Nobel Prize-winning Indian writer, tell of children's occasional inexplicable cruelty toward the class that raised them.

Passage A—from the Narrative of James Curry, former slave (1840)

My mother was a cook in the house for about twenty-two years. She cooked for from twenty-five to thirty-five, taking the family and the slaves together. The slaves ate in the kitchen. After my mistress's death, my mother was the only woman kept in the

(5) house. She took care of my master's children, some of whom were then quite small, and brought them up. One of the most trying scenes I ever passed through, when I would have laid down my life to protect her if I had dared, was this: after she had raised my master's children, one of his daughters, a young

(10) girl, came into the kitchen one day, and for some trifle about the dinner, she struck my mother, who pushed her away, and she fell on the floor. Her father was not at home. When he came, which was while the slaves were eating in the kitchen, she told him about it. He came down, called my mother out, and, with a

(15) hickory rod, he beat her fifteen or twenty strokes, and then called his daughter and told her to take her satisfaction of her, and she did beat her until she was satisfied. Oh! it was dreadful, to see the girl whom my poor mother had taken care of from her childhood, thus beating her, and I must stand there, and did not

(20) dare to crook my finger in her defence.

Passage B—from *My Lord, the Baby* by Rabindranath Tagore (1916)

Raicharan was twelve years old when he came as a servant to his master's house. He belonged to the same caste as his master, and was given his master's little son to nurse. As time went on the boy left Raicharan's arms to go to school. From school

(25) he went on to college, and after college he entered the judicial service. Always, until he married, Raicharan was his sole attendant.

But, when a mistress came into the house, Raicharan found

(30) two masters instead of one. All his former influence passed to the new mistress. This was compensated for by a fresh arrival.

Anukul had a son born to him, and Raicharan by his unsparing attentions soon got a complete hold over the child. He used to toss him up in his arms, call to him in absurd baby language, put his face close to the baby's and draw it away again with a
(35)   grin.

Presently the baby was able to crawl and cross the doorway. When Raicharan went to catch him, he would scream with mischievous laughter and make for safety. Raicharan was amazed at the profound skill and exact judgment the baby showed when
(40)   pursued. He would say to his mistress with a look of awe and mystery: "Your son will be a judge someday."

New wonders came in their turn. When the baby began to toddle, that was to Raicharan an epoch in human history. When he called his father Ba-ba and his mother Ma-ma and Raicharan
(45)   Chan-na, then Raicharan's ecstasy knew no bounds. He went out to tell the news to all the world....

One afternoon the rain cleared. It was cloudy, but cool and bright. Raicharan's little despot did not want to stay in on such a fine afternoon. His lordship climbed into the go-cart.
(50)   Raicharan, between the shafts, dragged him slowly along till he reached the rice-fields on the banks of the river. There was no one in the fields, and no boat on the stream. Across the water, on the farther side, the clouds were rifted in the west. The silent ceremonial of the setting sun was revealed in all its glowing
(55)   splendor. In the midst of that stillness the child, all of a sudden, pointed with his finger in front of him and cried: "Chan-na! Pitty fow."

Close by on a mud-flat stood a large *Kadamba* tree in full flower. My lord, the baby, looked at it with greedy eyes, and
(60)   Raicharan knew his meaning.... But Raicharan had no wish that evening to go splashing knee-deep through the mud to reach the flowers. So he quickly pointed his finger in the opposite direction, calling out: "Oh, look, baby, look! Look at the bird." And with all sorts of curious noises he pushed the go-cart rapidly
(65)   away from the tree. But a child, destined to be a judge, cannot be put off so easily.... The little Master's mind was made up, and Raicharan was at his wits' end. "Very well, baby," he said at last, "you sit still in the cart, and I'll go and get you the pretty flower. Only mind you don't go near the water."
(70)   As he said this, he made his legs bare to the knee, and waded through the oozing mud toward the tree.

1. The numbers "twenty-five to thirty-five" (Passage A, line 2) refer to
   - (A) the age Curry's mother was when she was a cook.
   - (B) the number of people Curry's mother cooked for.
   - (C) the years during which Curry's mother cooked.
   - (D) a system of measurement now obsolete.
   - (E) the number of consecutive hours Curry's mother worked without a break.

2. The word "trying" (Passage A, line 7) means
   - (A) daring.
   - (B) troublesome.
   - (C) secure.
   - (D) binding.
   - (E) elementary.

3. The word "trifle" (Passage A, line 10) means
   - (A) knickknack.
   - (B) jest.
   - (C) unimportant thing.
   - (D) trace.
   - (E) toy.

4. By "take her satisfaction of her" (Passage A, line 16), Curry means
   - (A) please her.
   - (B) punish her until contented.
   - (C) give her trinkets.
   - (D) show her the correct way.
   - (E) pacify her.

5. The best description of Curry's feelings at this scene might be that of
   - (A) apathy.
   - (B) helplessness.
   - (C) horror.
   - (D) Both A and B
   - (E) Both B and C

6. In Passage B, the word "caste" (line 22) means
   - (A) job.
   - (B) performance.
   - (C) company.
   - (D) post.
   - (E) class.

7. The tone of paragraph 4, Passage B, is
   - (A)   ironic.
   - (B)   dark.
   - (C)   foreshadowing.
   - (D)   Both A and B
   - (E)   Both B and C

8. The word "despot" (Passage B, line 48) means
   - (A)   terminal.
   - (B)   arsenal.
   - (C)   repository.
   - (D)   outrage.
   - (E)   slavedriver.

9. In paragraph 5, Passage B, it becomes clear that the author thinks the child is
   - (A)   tyrannical and spoiled.
   - (B)   sweet and innocent.
   - (C)   loud and witless.
   - (D)   loving but foolish.
   - (E)   amusingly gregarious.

10. The word "mind" (Passage B, line 69) is used to mean
    - (A)   consider.
    - (B)   reason.
    - (C)   take care.
    - (D)   follow.
    - (E)   sense.

11. Like Passage A, Passage B tells of
    - (A)   a cook who becomes a child's nurse.
    - (B)   a man living as a house servant.
    - (C)   the early life of a slave.
    - (D)   inhuman conditions under colonialism.
    - (E)   a child's cruelty to a caretaker.

12. Unlike the main character in Passage A, the one in Passage B
    - (A)   seems to enjoy his job.
    - (B)   takes care of girls and boys.
    - (C)   does not earn a salary.
    - (D)   Both A and B
    - (E)   Both B and C

EXERCISE 3

William Hazlitt (1778–1830) was an essayist and literary critic known for his studies of the romantic poets and Elizabethan playwrights. This passage is from an essay entitled "On Familiar Style," first published in 1821.

It is not easy to write a familiar style. Many people mistake a familiar for a vulgar style, and suppose that to write without affectation is to write at random. On the contrary, there is nothing that requires more precision, and, if I may so say,
(5) purity of expression, than the style I am speaking of. It utterly rejects not only all unmeaning pomp, but all low, cant phrases, and loose, unconnected, *slipshod* allusions. It is not to take the first word that offers, but the best word in common use; it is not to throw words together in any combinations we please, but to
(10) follow and avail ourselves of the true idiom of the language. To write a genuine familiar or truly English style, is to write as any one would speak in common conversation, who had a thorough command and choice of words, or who could discourse with ease, force, and perspicuity, setting aside all pedantic and oratorical
(15) flourishes. Or to give another illustration, to write naturally is the same thing in regard to common conversation, as to read naturally is in regard to common speech. It does not follow that it is an easy thing to give the true accent and inflection to the words you utter, because you do not attempt to rise above
(20) the level of ordinary life and colloquial speaking. You do not assume indeed the solemnity of the pulpit, or the tone of stage-declamation: neither are you at liberty to gabble on at a venture, without emphasis or discretion, or to resort to vulgar dialect or clownish pronunciation. You must steer a middle course. You
(25) are tied down to a given and appropriate articulation, which is determined by the habitual associations between sense and sound, and which you can only hit by entering into the author's meaning, as you must find the proper words and style to express yourself by fixing your thoughts on the subject you have to
(30) write about. Any one may mouth out a passage with a theatrical cadence, or get upon stilts to tell his thoughts: but to write or speak with propriety and simplicity is a more difficult task. Thus it is easy to affect a pompous style, to use a word twice as big as the thing you wish to express: it is not so easy to pitch upon the
(35) very word that exactly fits it. Out of eight or ten words equally common, equally intelligible, with nearly equal pretensions, it is a matter of some nicety and discrimination to pick out the very one, the preferableness of which is scarcely perceptible, but decisive.

1. By "familiar" (line 1), Hazlitt means
   (A) public.
   (B) accepted.
   (C) informal.
   (D) well-known.
   (E) famous.

2. By "purity of expression" (line 5), Hazlitt means
   (A) sweet face.
   (B) religious speech.
   (C) innocent statements.
   (D) pious manner.
   (E) clear wording.

3. The word "cant" (line 6) means
   (A) tilted.
   (B) inclined.
   (C) sung.
   (D) jargonistic.
   (E) negative.

4. Hazlitt compares writing a familiar style to
   (A) ascending a pulpit.
   (B) wearing an old shoe.
   (C) writing a letter.
   (D) writing in a journal.
   (E) speaking naturally.

5. The word "perspicuity" (line 14) means
   (A) clarity.
   (B) stuffiness.
   (C) pedantry.
   (D) insensitivity.
   (E) sweat.

6. The word "colloquial" (line 20) means
   (A) oratorical.
   (B) pleasant.
   (C) worldly.
   (D) religious.
   (E) everyday.

7. Hazlitt believes that a writer must "steer a middle course" (line 24) between
   (A) familiar and unfamiliar.
   (B) theatrics and bombast.
   (C) clowning and sobriety.
   (D) vulgarity and pomposity.
   (E) discrimination and judgment.

8. The general tone of this passage is
   (A) disdainful.
   (B) reverent.
   (C) scholarly.
   (D) witty.
   (E) pompous.

9. How might you paraphrase Hazlitt's final sentence?
   (A) Common, everyday words may be pretentious, but it is nice to choose the correct one.
   (B) Common language is often discriminated against, but a writer should be decisive when choosing it.
   (C) It hardly matters which word you choose when all your choices have similar meanings and usages.
   (D) Judgment will help you decide whether to use a common word or one with more pretensions.
   (E) Choosing the word with the precise shade of meaning you desire is difficult but indispensable.

10. Hazlitt's main idea seems to be that
    (A) writing in a familiar style is harder than it looks.
    (B) it is easier to write familiarly than vulgarly.
    (C) the common touch should be used only with commoners.
    (D) familiar language is only appropriate on certain occasions.
    (E) an author must be consistent in style and tone.

Exercise 4

Throughout history, people have found themselves at the mercy of unyielding rulers to whom they have had to beg for mercy. The letters below were written perhaps 1,800 years apart, yet each is a heartfelt plea to a man in a position of power.

Passage A—from Agrippina to her son, the emperor Nero, responding to charges of treason

Don't you know, my son, the affection all mothers naturally bear their children? Our love is unbounded, incessantly fed by that tenderness unknown to all but ourselves. Nothing should be more dear to us than what we have bought with the risk of our
(5) lives; nothing more precious than what we have endured such grief and pain to procure. These are so acute and unbearable that if it were not for the vision of a successful birth, which makes us forget our agonies, generation would soon cease.

Do you forget that nine full months I carried you in my
(10) womb and nourished you with my blood? How likely is it, then, that I would destroy the dear child who cost me so much anguish to bring into the world? It may be that the just gods were angry at my excessive love of you, and used this way to punish me.

Unhappy Agrippina! You are suspected of a crime of which
(15) nobody could really think you guilty.… What does the title of empress mean to me, if I am accused of a crime that even the basest of women would abhor? Unhappy are those who breathe the air of the court. The wisest of people are not secure from storms in that harbor. There even a calm is dangerous. But why
(20) blame the court? Can that be the cause of my being suspected of parricide?…

Tell me, why should I plot against your life? To plunge myself into a worse fate? That's not likely. What hopes could induce me to build upon your downfall? I know that the lust for
(25) empire often corrupts the laws of nature; that justice has no sword to punish those who offend in this way; and that ambition disregards wrong so long as it succeeds in its aim.… Nay, to what deity could I turn for absolution after I had committed so black a deed?…

(30) What difficulties have I not surmounted to crown your brow with laurels? But I insult your gratitude by reminding you of my services. My innocence ought not to defend itself but to rely wholly on your justice.

Farewell

Passage B—from Elizabeth Barrett Browning to Napoleon III, pleading for mercy for a fellow artist

(35) Sire,

I am only a woman and have no claim on your Majesty's attention except that of the weakest on the strongest. Probably my very name as the wife of an English poet and as named itself a little among English poets, is unknown to your Majesty.

(40) I never approached my own sovereign with a petition, nor am skilled in the way of addressing kings. Yet having, through a studious and thoughtful life, grown used to great men (among the Dead at least) I cannot feel entirely at a loss in speaking to the Emperor Napoleon.

(45) And I beseech you to have patience with me while I supplicate you. It is not for myself nor for mine.

I have been reading with wet eyes and a swelling heart (as many who love and some who hate your Majesty have lately done) a book called the 'Contemplations' of a man who has sinned deeply against you

(50) in certain of his political writings, and who expiates rash phrases and unjustifiable statements in exile in Jersey. I have no personal knowledge of this man; I never saw his face; and certainly I do not come now to make his apology. It is indeed precisely because he cannot be excused, that, I think, he might worthily be forgiven. For this man, whatever else

(55) he is not, is a great poet of France, and the Emperor who is the guardian of her other glories should remember him and not leave him out.

Ah sire, what was written on "Napoleon le petit" does not touch your Majesty; but what touches you is, that no historian of the age should have to write hereafter, "While Napoleon the

(60) Third reigned Victor Hugo lived in exile." What touches you is that when your people count gratefully the men of commerce, arms and science secured by you to France, no voice shall murmur, "But where is our poet?" ... What touches you is, that when your own beloved young prince shall come to read these

(65) poems (and when you wish him a princely nature, you wish, sire, that such things should move him) he may exult to recall that his imperial father was great enough to overcome this great poet with magnanimity....

I am driven by an irresistible impulse to your Majesty's feet to ask

(70) this grace. It is a woman's voice, Sire, which dares to utter what many yearn for in silence. I have believed in Napoleon the Third. Passionately loving the democracy, I have understood from the beginning that it was to be served throughout Europe in you and by you. I have trusted you for doing greatly. I will trust you besides for pardoning nobly. You will be

(75) Napoleon in this also.

Elizabeth Barrett Browning

1. Agrippina's first two paragraphs (Passage A) appeal to Nero's
   (A) remembrance of his youth.
   (B) power as a leader.
   (C) love of women.
   (D) belief in the gods.
   (E) filial feelings.

2. "Storms in that harbor" (Passage A, line 19) is a metaphor referring to
   (A) tempests in teapots.
   (B) political upheavals at court.
   (C) adventurers in government.
   (D) pirates at sea.
   (E) Nero's early life as a sailor.

3. When she says that "ambition disregards wrong" (Passage A, lines 26–27), Agrippina means that
   (A) it is right to grasp power.
   (B) excessive ambition is wrong.
   (C) ambitious people commit crimes.
   (D) wickedness comes with rank.
   (E) few kings are kind.

4. Agrippina's final paragraph hints at her
   (A) desire for the crown.
   (B) dislike of the present queen.
   (C) gratitude toward Nero.
   (D) trust in the gods.
   (E) manipulation of Nero's career.

5. When Browning claims to be "used to great men" (Passage B, line 42), she means that she
   (A) has studied heroic lives.
   (B) knows a great many kings.
   (C) has been ill-used by her sovereign.
   (D) grew up in a famous house.
   (E) has a famous husband.

6. The word "supplicate" (Passage B, lines 45–46) means
   (A) astound.
   (B) consume.
   (C) petition.
   (D) render.
   (E) depose.

7. Browning suggests the Emperor should forgive Hugo because
   (A) his crime is not great.
   (B) she knows him personally.
   (C) no one deserves exile.
   (D) he is a great French poet.
   (E) his deed is excusable.

8. The word "touch" as it is used throughout paragraph 4, Passage B, means
   (A) caress.
   (B) meet.
   (C) affect.
   (D) move.
   (E) feel.

9. Unlike Browning, Agrippina is pleading
   (A) for mercy.
   (B) for her own life.
   (C) for a greater cause.
   (D) Both A and B
   (E) Both B and C

10. Unlike Agrippina, Browning
    (A) admits her own weakness.
    (B) apologizes.
    (C) denies the crime.
    (D) Both A and B
    (E) Both B and C

ANSWER KEY AND EXPLANATIONS

Level D

Exercise 1

1. C	3. C	5. C	7. C
2. C	4. A	6. E	8. D

1. **The correct answer is (C).** Does the author portray Copland's music in a very negative or very positive light? Neither, so (A) and (E) are out. The author actually just describes the reactions of others to Copland's music and interjects little opinion of his or her own. That eliminates (D). Then again, the author is not *clinically objective* in tone (just think, the passage does not sound like a science passage). That makes (C) the best choice.

2. **The correct answer is (C).** The virtuoso passages are passages only a virtuoso could play—essentially, difficult. Eliminate (E). There is no negative judgment of that quality in the passage. That eliminates all but (C), which is the answer.

3. **The correct answer is (C).** The different fates were that the *Piano Variation* was known by many pianists, but played by few in concert, and the *Symphonic Ode* was largely unknown because it was too difficult. Choice (C) says as much, and so is the answer.

4. **The correct answer is (A).** In the passage, Koussevitzky is first mentioned in connection to the difficulty of playing the *Symphonic Ode*. The passage tells you that even he, a "champion" of Copland's music, did not conduct the piece until it had been simplified. Choice (A) correctly points this out. Don't be tricked by the difficult name into answering that he was European.

5. **The correct answer is (C).** The second paragraph begins, "Perhaps as a reaction to the performance problems of the *Symphonic Ode,* Copland's next two orchestral works deal in shorter units of time." So the author thinks that the pieces immediately subsequent to the *Symphonic Ode* were made shorter because the Ode was not being performed. Choice (C) says the same. Choice (B) is tempting but the passage explicitly states that it was the length and not the complexity that Copland adjusted in the subsequent pieces.

6. **The correct answer is (E).** This sentence is essentially saying that, although brief, these works were also very difficult to

perform. The answer is (E). This is essentially a vocabulary question, asking you to define "agile."

7. **The correct answer is (C).** First off, what does the passage state about Copland's views of the Americas and music? It says that Copland, "envisioned 'American music' as being music of the Americas." In other words, he thought they were related, or should be. Choices (A), (B), and (E) run contrary to this meaning. Choice (D) is irrelevant. The answer is (C).

8. **The correct answer is (D).** The Mexican material is more accessible to audiences. The opposite of accessible is inaccessible. Choice (D) should look good to you right away. Don't get confused by (C). The emphasis in the sentence is on audiences, not musicians.

Exercise 2

1. B	4. B	7. A	10. C
2. B	5. E	8. E	11. E
3. C	6. E	9. A	12. A

1. **The correct answer is (B).** The phrase is literal: "She cooked for from twenty-five to thirty-five [people]."

2. **The correct answer is (B).** The scene troubled Curry. None of the other choices makes sense.

3. **The correct answer is (C).** It was some unimportant thing about the dinner that caused the girl to strike Curry's mother.

4. **The correct answer is (B).** This archaic phrase may be deciphered by plugging the choices into the context.

5. **The correct answer is (E).** He was certainly not *apathetic,* or indifferent, even if he did not dare to respond. Curry felt both *helpless,* (B), and *horrified,* (C).

6. **The correct answer is (E).** Raicharan does not have the same *job,* (A), as his master, but he does belong to the same class, even if he is acting as a servant.

7. **The correct answer is (A).** It is too humorous to be called "dark," (B), and it does not appear to foreshadow anything, (C). However, the description of baby activities as "an epoch in human history" is surely ironic.

8. **The correct answer is (E).** Choices (A) to (C) are synonyms for *depot.* The child is a young slave-driver.

9. **The correct answer is (A).** By referring to the child as "my lord," "his lordship," and "little despot," the author makes his feelings clear.

10. **The correct answer is (C).** Simply substituting the choices in the sentence gives you the correct response.

11. **The correct answer is (E).** The introduction gives you a big hint. Only Passage A fits (A) and (C). Choice (B) relates only to Passage B. Colonialism, (D), is only potentially an issue in Passage B, and "inhuman conditions" is somewhat exaggerated, anyway. Choice (E) is the only choice that fits both passages.

12. **The correct answer is (A).** We never have a sense how the characters in Passage A feel about their job, but it is unlikely to be positive. Raicharan, on the other hand, dotes on his young charge. He does not take care of girls, (B), and the characters in Passage A do not earn a salary, (C).

Exercise 3

1. C	3. D	5. A	7. D	9. E
2. E	4. E	6. E	8. D	10. A

1. **The correct answer is (C).** Each choice is a possible synonym for *familiar,* but only *informal* has the correct shade of meaning.

2. **The correct answer is (E).** Rereading the sentence in which this phrase appears should make your choice evident.

3. **The correct answer is (D).** Familiar style, says Hazlitt, rejects pomp, but it also rejects low, *cant* phrases—jargon.

4. **The correct answer is (E).** "To write a genuine familiar . . . style . . . is to write as any one would speak in common conversation" (lines 10–12).

5. **The correct answer is (A).** The fact that Hazlitt is listing *good* qualities of writing should allow you to eliminate all but (A) here.

6. **The correct answer is (E).** The parallel is with "ordinary life," so *everyday* seems a reasonable choice.

7. **The correct answer is (D).** This is a main theme of the passage, and its focus is clear if you reread the sentence that precedes the reference. Hazlitt does not think writing should be pompous *or* vulgar, but somewhere in between.

8. **The correct answer is (D).** He is saying something he believes, but Hazlitt tempers his lecture with lines such as "any one may . . . get upon stilts to tell his thoughts" and "it is easy . . . to use a word twice as big as the thing you wish to express."

9. **The correct answer is (E).** It may be a hard sentence to wade through, but understanding it is key to understanding the passage.

10. **The correct answer is (A).** He does *not* believe (B), and there is no evidence to support (C). He never says (D) or (E), although he may well believe them.

Exercise 4

1. E	3. C	5. A	7. D	9. B
2. B	4. E	6. C	8. C	10. A

1. **The correct answer is (E).** She reminds him that she is his mother and loves him as such, that she bore him and nourished him—Agrippina is appealing to Nero's feelings as a son.

2. **The correct answer is (B).** Reading the line that precedes this line will help you understand that Agrippina is referring to court and the dangers that lie there.

3. **The correct answer is (C).** Agrippina lists the things she "knows": that "lust for empire often corrupts" and that "ambition disregards wrong," but she does not admit her own wrongdoing.

4. **The correct answer is (E).** While saying she won't do so, Agrippina reminds Nero of all she has done to put him where he is today.

5. **The correct answer is (A).** Although she is not "skilled in the way of addressing kings," Browning has, through her study, "grown used to great men," especially those who are dead!

6. **The correct answer is (C).** This line announces Browning's purpose: to petition the king.

7. **The correct answer is (D).** She never says (A), and she denies (B). She never says (C), and she contradicts (E). The only reason Napoleon III should forgive Hugo is because Napoleon should not be remembered as the king who exiled France's great poet.

8. **The correct answer is (C).** The writing for which Hugo was condemned should not affect so great a personage; what should affect him is his reputation and his son's opinion.

9. **The correct answer is (B).** Both plead for mercy, (A), but only Agrippina pleads her own cause.

10. **The correct answer is (A).** Neither one apologizes, (B), and only Agrippina denies the crime, (C). Browning, unlike Agrippina, speaks from what she calls a position of weakness.

CHECK OUT

Before you go on to the next chapter, can you

- Explain the three different types of passage-based reading questions and discuss strategies for answering each type of question?

- State the areas where you are strong in answering passage-based reading questions and the areas in which you need more work?

PART IV

TAKE IT TO THE NEXT LEVEL

Top Techniques for Critical Reading

WHAT MAKES A TOUGH SENTENCE COMPLETION QUESTION?

Most of the 19 sentence completions you'll encounter on the SAT will be no-brainers for you. One feature that makes for a no-brainer question is easy vocabulary. Another feature that makes for a "gimmee" question is a short, simple sentence—an easily understood statement that doesn't take too many twists or turns as it goes. Here's an example of the kinds of straightforward, easy-to-understand sentences and answer choices that you'll find in comparatively easy sentence completion questions:

Example:

Many stage actors are intimidated by the ---- of drama critics, whose reviews can determine the fate of a play in a single night.

(A) tastes
(B) power
(C) expertise
(D) criticism
(E) reviews

The correct answer is (B). Of the five word choices, the one that it makes most sense to be "intimidated by" is *power*. And this word makes perfect sense in the context of the sentence: the ability to determine the fate of a play in a single night is a good description of a certain type of *power*. Just for the record, here's why none of the four wrong-answer choices can compete with (B):

(A) It makes no sense to be intimidated by tastes, so you can easily eliminate (A) without even considering the second part of the sentence.

(C) Although it might make sense to be intimidated by someone's *expertise* (knowledge or skill gained from experience), this kind of intimidation doesn't make as much sense as choice (B) when you consider the second part of the sentence as well.

(D) It makes no sense to be intimidated by "*criticism* of drama critics," a phrase suggesting that it is the drama critics who are being criticized.

(E) This choice provides a completion that results in the redundant, and very awkward, use of the word *reviews*.

No knowledge of rocket science is needed to handle questions like this one! And, believe it or not, you'll find some SAT sentence completions to be even easier. Don't worry, we won't waste any more time in this lesson on no-brainers. From here on, we'll handle only the tougher questions.

To crank up the difficulty level of the drama-critic question you just looked at, the test-makers might:

- Use more advanced vocabulary (in the sentence as well as in the answer choices)

- Provide "runner-up" answer choices that require closer judgment calls

- Add a second blank

Here's a souped-up variation on the drama-critic question, made tougher in all three ways:

Example:

Friends of the theater have long decried the ---- of big-city drama critics, whose reviews can determine the ---- of a play in a single night.

(A) tactlessness .. popularity
(B) callous indifference .. outcome
(C) incisive judgment .. attendance
(D) disingenuousness .. success
(E) unfettered sway .. fate

The correct answer is (E). To handle this more difficult version of the question, it helps to know that the word *decry* means "to discredit or criticize." It wouldn't make much sense for "friends of the theater" to discredit or criticize a drama critic's *incisive judgement*. (The word *incisive* in this context means keen or sharp.) So, you can at least eliminate choice (C), without even considering the second blank. But the remaining four choices for completing the first blank all make sense as characteristics of big-city drama critics as seen by friends of the theater. (Of course, it helps to know that *disingenuousness* means insincerity and that *unfettered sway* means unconstrained influence or power.) So, you'll need to consider the second blank.

Choice (B) doesn't make sense for the second blank. It's the playwright, not the critic, that determines the *outcome* of a play. Therefore, you can narrow your choices to (A), (D), and (E), all of which make sense for completing the second blank. (A drama critic's review can determine a play's *popularity*, *success*, or *fate*.) But of the three choices, (E) makes the most sense when you consider the completed sentence. Regardless of which word (*popularity*, *success*, or *fate*) you use to complete the second blank, the second part of the sentence provides a better description of *unfettered sway* than either *tactlessness* or *disingenuousness*. In other words, with (E), the sentence as a whole is more consistent and cohesive.

If you were paying attention to the analysis of the preceding question, you noticed some pretty subtle distinctions between the best answer choice and the others. That's exactly how many of the toughest sentence completion questions earn their stripes. By tuning in to these subtleties, you'll be ready for the toughest completions the test-makers can dish out.

Test-makers have another way to boost the difficulty level of sentence completions: they construct longer, more complex sentences that contain "signpost" words. These words connect the sentence's parts together to form a cohesive whole that makes sense with the right completion. We'll examine the test-makers' four favorite types of connections, and their signposts, later in this lesson.

STRATEGIES FOR SENTENCE COMPLETION QUESTIONS

Here you'll learn some strategies that you can use for handling sentence completion questions. But first, attempt each of the following "tougher than average" sample questions. Then, carefully read the explanations, which reveal some of these strategies.

Example 1:

Sleep researchers now view sleep as involving degrees of detachment from the surrounding world, a ---- whose rhythm is as unique and as consistent as a signature.

(A) realm
(B) progression
(C) science
(D) restfulness
(E) condition

The correct answer is (B). The sentence as a whole seems to suggest that sleep is a dynamic process involving a series of different stages defined by degree of detachment. Notice that the purpose of the second clause is to describe, or restate, what sleep is. This observation is key in getting to the correct answer. The missing word refers to "sleep," so perhaps a word such as state or *condition* might occur to you as a logical completion. Choices (C) and (D) make no sense as characterizations of sleep, so eliminate them. Notice also that "rhythm" is mentioned as a feature or trait of the missing word ("---- whose rhythm ..."). To describe a *realm* as having a rhythm makes no sense, so eliminate (A). You've narrowed the choices down to (B) and (E). Read the sentence with each word in turn. Ask yourself which word is more appropriate and effective in conveying the thrust of the sentence—that sleep is a dynamic process involving a series of different stages. The word *progression* clearly drives home this notion more pointedly and effectively than the word *condition*.

Example 2:

African-American legislators today not only ---- their constituencies but also serve as proxies in the democratic process for all African Americans; yet the records of some of them ---- their struggle to extend certain ideals to encompass all citizens.

(A) serve .. describe
(B) abandon .. affirm
(C) promote .. criticize
(D) represent .. belie
(E) influence .. discredit

The correct answer is (D). Notice that the sentence changes direction midway through. This change is signaled by the key word "yet," which provides a clue that the second part of the sentence sets up a contrast or contradiction to the first part. The words "not only ... but also" are important clues that the first blank must complement the phrase "serve as proxies . ..." (Proxy means substitute.) A negatively charged word such as "harm," "ignore," or "disagree with" would make no sense in the first blank; however, a word such as *serve*, *represent*, or aid would fit nicely. The meaning of the second clause should reflect a contrast to that of the first one. Therefore, a word such as "ignore," "de-emphasize," or "trivialize" would make sense here. Here's a good paraphrase of the sentence that shows the idea that it is probably trying to convey:

In doing their jobs, these legislators have helped (aided) all African Americans, yet the records of some of them don't reflect (they ignore) the efforts of these legislators as a group. Now analyze each answer choice to see how effectively it conveys these ideas:

(A) *Served* fits nicely, but *describe* fails to establish the necessary contrast between the two parts of the sentence. Eliminate (A).

(B) *Abandoned* doesn't fit, because it doesn't complement "served as proxies…." You can eliminate (B) even without considering the second word (*affirm*).

(C) *Promoted* and *criticize* each seem to make sense in context, and together they set up a sense of contrast between the two clauses. So (C) is in the running. However, it is the goals or interests of a constituency, not the constituency itself that an elected representative promotes. So *promoted* sets up an improper idiomatic expression. What's more, for the word *criticize* to establish a clear contrast, the first clause should at least suggest the opposing notion of approval, but it doesn't. Even though the "flavor" of *criticize* is in the right direction, it is not a perfect fit in the context of the sentence as a whole.

(D) *Represented* fits nicely. If you don't know what *belie* means, perhaps you can guess based on its root "lie" (falsehood), which provides the sort of contrast between the two clauses you're looking for. To *belie* is to misrepresent or contradict. For example, a smile belies sadness. Similarly, a biography can belie the struggle described in the sentence, perhaps by mis-describing it as an easier effort than it has in fact been. (D) appears to be a logical answer choice.

(E) *Influence* establishes a different meaning for the first clause than the one you're inferring. But *influence* does make some sense in the first clause. *Discredit* makes sense as well and sets off the necessary contrast between the two clauses. However, this version of the sentence inappropriately *discredits* a "struggle," while it makes better sense to discredit the "strugglers." You can eliminate (E) based on this defect alone. What's more, although the word *influence* makes sense in context, it doesn't establish the close parallel in ideas that the correlative phrases "not only … but also …" call for. (D) is better in this respect.

If you read the explanations for the preceding two questions, you already picked up some valuable ideas for gaining a tactical advantage on SAT sentence completion questions. Here, you'll review those ideas and pick up some additional ones. These strategies will help you gain insights into sentence completions so that you can handle them efficiently, while avoiding the kinds of blunders that average test-takers might make.

First, try to understand the sentence, paying particular attention to "signpost" words and phrases that connect parts of the sentence together.

Initially, read the sentence in its entirety, without worrying about how to fill in the blanks yet. Try to get a feel for the topic and the "thrust" of the sentence. Ask yourself about the point the sentence is trying to make. Pay particular attention to key, or *signpost,* words that indicate any of the following:

- A contrast (pointing out a difference, contradiction, or distinction)
- A similarity (pointing out how two things are analogous or otherwise the same)
- A restatement (paraphrasing, describing, or clarifying)
- An effect (pointing out a conclusion, consequence, or result of a cause or influence)

Signpost words can tell you where the sentence is going. Is it continuing along one line of thought? If so, you're looking for a word that supports that thought. Is it changing direction in midstream? If so, you're looking for a word that sets up a contrast between the thoughts in the sentence.

Words that signal blanks that go with the flow:	Words that signal blanks that shift gears:
and	but
also	yet
consequently	although
as a result	on the other hand
thus	in contrast
hence	however
so	nevertheless
for example	

Example 1:

Take another look at the sentence in Example 1. The sentence as a whole seems to suggest that sleep is a dynamic process involving a series of different stages defined by degree of detachment. Notice that the purpose of the second clause is to describe what sleep is. This observation is key in getting to the correct answer.

Example 2:

In reading the sentence in Example 2, you should have noticed that it changes direction midway through. This change is signaled by the keyword *yet*, which provides a clue that the second part of the sentence sets up a contrast or contradiction to the first part. You can bet that this structural clue will be crucial in determining the best answer.

As a starting point, complete the sentence with your own words before looking at the answer choices.

Filling in the blank(s) with your own words first will help get your mental wheels turning and get you into the question. If you use this approach, you'll have a much easier time spotting "sucker bait" answer choices (and you'll see plenty of them in sentence completions). If the question includes two blanks, be sure that your two "homegrown" words make sense considered together.

Keep in mind that filling in the blanks with your own words is only a starting point. Don't expect to find your answer verbatim among the choices because most SAT sentence completions are not that easy.

Example 1:

The words "not only ... but also" in the first sentence provide clues that the first blank must complement the phrase "served as proxies ...." The word "aided" fits nicely. Because the sentence's second clause should set up a contrast to the first one, a word such as "ignore" makes sense. With these two words, you now make overall sense of the sentence, and you can eliminate conflicting answer choices.

If you were filling in the blank yourself (without the aid of the answer choices), what word would you use? The missing word refers to "sleep," so perhaps a word such as *state* or *condition* might occur to you as a logical completion. While choice (E) provides the word "condition," another choice turned out to be better.

DON'T WASTE TIME TRYING TO MAKE SENSE OF ANSWER CHOICES THAT DON'T FIT.

For any sentence completion question, you're bound to find at least one or two choices that make little or no sense in the context of the sentence. Clear those away first, so that you can focus your attention on the viable candidates. If the sentence contains two blanks, you can eliminate any answer choice in which one of the words considered alone makes no sense.

Example 1:

The correct answer must make sense as a characterization of sleep. Choices (C) and (D) obviously make no sense, so you can easily eliminate them. It makes no sense to describe a "realm" as having a rhythm, so you can also eliminate choice (A).

Example 2:

You can eliminate choice (B) because *abandon* doesn't make sense in the first clause. You don't even need to analyze the second word (*affirm*).

DON'T STOP SHORT OF CONSIDERING EACH AND EVERY ANSWER CHOICE.

Okay, you've thought up your own answer first, and one of the five choices looks perfect. Should you select it and move on, without considering the others? No! Remember: the qualitative difference between the best and second best answer can be subtle.

Example 1:

If choices (B) and (E) were switched, you might have been tempted to select (B) without considering other choices. But you would have been wrong!

Example 2:

Choice (C) seemed to fit okay, but if you selected it and moved on without considering later choices, you'd have missed the best answer, choice (D).

DON'T CHOOSE AN ANSWER TO A DUAL-BLANK QUESTION JUST BECAUSE ONE OF THE WORDS IS A PERFECT FIT.

As often as not, one word that fits perfectly is paired with another word that doesn't fit well at all. When it comes to dual-blank questions, this is the test-makers' favorite trap. Don't fall for it!

Example 2:

The word *serve* in choice (A) is a perfect fit for the first blank; yet, (A) is not the correct answer choice.

DON'T CHOOSE AN ANSWER JUST BECAUSE IT CONTAINS A TOUGH WORD.

Expect to encounter some tough vocabulary words in later sentence completion questions. But don't choose an answer just because it includes a difficult word. By the same token, don't rule it out for this reason. That's not how the test-makers design sentence completions. Instead, try to take your best guess as to what the word might mean (perhaps it looks a bit like a familiar word). A reasoned guess is better than an unreasoned one, right?

Example 2:

The word *belie* happened to be part of the best answer; but that's just the way this question turned out. Don't generalize from this single example!

CHOOSE BETWEEN THE BEST CHOICES BY CHECKING FOR IDIOM, USAGE, AND AWKWARDNESS.

Don't forget that the test-makers are covering not just overall sentence sense but also word usage (whether a word is used properly) and idiom (how ideas are expressed as phrases). If you're having trouble deciding between choices, check for these two problems, and eliminate any answer choice that makes any part of the sentence confusing or awkward.

Example 2:

Both (C) and (E) contain subtle usage and idiom problems that distinguish them from the best answer choice (D).

THE TEST-MAKERS' FAVORITE SENTENCE CONNECTIONS

Earlier in this chapter, we looked at how advanced vocabulary and subtle distinctions between best and second-best answer choices can make for tougher sentence completion questions. Yet another feature that makes for a tougher question is a sentence with a complex logical structure. In this kind of sentence, signpost words are included to connect the sentence's parts together to form a complete idea that makes sense (assuming the right words are used to fill in the blanks). For the remainder of this lesson, we'll focus on the test-makers' four favorite types of connections and the signpost words used for each type.

The test-makers are rather predictable when it comes to how they construct complex sentences that contain signpost words. Once you see enough of these sentences, you'll begin to recognize certain patterns in how parts of the sentences connect together logically. Here are the types of connections that you're most likely to encounter and should learn to recognize:

- Contrast
- Similarity
- Restatement
- Cause and effect

Not every tough sentence completion question will illustrate one of these four connections; but most will.

CONTRAST

In a sentence fitting this pattern, one part of a sentence contains an idea that contrasts with, or is opposed to, an idea in another part of the sentence. Here's an example:

Example:

Whereas Wordsworth wrote his best poetry during ----, Yeats wrote some of his finest poems when he was over seventy years old.

(A) illness
(B) war
(C) youth
(D) marriage
(E) convalescence

The correct answer is (C). What is there about the sentence that tells you to look for a contrast? It's the word "whereas," isn't it? Without this word, you can't make the contrast connection. If you doubt this, think about how you'd fill in the blank without the word, as in this variation:

Wordsworth wrote his best poetry during ----, *and* Yeats wrote some of his finest poems when he was over seventy years old.

The single word "whereas" makes all the difference. It tells you that a contrast is coming. In other words, the first part of the sentence tells you something about Wordsworth that *should contrast* with what the second part of the sentence tells you about Yeats. Since the second part says that Yeats wrote his best poetry when he was old ("over seventy years old"), Wordsworth must have written his best poetry when he was young. The only answer choice that provides this contrast is (C).

Here are some other signpost words used to signal a contrast connection:

although	however	on the other hand
but	nevertheless	unlike
by contrast	nonetheless	yet
despite		

For the sentence involving Wordsworth and Yeats, you can use almost any word from the preceding list instead of "whereas" to set up the same contrast. Some you can use to introduce the first part of the sentence; others you can use to introduce the second part of the sentence. Try each one to see if it fits (and, if so, where).

SIMILARITY

In a sentence fitting this pattern, one part describes something that is similar to something described in another part of the sentence. Here's an example:

Example:

Just as musicians in the 1970s were amazed by the powers of the electronic synthesizer, musicians during the time of Bach ---- the organ, the technical wonder of its day.

- (A) were reluctant to play
- (B) marveled at
- (C) were intimidated by
- (D) were anxious to master
- (E) misunderstood

The correct answer is (B). In this sentence, the words "just as" tell you that the two parts of the sentence are describing similar situations. In other words, musicians during Bach's time reacted to the organ in the same way that musicians in the 1970s reacted to the synthesizer. The sentence indicates that musicians of the 1970s "were amazed by" the synthesizer, so the words for the blank should express something similar about the reaction to the organ. Only choice (B), *marveled at*, provides the similarity, so it's the best answer choice.

Here are some other words and phrases that act as similarity signposts:

as	like	similarly
in the same way	likewise	

Try redrafting the sentence about synthesizers using each of these signposts instead of the words "just as." Notice that some words work only to begin the first clause, whereas others work only to begin the second clause.

RESTATEMENT

In a sentence fitting this pattern, one part paraphrases, defines, or clarifies what is said in another part of the sentence. Here's an example:

Example:

Public attitudes toward business ---- are somewhat ----; most people resent intrusive government rules, yet they expect government to prevent businesses from defrauding, endangering, or exploiting the public.

(A) ethics .. divided
(B) investment .. confused
(C) practices .. emotional
(D) regulation .. ambiguous
(E) leaders .. skeptical

The correct answer is (D). As you read the sentence as a whole, you get the distinct idea that the second part is intended to elucidate (clarify or explain) the first part. What provides the clue for this connection? In this sentence, there are two keys: the semicolon and the syntax. The first part is much briefer than the second, and there are no connecting words that signal anything but restatement.

Think of the brief phrase as a dictionary entry, and the longer phrase as its definition. A dictionary might separate the entry from its definition with a colon; here a semicolon serves a similar purpose.

In this sentence, the second part (following the semicolon) describes in some detail the public's attitude about government rules for business. As you can see, the attitude described is self-contradictory in that the same person typically has conflicting expectations when it comes to government rules for business. (Notice the keyword "yet," which signals the contradiction.) Try starting with the second blank.

You're looking for a word that accurately captures the public attitude. Choices (A), (B), and (D) work best; *divided*, *confused*, and *ambiguous* all convey the general idea that the public wants two things that don't go together very well. For the first blank, you want a word that describes what the second part of the sentence also describes. Choice (D) appears to be the best fit; the sentence as a whole has to do with "business *regulation*," that is, the rules laid down by government for business. Two other choices, (A) and (C), work okay for the first blank. But *ethics* is a bit too specific, while *practices* is a bit too vague. (You can already eliminate choice (C) based on the second missing word.) So, the best answer choice is (D).

As you just saw, the semicolon without a connector word might provide a wordless warning that a restatement might be taking place. Also, look for these keywords and phrases, which often mark restatement connections:

in fact	in short	that is
in other words	namely	

Three of these markers could easily be inserted into the sentence about business regulation to strengthen the signal that a restatement is taking place. Try redrafting the sentence with the addition of each marker in turn to find out which three work.

CAUSE AND EFFECT

In a sentence fitting this pattern, one part describes something that causes, produces, or influences what's described in another part.

Example:

When waging election campaigns against challengers, most incumbent politicians have significant ---- as a result of the power and recognition that are typically part and parcel of holding public office.

(A) propensities
(B) expenses
(C) contributions
(D) budgets
(E) advantages

The correct answer is (E). In this sentence, the operative phrase is "as a result." What precedes this phrase describes the effect, or result, of the "power and recognition" that goes with holding an official position in the government. Or, put another way, the power and recognition of public office causes or influences what the earlier part of the sentence intends to describe. Logically, what effects would be caused by the power and recognition of public office? One natural effect would be to make it easier to run for reelection, if only because the current office holder is already well known. So, *advantages* is an apt expression of this natural effect. The most tempting wrong answer choices are probably (C) and (D). However, significant *contributions* or *budgets* wouldn't necessarily be logical, or natural, effects of having power and recognition, would they? A candidate with a lot of power and recognition could perhaps spend as much, or as little, as he would like. What's more, the phrase "have ... *contributions*" is an awkward idiom. (A more effective and clearer phrase is "receive *contributions*.") So, on this count as well, choice (C) cannot be the best one.

To understand the preceding sentence, it helps to know that an "incumbent politician" is one who is already in office. Even if you don't know what "incumbent" means, you can still make an educated guess based on the sentence as a whole. "Incumbent politicians" are depicted here as running against "challengers," and a "challenger" is typically a person who goes up against a current title holder. So, it would be a good guess that an incumbent candidate is the current office holder.

In the preceding example, the words "as a result" mark the cause-and-effect connection. Here are some other signposts that mark this kind of connection:

because	leads to	since
hence	produces	therefore
consequently	results in	thus
due to		

You can redraft the sentence about incumbent candidates using any of these signposts instead of "as a result." You'll find that you can plug in some as substitutes for "as a result," but others require that you restructure the sentence.

WHAT ARE THE TRICKIEST TYPES OF PASSAGE-BASED READING QUESTIONS?

As SAT reading passages go, this next one is not especially difficult to understand. What you'll be focusing on here are not tough passages, but rather tough questions.

Example:

Francis Bacon was a sixteenth-century philosopher of science. The passage below explores the link between his thinking and that of the modern-day scientific establishment.

Francis Bacon contributed to the scientific enterprise a prophetic understanding of how science would one day be put to use in the service of technology, and how such a symbiosis between the two would radically impact both man and his surroundings.

(5) As inseparable as they are today, it is hard to imagine science and technology as inhabiting separate domains. But in Bacon's world of the sixteenth century, science was not generally viewed as a practical instrument for improving the physical conditions of life. Anticipating Jules Verne and H.G. Wells* by

(10) 300 years, Bacon foresaw not only the extent to which science would contribute to the enlargement of technology, but also how technology would come to be seen as the ultimate justification of science.

There is little doubt that others before Bacon understood

(15) that discovering the mysteries of air, water, fire, and earth could lead to useful applications. But Bacon's systematic elaboration of the promise of joining science with technology was a major leap forward in closing the gap between the two endeavors. He, more than any before him, stressed the need for collective organiza-

(20) tions for scientific inquiry and application—the forerunners of our vast government, academic, and corporate-sponsored research and development departments. Bacon did not ignore the necessity for creative and dedicated individuals to spur science onwards. Rather, he declared that such individuals

(25) would need the help of state aid, corporate organization, official conferences and publications, and regulated social and pecuniary incentives in order for their experiments and insights to have the widest possible application.

The danger that Bacon did not foresee was that corporate

(30) influences could restrict the opportunities of the individual

*Nineteenth-century science fiction writers.

(35)

scientist, and that a time could come when no scientific work would be possible without corporate support. The most important ramification of these new conditions is that the judgment and moral grounding possible of individual scientists must now compete with the concerns of industrial collectives. Entangled within the scientific/technological system, the modern scientist has jeopardized the qualities once exalted as the very

(40) hallmarks of science: the detachment from worldly gains and the disinterested pursuit of truth. Influenced by political and economic pressures, scientists have less and less power to enact any controls over the scientific establishment that pursues the Baconian ideals of riches and power over another of his stated

(45) uses for science, "the relief of man's estate." Scientists are losing the power to say "No."

No one questions the immense benefits already conferred by science's efficient methodology. However, since individual scientists must now choose between improving standards of

(50) living and obtaining financial support for their research, there is cause for concern. In light of current circumstances, we must ask certain questions about science that Bacon, from a sixteenth-century perspective, could not possibly have put to himself.

ASSUMPTION QUESTIONS

Assumption questions ask you to fill in gaps in the author's argument or in a position put forth by some other character in the passage. An assumption is an unstated yet necessary part of an argument. These questions can be difficult because, in order to recognize the assumption required to hold the argument together, you must understand both the conclusion that's drawn and the evidence offered in support of it.

An SAT assumption question usually contains some form of the word *assumption* or *assume*. Here are a few typical examples:

> The author's discussion about ... assumes that

> The author's argument is based on the assumption that...

An assumption in a passage will not necessarily be the author's. It might instead be an assumption made by a character or other person discussed in the passage.

When you see an assumption question, you should follow these three steps:

1. Focus on the point established (the conclusion) and the evidence used to support it.

2. Look for a link between the evidence and the conclusion that is necessary to the logic yet not explicitly stated in the passage.

3. Eliminate choices that are outside the scope of the argument. In order for something to be necessary to an argument, it must first be relevant.

Now, apply these steps to a question that relates to the passage about Francis Bacon. Use the line reference to find the phrase in question, and read the entire sentence carefully. As you read it, try to figure out what the author is NOT saying that nevertheless must be true for the argument in that sentence to make sense. That unstated premise is the assumption.

Example:

In stating the case for his "cause for concern" (line 51), the author assumes that

(A) individual scientists have sacrificed all power of choice with regard to the direction of their research.

(B) it is not in the financial interest of the scientific establishment to improve standards of living.

(C) science's efficient methodology has led to the solution of most of society's problems.

(D) no scientists will choose to devote their time to improving standards of living.

(E) non-scientists are incapable of improving their own standard of living.

The correct answer is (B). The author is concerned that scientists will have to choose between improving standards of living and getting money from the scientific establishment for their research. But if scientists receive money from the establishment for projects that will improve the standards of living, then this concern is not so well-founded. In making his argument, the author must *assume* that the scientific establishment does not have an interest in improving standards of living. If it *did,* then the author's concern would make less sense. Let's examine the other four choices to see why none can compete with choice (B):

(A) The author need not assume that scientists have sacrificed all control over their work. In fact, the argument in question indicates that scientists still have a choice regarding what they do. The author is concerned because it is a choice that may not bode well for society, but his concern does not rely on the notion in choice (A).

(C) The reference to "science's efficient methodology" comes from the previous sentence and is just there to acknowledge science's achievements before the author states his concern. This concern does not rely on the notion that science has solved most of society's problems, so choice (C) is not the assumption we're looking for here.

(D) The argument in question indicates that scientists still have a choice regarding what they do. The author's concern does not rely on the idea that not one single scientist will choose to improve standards of living. A handful may, and the author would still be concerned because the nature of the choice that has arisen in the modern scientific community does not bode well for society overall. So, choice (D) is not the necessary assumption we seek.

(E) This choice is not the assumption you're looking for because non-scientists are outside the scope. The passage, and the specific concern that's the focus of this question, concerns only the situation of scientists.

ADDITIONAL INFORMATION QUESTIONS

Additional information questions ask you to recognize an additional fact that would make an argument within the passage either more or less convincing—that is, stronger or weaker. These two question types are tougher than average because they require you to challenge the text and to think for yourself as an active reader rather than passively assimilate what's on the page.

An SAT "strengthen" question typically contains a word such as *support* or *strengthen*, as in these two question stems:

> Which of the following, if true, would provide the most direct support for the author's assertion that ----?
> *a specific claim made by the author*

> Which of the following statements, if true, would best strengthen the contention that ----?
> *a specific point mentioned in the passage*

To identify a "weaken" question on the SAT, look for a word such as *weaken*, *undermine*, *contradict*, or *refute*, as in these two question stems:

> Which of the following statements, if true, would contradict most directly the author's claim that ----?
> *a specific claim made by the author*

> Which of the following, if true, would most seriously weaken the author's argument ----?
> *a specific conclusion made by the author*

To handle a strengthen or weaken question, follow these three steps:

1. Make sure you're clear on the argument. You won't have much luck strengthening or weakening an argument that you don't understand.

2. Look for assumptions in the argument. Often, the key to strengthening or weakening an argument lies in building up or breaking down an author's central assumption.

3. Beware of choices that are true but that don't have the desired effect. A choice may perfectly reflect what's in the passage, but if it doesn't strengthen or weaken the argument (whichever you're asked to do), then it cannot be correct. Don't select a choice simply because it seems "true"; that may not be good enough.

Apply these steps to the following weaken question about the Francis Bacon passage. To handle the question, find the relevant text and reread what the author says about what Bacon didn't foresee—that is, what Bacon missed in his analysis. Keep in mind that you're being asked to weaken the *author's* point, not any arguments that Bacon himself makes. Therefore, get into the mindset of challenging the author as you go back to read this part of the passage.

Example:

The author's assertion regarding what "Bacon did not foresee" (line 29) would be most seriously weakened if it were determined that Bacon

(A) outlined the mechanisms of corporate support necessary to adequately fund scientific research.

(B) stated in his writings that the economic and political requirements for a stable society were intertwined with the efficient functioning of the scientific establishment.

(C) suggested that passionate and creative people were indispensable to the advancement of the scientific enterprise.

(D) was generally perceptive regarding most scientific topics.

(E) warned of the dangers to scientific inquiry that would result if collective organization became an integral part of scientific research.

The correct answer is (E). Paraphrasing the text, the author says that Bacon didn't realize that corporate/institutional support would become so essential to science that no science would be possible without it. If, however, we find that Bacon *did* in fact warn of the dangers to science of such corporate control ("collective organization"), then the author's argument here would carry much less weight. Choice (E) is the best "weakener" of the bunch. Let's examine the other four choices to see why none can compete with choice (D):

(A) The author credits Bacon with the idea that corporate support would be necessary for science to flourish. If it were determined that somewhere Bacon spells out just what that support would consist of, that would still do nothing to damage the author's claim that Bacon missed the point that such corporate control of science could have negative consequences.

(B) It wouldn't be surprising to find the claim stated in choice (B) in Bacon's writings, considering what we know about his ideas from the passage. However, this wouldn't in any way damage the author's claim that Bacon missed the point that corporate control of science could have negative consequences.

(C) The author states that "Bacon did not ignore the necessity for creative and dedicated individuals to spur science onwards," so it wouldn't be surprising to find the suggestion described in choice (C) in Bacon's writings. However, this wouldn't in any way damage the author's claim that Bacon missed the point that corporate control of science could have negative consequences.

(D) Based on the passage, Bacon seems to be a fairly perceptive fellow, so we wouldn't be surprised to find he was totally up on his science. However, as with all the other wrong choices here, this in no way hurts the author's argument that Bacon missed the point that corporate control of science could have negative consequences. That's the claim we're trying to weaken, and choice (D) doesn't do it.

APPLICATION QUESTIONS

Application questions ask you to relate ideas and situations described in the passage to outside scenarios. In other words, they test whether you can understand how examples represented in the passage might be applied in a different context. Application questions are inherently difficult because the choices involve situations foreign to the topic of the passage, and a leap is required on your part to connect the correct choice to the relevant idea or example in the passage. Here is what application questions typically look like:

As described in the passage, ---- is most nearly analogous to which of the following?

something the author describes

Which of the following best exemplifies ----?

something mentioned in the passage

Which of the following would the author consider to be most similar to ----?

something mentioned in the passage

When you see an application question, you should follow these three steps:

1. Go back to the example or idea in question and reread it to make sure you have a firm grasp of it.

2. Put the example or idea into general terms. This helps because it is the general logic of the example that somehow relates to the correct answer choice.

3. Test the choices to see whether each one matches the example or idea in question. Beware of choices that distort the meaning of the example.

Now, try to answer an application question about the Francis Bacon passage. Remember that the key to an application question is to generalize a situation and recognize it in another context. Think about the plight of the modern scientist and try to put it into general terms. Then, check the choices to see which one corresponds best to such a scenario.

Example:

The situation of the modern scientist as described in the passage is most nearly analogous to that of

(A) a painter who participates in an artistic community in order to gain exposure for his works.

(B) a doctor who is required to attend a yearly conference in order to keep up with developments in her field.

(C) a musician who needs to alter her vision for a recording project in order to maintain the support of her record company.

(D) an executive who is fired for disobeying company policy.

(E) a union member who organizes a strike to protest against poor working conditions.

The correct answer is (C). According to the author, the modern scientist depends on support from a large organization that forces him to conduct his work according to the demands of the organization. Similarly, the musician in choice (C) depends on a record company that forces her to change what she wants to create in order to please the company. Choice (C) offers the best analogy to the author's description of the modern scientist's plight. Let's examine the other four choices to see why none can compete with choice (C):

(A) According to the author, the modern scientist depends on support from a large organization that forces him to conduct his work according to the demands of the organization. This results in a problem for the scientist, whereas the painter in choice (A) benefits from his attachment to the artistic community.

(B) According to the author, the modern scientist depends on support from a large organization that forces him to conduct his work according to the demands of the organization. A doctor required to attend a conference is not in the same situation because nothing implies that the doctor must alter, against her will, the way she goes about practicing medicine.

(D) According to the author, the modern scientist depends on support from a large organization that forces him to conduct his work according to the demands of that organization. A fired executive need not fit into the same general category. Maybe he deserves to be fired, maybe not, but either way a company has a right to determine how its employees should behave. However, the scientist, according to the author, was once independent and needs to be independent for society to benefit. The predicament of the scientist that the author laments is therefore not similar to the situation of a fired executive.

(E) According to the author, the modern scientist depends on support from a large organization that forces him to conduct his work according to the demands of the organization. That's the situation we need to mirror. A union worker organizing a protest doesn't match the scenario in the question stem. We never hear about scientists fighting back—the author simply voices his concern regarding their ability to work independent of corporate influence.

METHOD QUESTIONS

Method questions ask you to recognize what the author is doing in the passage or how the author goes about making her points. Some method questions ask for the author's overall approach in the passage, while others ask about how a specific point is made or about the structure of a particular paragraph. Method questions can be difficult because the answer choices are usually stated very generally, and it's up to you to connect the general wording of the choices with what's going on in the passage.

A method question can come in many different forms. Here are just a few examples of what the question stem might look like:

> Which of the following best describes the approach of the passage?
>
> In the last paragraph, the author proceeds by ...
>
> How does the fourth paragraph function in relation to the third paragraph?
>
> Which of the following most accurately describes the organization of the second paragraph?
>
> Which of the following techniques is used in the last sentence of paragraph 3?

When you see a method question, you should follow these three steps:

1. Let the question guide you to the appropriate area of the passage and reread that section carefully.

2. Focus on what the author is doing—don't get bogged down in details. Method questions concern how the author makes his/her points, not what those points are. The latter is the subject of detail and inference questions.

3. Test the choices rigorously. Every word in the correct choice must be consistent with what's going on in the passage. Wrong choices contain elements that go against the author's approach or that are simply not represented in the passage.

Now, apply these steps to a method question about the Francis Bacon passage. The final paragraph is short enough to skim quickly before checking out the choices. But read it with a very specific goal in mind—to see what the author is doing in these few lines. Don't get bogged down in details—they really won't help you here. Test the choices, making sure every word of the choice you select matches what's going on in this part of the passage.

Example:

Which of the following most accurately describes the organization of the last paragraph of the passage?

(A) An assertion is made and is backed up by evidence.
(B) A viewpoint is expressed and an opposing viewpoint is stated and countered.
(C) An admission is offered and followed by a warning and recommendation.
(D) Contradictory claims are presented and then reconciled.
(E) A problem is outlined and a solution is proposed and defended.

The correct answer is (C). The notion that no one questions the benefits of science does qualify as an admission in the context of the paragraph; that is, the author admits that science has given humankind enormous benefits, but then goes on to voice his concern regarding the current state of the scientific enterprise. Note how the contrast signal word "however" screams at us that some kind of change must come after the author admits that science has conferred immense benefits, and indeed, what comes next is, as choice (C) puts it, a warning: there is cause for concern. The recommendation that rounds out choice (C) appears in the final sentence, highlighted by the words "we must ask certain questions ..." Every element in choice (C) is present and accounted for, so choice (C) correctly describes the organization of the paragraph. Let's examine the other four choices to see why none can compete with choice (C):

(A) This choice says that the paragraph begins with an assertion, and we can surely accept that: the assertion that no one questions the benefits of science. Is this then backed up by evidence? No. The contrast signal word "however" alerts us that some kind of change is coming, it does not provide evidence for the statement in the first sentence. And indeed, the rest does go off in a different direction.

(B) This choice doesn't reflect what's going on here. It says that the final paragraph begins with a viewpoint, and we can surely accept that: the view that no one questions the benefits of science. But does an opposing viewpoint follow— that is, an argument against the benefits of science? No, the author doesn't go there. He is concerned about the way science is now conducted. He doesn't mention or counter the position that tries to downplay what science has already accomplished.

(D) This choice is incorrect because there are no contradictory claims here. The author admits that science has given humankind enormous benefits, but then goes on to voice his concern regarding the current state of the scientific enterprise. These things aren't contradictory, and nothing in the paragraph contradicts either of these things, so choice (D) can't be correct.

(E) It's fair to say that a problem is outlined—the problem that securing financial support for scientific work might get in the way of scientists improving standards of living. But does the author propose a solution? No. He recommends that serious questions be asked about the problem, but offers no solution of his own. Even if you view his recommendation as a solution, you still have to bog down on the "defended" part of choice (E). The passage ends before any kind of defense of his recommendation is offered.

SIX NEXT-LEVEL TECHNIQUES FOR EFFECTIVE READING

Even if you're a voracious reader who's already developed the kinds of effective reading habits that will serve you well in SAT critical reading, it can't hurt to review the basic reading techniques that apply most directly to the SAT.

Don't expect to just walk into the SAT testing room and apply the techniques you'll learn about here without practicing them first. You need to try them out first, during your SAT practice testing, until you become comfortable with them.

Most test-takers approach critical reading passages *passively*. They give equal time and attention to every sentence in a passage, reading the passage from beginning to end without interruption and with very little thought as to what particular information is most important in order to respond to the specific questions. This strategy is actually better characterized as a *non*-strategy. What's the result? The test-taker might remember some scattered facts and ideas, which will help him/her respond correctly to some easier questions.

But the passive mindset won't take the test-taker very far when it comes to tougher questions. As you're no doubt aware of by now, harder critical reading questions are tougher because they measure your ability to *understand* the ideas in the passage rather than to simply *recall* information. In order to understand a passage, you must be able to (1) identify the thesis (or main idea) and the author's primary purpose and (2) follow the author's line of reasoning from paragraph to paragraph. Both tasks require an *active* frame of mind in which you constantly interact with the text as you read.

1. Mark up the passage. (That's what your pencil is for!)

Selective *annotating* (e.g., circling and underlining key words and phrases) serves three important purposes:

1. It helps you to maintain an active frame of mind considering you are shopping for ideas and information that are sufficiently important to earmark.

2. It provides a pre-written outline. After you read (and annotate) the entire passage, reviewing the annotated words and phrases is an effective way to recap the passage for yourself.

3. If you need to refer to the passage as you answer the questions, effective annotating helps you quickly locate the information you need.

What sort of information should you annotate? If you under-annotate, you cannot effectively recap the passage by reviewing your annotations. On the other hand, if you over-annotate, your annotations lose their meaning, and you might as well not have annotated at all. Here are some suggestions for finding just the right balance:

- Mark areas of discussion that you may need to locate again to answer one or more of the questions.

- Instead of underlining complete sentences, select key words or phrases that "trigger" for you the idea or point that is made in this sentence or this part of the paragraph.

- Mark structural connectors—key words that connect the logical building blocks of the passage.

- In chronological passages, mark historical benchmarks and divisions—centuries, years, decades, or historical periods—that help to form the structure of the author's discussion.

- Use arrows to physically connect words that signify ideas that are connected; for example:

  —To clarify cause and effect in the natural sciences or in the context of historical events

  —To indicate who was influenced by whom in literature, music, psychology, etc.

  —To connect names (philosophers, scientists, authors, etc.) with dates, events, other names, theories, schools of thought, works, etc.

—To indicate the chronological order in which historical events occurred

- Create your own visual cues to earmark possible thesis statements, major supporting points, and points of author disagreement.

2. MAKE MARGIN NOTES AND (FOR SOME PASSAGES) OUTLINES.

In the left-hand margin, make shorthand notes to summarize paragraphs, earmark areas of discussion, and otherwise provide signals for yourself so that you can locate details more quickly and recap the passage more effectively. Keep your notes as brief as possible; two or three words should provide a sufficient cue.

Don't bother constructing a formal outline of the passage. This takes more time than it's worth. Instead, rely on your margin notes and annotations to indicate the flow of the discussion. For certain high-density passages, however, some organized notes—a "mini-outline"—may be necessary to organize information. Shorthand notes at the bottom of the page may help to keep particular details straight in your mind. The following scenarios typically call for the mini-outline:

- If the passage categorizes or classifies various phenomena, notes may help clarify which phenomena belong in which categories.

- If the passage mentions numerous individual names (of authors, artists, political figures, etc.), use notes to link them according to influence, agreement or disagreement, and so forth.

3. PAY ATTENTION TO THE OVERALL STRUCTURE OF THE PASSAGE.

Different types of reading passages are organized in different ways. For example:

- A passage that traces historical causes or consequences will probably be organized chronologically.

- A passage that critiques a theory will probably describe the theory first, and then explain its problems, one at a time.

- A passage that draws a comparison (pointing out similarities and differences) between two things might first list similarities, then differences.

- A passage that describes a classification system will probably begin by defining the main class, then branch out to each sub-class level.

Understanding how the passage is organized—in other words, recognizing its structure—will help you to articulate the passage's main idea and primary purpose, to understand the author's purpose in mentioning various details, and to distinguish between main points and minor details—all of which will help you answer the questions.

4. LOOK FOR STRUCTURAL CLUES OR "TRIGGERS."

Triggers are key words and phrases that provide clues about the structure and organization of the passage and the direction in which the discussion is flowing. The lists below contain many common trigger words and phrases. Underline or circle trigger words as you read the passage. Review your annotations to help you recap the passage and see its structure and organization.

- These words precede an item in a list (e.g., examples, classes, reasons, or characteristics):

   —*first, second* (etc.)

   —*in addition, also, another*

- These words signal that the author is contrasting two phenomena:

   —*alternatively, by contrast, however, on the other hand, rather than, while, yet*

- These words signal a logical conclusion based upon preceding material:

   —*consequently, in conclusion, then, thus, therefore, as a result, accordingly*

- These words signal that the author is comparing (identifying similarities between) two phenomena:

   —*similarly, in the same way, analogous, parallel, likewise, just as, also, as*

- These words signal evidence (factual information) used to support the author's argument:

   —*because, since, in light of*

- These words signal an example of a phenomenon:

   —*for instance, e.g., such as, ... is an illustration of*

5. DON'T GET BOGGED DOWN IN DETAILS AS YOU READ.

SAT reading passages are packed with details: lists, statistics and other numbers, dates, titles, and so forth. If you try to absorb all of the details as you read, you'll not only lose sight of the main points but also lose reading speed. Don't get bogged down in the details; gloss over them. In the left-hand margin, note where particular examples, lists, and other details are located. Then, if a particular question involving those details is included, you can quickly and easily locate them and read them more carefully.

6. SUM UP THE PASSAGE AFTER YOU READ IT.

After reading the entire passage, take a few seconds to recap it. What was the author's main point and what were the major supporting points? Remind yourself of the flow of the discussion without thinking about all the details. Chances are, you'll be able to answer at least one or two of the questions based just on your recap.

SUMMING IT UP

Many passages have a conclusion, so it's only right that our chapter about passages has one, too. Most of the techniques discussed here are things that you do in some form already. This chapter has shown how strategies such as "using context" and "finding the main idea" apply to the reading section of the SAT. When you work on the practice passages in this book, focus on using these techniques. Cover the answer choices of a sentence completion problem while you come up with your own word. Jot down quick summaries of a passage while you're reading it. These techniques are highly effective, and all you need to do is practice them to the point where they become second nature. When you get to that level of comfort, you will see how beneficial they are in answering easy, medium, and hard problems.

PART V
FOUR CRITICAL READING PRACTICE TESTS

ANSWER SHEET PRACTICE TEST 2

1 (A) (B) (C) (D) (E)   6 (A) (B) (C) (D) (E)   11 (A) (B) (C) (D) (E)   16 (A) (B) (C) (D) (E)
2 (A) (B) (C) (D) (E)   7 (A) (B) (C) (D) (E)   12 (A) (B) (C) (D) (E)   17 (A) (B) (C) (D) (E)
3 (A) (B) (C) (D) (E)   8 (A) (B) (C) (D) (E)   13 (A) (B) (C) (D) (E)   18 (A) (B) (C) (D) (E)
4 (A) (B) (C) (D) (E)   9 (A) (B) (C) (D) (E)   14 (A) (B) (C) (D) (E)   19 (A) (B) (C) (D) (E)
5 (A) (B) (C) (D) (E)   10 (A) (B) (C) (D) (E)   15 (A) (B) (C) (D) (E)   20 (A) (B) (C) (D) (E)

Critical Reading Practice Test 2

20 Questions • 25 Minutes

Directions: Each of the following questions consists of an incomplete sentence followed by five words or pairs of words. Choose that word or pair of words which, when substituted for the blank space or spaces, best completes the meaning of the sentence. Mark the letter of your choice on your answer sheet.

Example:

In view of the extenuating circumstances and the defendant's youth, the judge recommended ----.

(A) conviction
(B) a defense
(C) a mistrial
(D) leniency
(E) life imprisonment

Ⓐ Ⓑ ● Ⓓ Ⓔ

1. Friends of the theater have long decried the ---- of the New York drama critics, whose reviews can determine the fate of a play in a single night.

    (A) insensitivity
    (B) provinciality
    (C) intelligence
    (D) power
    (E) inaccuracy

2. The ---- manner in which the teacher candidate addressed the school board was a key factor in his rejection; the school board members agreed that enthusiasm is an essential quality in a teacher.

    (A) pretentious
    (B) solicitous
    (C) superficial
    (D) perfunctory
    (E) combative

3. Her ---- writing style made it difficult to follow her thought processes—no surprise to her colleagues, who were familiar with her ---- manner of speech.

    (A) precise .. arcane
    (B) laborious .. tedious
    (C) trite .. flippant
    (D) convoluted .. circumlocutory
    (E) ambiguous .. affected

4. The new team member's ---- was an encouragement to the rest of the team, who had become ---- by the string of defeats.

    (A) enthusiasm .. elated
    (B) vigor .. inundated
    (C) ebullience .. dispirited
    (D) dourness .. undone
    (E) excessiveness .. downcast

5. Advertising can increase sales of a ---- product, but it cannot create demand for a bad one; consumers may buy a ---- item because of advertising—but only once.

    (A) good .. new
    (B) reliable .. costly
    (C) useful .. valuable
    (D) needless .. single
    (E) well-made .. badly made

6. Like Truman, who was never considered a major national figure until Roosevelt's death made him president, Ford attained national prominence only after ---- thrust him into the presidency.

    (A) personal ambition
    (B) outside circumstances
    (C) popular acclaim
    (D) political intrigue
    (E) public demand

7. Thus far, predictions that global ---- would lead to mass starvation have proven false; however, in the years to come, population ---- may yet prove to be one of the world's greatest problems.

    (A) pollution .. expansion
    (B) overcrowding .. growth
    (C) poverty .. density
    (D) deforestation .. control
    (E) warfare .. stabilization

8. Amelia Earhart's hope of being the first woman to fly around the globe was ---- when she disappeared in the middle of her ---- journey.

   (A) thwarted .. ill-fated
   (B) realized .. triumphant
   (C) fulfilled .. historic
   (D) controversial .. hazardous
   (E) postponed .. famous

9. The idea of "children's literature" ---- in the late eighteenth century, when educators first decided that children needed special ---- of their own.

   (A) emerged .. books
   (B) changed .. reading
   (C) grew .. treatment
   (D) developed .. training
   (E) receded .. teaching

10. In some of the poorest neighborhoods of New York City, community gardens are springing up as ---- the filth and desolation of their urban surroundings.

    (A) an affirmation of
    (B) a validation of
    (C) a reaction to
    (D) an amplification of
    (E) a celebration of

Directions: Each reading passage below is followed by a set of questions. Read the passage and answer the accompanying questions, basing your answers on what is stated or implied in the passage. Mark the letter of your choice on your answer sheet.

Questions 11–12 are based on the following passage.

Richard III was without any doubt whatsoever the most evil man to have worn the crown of England. Attached to his name are so many crimes, and crimes so heinous and unnatural, that it is scarcely credible that such a monster could exist. He not

(5) only committed murder on a number of occasions, but many of those he murdered he had either sworn to protect or should have been expected to defend with his last ounce of strength if he had anything approaching human feelings. First on the list of crimes was the death of his sovereign, Henry VI. Granted that Henry

(10) had been deposed by Richard's brother, and hence could not easily claim Richard's loyalty.

11. The word *heinous* in line 3 means

    (A) awful.

    (B) secretive.

    (C) bloody.

    (D) deceitful.

    (E) dishonest.

12. The author calls Richard a "monster" because

    (A) Richard murdered people.

    (B) Richard did not allow honor or family feeling to hold him back.

    (C) Richard was overly ambitious.

    (D) all early English kings were ruthless.

    (E) Richard supported Henry VI against his own brother.

Questions 13–14 are based on the following passage.

A bill is the form used for most legislation in the United State Congress. Only constitutional amendments and procedural issues affecting the House and Senate are adopted by a resolution, rather than a bill. Bills can be written to be permanent

(5) or temporary, general or special. A bill originating in the House of Representatives is designated by the letters "H.R.," signifying "House of Representatives," followed by a number that it retains throughout all its parliamentary stages. The number on the bill is determined by the order in which it was submitted

(10)   during a particular session. Bills are presented to the President
         for action when approved in identical form by both the House of
         Representatives and the Senate.

13. From the passage, it can be inferred that a bill that is designated
    as H.R. 1 is the first bill

    (A)   voted upon by the House of Representatives in a particular
          session of Congress.
    (B)   submitted to the House of Representatives in a particular
          session of Congress.
    (C)   sent to the Senate from the House of Representatives in a
          particular session of Congress.
    (D)   originating in the House of Representatives signed by the
          President in a particular session of Congress.
    (E)   debated on the floor of the House of Representatives in a
          particular session of Congress.

14. It is implied in the passage that once a bill is passed in the House
    of Representatives it might be sent to which of the following two
    places?

    (A)   Senate, conference committee
    (B)   Senate, House committee
    (C)   Senate, President
    (D)   President, Supreme Court
    (E)   President, Congress

Questions 15–16 are based on the following passage.

         Native American views of nature have important parallels in
         contemporary ecology. Through traditional customs and symbols
         like the medicine wheel, a circular arrangement of stones is
         often interpreted as representing the relationship between
(5)   Earth, air, water, and fire, Native Americans have long rec-
         ognized and celebrated the connectedness among all natural
         things. Indeed, the Native American view of the world has
         always been consistent with that of Earth ecology—that Earth is
         a single system of interconnected parts.

15. The symbol of the medicine wheel is given as a(n)

    (A)   illustration of how Native Americans view Earth as an
          interconnected system.
    (B)   example of the Native American understanding of the four
          elements.
    (C)   example of the interrelatedness of the four basic elements.
    (D)   critique of contemporary ecological understandings of Earth.
    (E)   contrast to contemporary ecological understandings of
          Earth.

16. Given what the passage states about Native American views of nature, which of the following scenarios most accords with a Native American view?

    (A) Studying a microorganism removed from its habitat.
    (B) Studying Earth through satellite images.
    (C) Studying only animals and substances with spiritual symbolism.
    (D) Studying a specific organism's interrelationships with its habitat.
    (E) Studying a habitat as a whole.

Questions 17–20 are based on the following passage.

Big earthquakes are naturally occurring events well outside the powers of humans to create or stop. An earthquake is caused by a sudden slip on a fault. Stresses in the earth's outer layer push the sides of the fault together. The friction across the surface
(5) of the fault holds the rocks together so they do not slip immediately when pushed sideways. Eventually enough stress builds up and the rocks slip suddenly, releasing energy in waves that travel through the rock to cause the shaking that we feel during an earthquake. Earthquakes typically originate several tens
(10) of miles below the surface of the earth. It takes many years—decades to centuries—to build up enough stress to make a large earthquake, and the fault may be tens to hundreds of miles long. The scale and force necessary to produce earthquakes are well beyond our daily lives. Likewise, people cannot prevent earth-
(15) quakes from happening or stop them once they've started—giant nuclear explosions at shallow depths, like those in some movies, won't actually stop an earthquake.

   The two most important variables affecting earthquake damage are the intensity of ground shaking caused by the quake
(20) and the quality of the engineering of structures in the region. The level of shaking, in turn, is controlled by the proximity of the earthquake source to the affected region and the types of rocks that seismic waves pass through en route (particularly those at or near the ground surface). Generally, the bigger and
(25) closer the earthquake, the stronger the shaking. But there have been large earthquakes with very little damage either because they caused little shaking or because the buildings were built to withstand that shaking. In other cases, moderate earthquakes have caused significant damage either because the shaking was
(30) locally amplified or more likely because the structures were poorly engineered.

17. The word *fault* (line 3) means

    (A) error.
    (B) the place where two rock plates come together.
    (C) criticize.
    (D) responsibility.
    (E) volcanic activity.

18. The amount of shaking during an earthquake is determined by

    (A) the amount of damage.
    (B) how soon people take action to stop the earthquake.
    (C) how close the epicenter of the earthquake is to the area.
    (D) how well the offices and homes have been built in the region.
    (E) the duration of the quake.

19. This passage was most likely written to

    (A) explain some basic facts about the causes and effects of earthquakes.
    (B) reassure people who are considering moving into regions prone to earthquakes that they will be safe from harm.
    (C) teach people the methods they need to alleviate earthquake damage.
    (D) persuade people to allocate more funding to earthquake research.
    (E) describe the damage that earthquakes can cause and the reason for varying degrees of damage.

20. You can conclude from this passage that

    (A) all earthquakes are equally dangerous.
    (B) there are steps that people can take to prevent or at least mitigate earthquakes.
    (C) earthquakes occur all over the world.
    (D) very little is known about earthquakes.
    (E) scientists understand a great deal about the origins of earthquakes but are powerless to stop them.

STOP

IF YOU FINISH BEFORE THE TIME IS UP,
GO BACK AND CHECK YOUR WORK.

ANSWER KEY AND EXPLANATIONS

1. D	5. E	9. A	13. B	17. B
2. D	6. B	10. C	14. C	18. C
3. D	7. B	11. A	15. A	19. A
4. C	8. A	12. B	16. E	20. E

1. **The correct answer is (D).** The missing word must fit the description of the critics given in the second half of the sentence. If they "can determine the fate of a play in a single night," then clearly they have a lot of *power*.

2. **The correct answer is (D).** Remember that a semicolon (;) often indicates that the two halves of the sentence restate or paraphrase the same idea. The second half of this sentence tells us that the members of the school board wanted "enthusiasm" in a teacher candidate. Therefore, the word that describes the candidate they rejected should mean the opposite of "enthusiastic." *Perfunctory* fits the bill.

3. **The correct answer is (D).** Since both blanks here describe something similar—the way this unnamed person communicates—the two words should be near-synonyms. And the words "difficult to follow her thought processes" make it clear that both missing words should mean "hard to understand, unnecessarily complicated."

4. **The correct answer is (C).** On this dual-blank sentence, let's do the first blank first since we know that the blank was *an encouragement to the rest of the team.* Good spirits would be an encouragement to the rest of the team. You can eliminate (D) and (E). As for the second blank, what does a string of defeats do to a team? It discourages them. (A), *elated,* does not match this. Nor does (B), *inundated.* But (C), *dispirited,* fits well and you've already eliminated (D) and (E). Choice (C) is the best answer.

5. **The correct answer is (E).** Both halves of the sentence make much the same point—that people buy good products but not bad ones. Only the words in choice (E) fit this idea.

6. **The correct answer is (B).** Obviously, the structure of this sentence involves similarity. We want a phrase to fit in the blank that matches the description of how both Truman and Ford attained prominence. You don't need to know history; just realize that Ford's case must have resembled Truman's, in which pure accident (or *outside circumstances*) made him president.

7. **The correct answer is (B).** The word "however" tells you that the two halves of the sentence contrast with each other. The first half says that "predictions" of "mass starvation have proven false"; the

second half says that, in the future, (something) "may yet prove to be one of the world's greatest problems." Thus, the contrast involves the idea that a problem which doesn't exist now may come to exist in the future; the same problem is discussed in both parts of the sentence. Choice (B), then, makes sense because "global *overcrowding*" and "population *growth*" describe the same problem.

8. **The correct answer is (A).** If she disappeared during the journey, then clearly her hope of flying around the globe was *thwarted,* choice (A). *Ill-fated* is the logical word to use to describe a trip that ends this way (worse than losing your luggage).

9. **The correct answer is (A).** If it wasn't until the late eighteenth century that educators decided children needed *books* of their own, then that must have been when the idea of children's literature *emerged*, choice (A).

10. **The correct answer is (C).** Only *reaction* makes sense as a description of the relationship between a garden and surroundings that are full of "filth and desolation."

11. **The correct answer is (A).** Richard is *heinous* (awful), shown by the synonyms "evil" and "unnatural."

12. **The correct answer is (B).** You can infer this answer because Richard murdered many people, even those he should have protected—such as King Henry VI.

13. **The correct answer is (B).** The passage says that H.R. means House of Representatives and that the number is given according to, "the order it was submitted in a particular session." (lines 9–10) So the 1 means that it was submitted first in a particular session. Choice (B) is the correct answer.

14. **The correct answer is (C).** This is a tricky question. The major clue is that only three entities are mentioned in the passage: the House of Representatives, the Senate, and the President. You should suspect then that the answer will be the Senate and the President since those are the only other two entities mentioned in the passage. You can get confirmation for this hunch in the sentence that says "Bills are presented to the President for action when approved in identical form by both the House of Representatives and the Senate." Bills must pass both houses, so if the bills originate in the house, they have to go to the Senate before reaching the President. The answer is (C).

15. **The correct answer is (A).** The paragraph is about how Native Americans have "long recognized and celebrated the connectedness among all natural things." The medicine wheel illustrates this point because it emphasizes the connectedness of the four basic elements. So (A) is the best choice.

16. **The correct answer is (E).** Remember the Native American view stated in the passage is that all natural things are connected; so we should expect that the scenario will demonstrate this belief. Choice (A) is specifically opposed to that. Choice (C) is also, to a lesser degree. Choice (B) is neutral toward the Native American idea—it neither contradicts it nor realizes it. Choices (D) and (E) are in accord with the Native American view because they recognize the connectedness of an organism and its habitat. However, (D) mentions studying a specific organism in its habitat, while (E) mentions studying a habitat as a whole. So, (E) is broader and, in this case, broader is better. The best answer is (E).

17. **The correct answer is (B).** Infer the answer from the context clues "the earth's outer layer push the sides of the fault together" and "friction across the surface of the fault holds the rocks together."

18. **The correct answer is (C).** The answer is directly stated: "The level of shaking, in turn, is controlled by the proximity of the earthquake source to the affected region and the types of rocks that seismic waves pass through en route (particularly those at or near the ground surface)."

19. **The correct answer is (A).** Using process of elimination, choices (B) and (C) are directly contradicted by information in the text. Choice (D) is never mentioned. The second half of choice (E) is correct, but not the first half. Thus, the only possible correct response is choice (A).

20. **The correct answer is (E).** Choices (A), (B), and (D) cannot be correct. Choice (D) is contradicted by information in the passage. Thus, the only possible correct response is choice (E).

ANSWER SHEET PRACTICE TEST 3

1 Ⓐ Ⓑ Ⓒ Ⓓ Ⓔ 6 Ⓐ Ⓑ Ⓒ Ⓓ Ⓔ 11 Ⓐ Ⓑ Ⓒ Ⓓ Ⓔ 16 Ⓐ Ⓑ Ⓒ Ⓓ Ⓔ
2 Ⓐ Ⓑ Ⓒ Ⓓ Ⓔ 7 Ⓐ Ⓑ Ⓒ Ⓓ Ⓔ 12 Ⓐ Ⓑ Ⓒ Ⓓ Ⓔ 17 Ⓐ Ⓑ Ⓒ Ⓓ Ⓔ
3 Ⓐ Ⓑ Ⓒ Ⓓ Ⓔ 8 Ⓐ Ⓑ Ⓒ Ⓓ Ⓔ 13 Ⓐ Ⓑ Ⓒ Ⓓ Ⓔ 18 Ⓐ Ⓑ Ⓒ Ⓓ Ⓔ
4 Ⓐ Ⓑ Ⓒ Ⓓ Ⓔ 9 Ⓐ Ⓑ Ⓒ Ⓓ Ⓔ 14 Ⓐ Ⓑ Ⓒ Ⓓ Ⓔ 19 Ⓐ Ⓑ Ⓒ Ⓓ Ⓔ
5 Ⓐ Ⓑ Ⓒ Ⓓ Ⓔ 10 Ⓐ Ⓑ Ⓒ Ⓓ Ⓔ 15 Ⓐ Ⓑ Ⓒ Ⓓ Ⓔ 20 Ⓐ Ⓑ Ⓒ Ⓓ Ⓔ

Critical Reading Practice Test 3

20 Questions • 25 Minutes

Directions: The incomplete sentences below are followed by five words or pairs of words. Choose that word or pair of words that, when substituted for the blank space or spaces, best completes the meaning of the sentence. Mark the letter of your choice on your answer sheet.

Example:

In view of the extenuating circumstances and the defendant's youth, the judge recommended ----.

(A) conviction
(B) a defense
(C) a mistrial
(D) leniency
(E) life imprisonment

Ⓐ Ⓑ Ⓒ ● Ⓔ

1. The neighborhood group's rendering of the proposed office complex ---- the ---- of the project: as they appeared on the drawing, the proposed office buildings appeared to dwarf the rest of the downtown area.

(A) minimized .. grandiosity
(B) accentuated .. beauty
(C) underscored .. vastness
(D) trivialized .. enormity
(E) revealed .. immensity

2. Twentieth-century Japan faced the question of how to ---- the best of modern civilization without losing the benefits of Japan's ---- way of life.

(A) reject .. ancient
(B) adopt .. outmoded
(C) assimilate .. traditional
(D) incorporate .. contemporary
(E) reshape .. historic

281

3. The proposal to forbid the use of indoor furniture on front porches has divided the town along ---- lines: the affluent feel the old couches are eyesores, while those who cannot afford new outdoor furniture are ---- about what they feel is an attempt to restrict their lifestyle.

   (A) political .. nonplussed
   (B) aesthetic .. dismayed
   (C) class .. pleased
   (D) racial .. angry
   (E) socioeconomic .. incensed

4. In his politics, Aristotle characterizes Plato's support of collectivism as ---- and ---- the unity of the city; not only would it be difficult to institute and enforce, but the absence of private property would lead to bickering among the citizens.

   (A) commendable .. deleterious to
   (B) controversial .. essential to
   (C) impractical .. detrimental to
   (D) divisive .. indifferent toward
   (E) unattainable .. supportive of

5. The bright coloration of American coot chicks is an anomaly: although colorful plumage is usually ---- to newborn birds because it may attract predators, among this species it appears to be ----, because parents are more likely to notice and care for brightly-colored offspring.

   (A) pernicious .. fatal
   (B) dangerous .. unnecessary
   (C) deleterious .. favorable
   (D) beneficial .. advantageous
   (E) detrimental .. helpful

6. Unlike the American worker, who expects to work for several different firms during his or her career, until recently the Japanese worker regarded employment as ---- commitment.

   (A) a lifetime
   (B) a significant
   (C) a bilateral
   (D) an economic
   (E) a moral

7. Andre's gift for music seemed to be ----; both his mother and grandfather before him had been famed concert pianists.

    (A) simulated
    (B) innate
    (C) accidental
    (D) inexplicable
    (E) prodigious

8. The many obvious lapses in the author's research make it ---- to accept the ---- of his conclusions.

    (A) easy .. accuracy
    (B) impossible .. meaning
    (C) attractive .. logic
    (D) questionable .. structure
    (E) difficult .. validity

9. Her wildlife movies unflinchingly capture the ---- of the animal kingdom: predators stalking their prey, singling out the weak, young, and very old as easy kills, and the cold-blooded killing is a necessity of life in the wild.

    (A) brutality
    (B) romance
    (C) color
    (D) mystery
    (E) grandeur

10. Although the Internet was originally created to facilitate scientific research and emergency communication, today most people consider it ---- enterprise, offering services marketed as sources of information and entertainment.

    (A) a commercial
    (B) a private
    (C) an obsolete
    (D) an insidious
    (E) an institutional

Directions: Each reading passage below is followed by a set of questions. Read the passage and answer the accompanying questions, basing your answers on what is stated or implied in the passage. Mark the letter of your choice on your answer sheet.

Questions 11–12 are based on the following passage.

Farmlands, wetlands, forests, and deserts that composed the American landscape in the early twentieth century have frequently been transformed during the past thirty years into mushrooming metropolitan areas as urbanization spreads across
(5) the country. Many metropolitan areas in the United States are growing at extraordinary rates. "Urban growth is a vital issue that requires our careful attention from local to global scales," said Barbara Ryan, USGS Associate Director of Geography. "It is not until we begin to take a broad census of the land itself—
(10) tracking landscapes from a spatial perspective in a time scale of decades—that we can grasp the scale of the changes that have already occurred and predict the impact of changes to come."

On average, between 1984 and 2004, Atlanta, Boston, Chicago, Denver, Houston, Las Vegas, Memphis,
(15) Minneapolis-St. Paul, Orlando, Phoenix, Pittsburgh, Raleigh-Durham, Reno-Sparks, Sacramento, Seattle-Tacoma, and Tampa-St. Petersburg averaged 173 square miles of additional urban land over the two decades, with Houston, Orlando, and Atlanta as the top three regions by area. The growth leaders by
(20) percentage change were Las Vegas (193 percent), Orlando (157 percent), and Phoenix (103 percent).

11. The tone of this passage is best described as
   (A) restrained ardor.
   (B) dour.
   (C) neutral.
   (D) fanatical.
   (E) biased.

12. You can infer from this article that
   (A) the author believes that further study on the issue of urban growth is needed.
   (B) the author heartily endorses urban growth.
   (C) the author is very much against urban sprawl and is actively working to limit it.
   (D) Seattle-Tacoma is getting overcrowded.
   (E) the author is inflating the change in land use to further his or her own agenda.

Questions 13–14 are based on the following passage.

The small hive beetle, Aethina tumida (Order Caleoptera;
Family Nitidulidae), was first discovered in Florida in June
of 1998 and has now been found in six other states, Georgia,
South Carolina, North Carolina, Pennsylvania, Ohio, and
(5)   Minnesota. To date, the beetle has not been found in Virginia,
but the movement of migratory beekeepers from Florida may
have transported the beetle to other states. Recent findings also
indicate transport of the beetles in packages.

The small hive beetle can be a destructive pest of honey bee
(10)   colonies, causing damage to combs, stored honey, and pollen. If
a beetle infestation is sufficiently heavy, they may cause bees
to abandon their hive. The beetles can also be a pest of stored
combs and honey (in the comb) awaiting extraction. Beetle
larvae may tunnel through combs of honey, causing discoloration
(15)   and fermentation of honey.

13. The small hive beetle is undesirable for all of the following
reasons EXCEPT the

   (A) harm it can cause to the honeycomb.
   (B) potential deleterious effects to store honey and pollen.
   (C) possibility that bees may flee the hive.
   (D) probability of the beetle attacking people and animals.
   (E) way it can stain and spoil honey.

14. This passage was most likely written to

   (A) help customers understand how difficult it is to raise
       commercial honey bees.
   (B) inform beekeepers about a menace that may be
       contaminating their hives.
   (C) warn consumers that the price of honey is likely to rise.
   (D) spark a federal bailout of the industry.
   (E) convince the Pure Food and Drug Administration to take the
       problem more seriously.

Questions 15–20 are based on the following passage.

Although often confused with each other, global warming and
ozone depletion are two separate problems threatening Earth's
ecosystem today. Global warming is caused by the build-up
of heat-trapping gases in the atmosphere. It was dubbed the
(5)   "greenhouse effect" because it is similar to a greenhouse in that
the sun's rays are allowed into the greenhouse but the heat
from these rays is unable to escape. Ozone depletion, however,
is the destruction of the ozone layer. Chemicals such as cholor-
fluorocarbons and methyl bromide react with ozone, leaving a

(10) "hole" in the ozone layer that lets dangerous UV rays through. Both are serious threats to life on Earth. While the greenhouse effect maintains the appropriate temperature for life on Earth, problems are exacerbated when the quantity of greenhouse gases in the Earth's atmosphere increases drastically. When this

(15) occurs, the amount of heat energy that is insulated within the Earth's atmosphere increases correspondingly and results in a rise in global temperature.

An increase of a mere few degrees Celsius does not appear very threatening. However, numbers can be deceiving. When

(20) you consider that the Ice Age resulted from temperatures only slightly cooler than those today, it is obvious that even very subtle temperature changes can significantly impact our global climate. Global warming threatens to desecrate the natural habitats of organisms on Earth and disturb the stability of our

(25) ecosystem. The climate changes that would result from global warming could trigger droughts, heatwaves, floods, and other extreme weather events.

Like most other environmental problems, humans are the cause of global warming. The burning of fossil fuels is largely

(30) responsible for the increase in the concentration of carbon dioxide in the atmosphere. Every time someone drives a car or powers their home with energy derived from power plants that use coal, carbon dioxide is released into the atmosphere. The atmospheric concentrations of carbon dioxide and methane have

(35) risen meteorically since preindustrial times, mainly due to the contributions of factories, cars, and large-scale agriculture. Even if we immediately stopped emitting greenhouse gases, we would continue to see the effects of global warming for decades because of the damage we have already inflicted.

(40) Despite the pessimistic outlook, there are things that can be done to reduce global warming. Although the problem may seem overwhelming, individuals can make a positive difference in combating global warming. Simple things like driving less, using public transportation, and conserving electricity generated by

(45) combustion of fossil fuels can help reduce the emissions of greenhouse gases. It is important to realize that it is not too late to make a difference. If everyone does what he or she can to reduce their contributions of greenhouse gases to the atmosphere, the efforts of people around the world will act in concert to thwart

(50) the progression of global warming. If the effort is not made immediately, the delicate global ecosystem could be thrown irreversibly out of balance, and the future of life on Earth may be jeopardized.

15. The "greenhouse effect" is

    (A) global warming.
    (B) another term for the Ice Age.
    (C) ozone depletion.
    (D) a chemical that is harming Earth.
    (E) a type of gas.

16. The greenhouse effect is so serious because

    (A) no one really understands it.
    (B) it has been going on for a very long time.
    (C) it cannot be reversed.
    (D) it interferes with the ecosystem and changes weather patterns.
    (E) it leads to the destruction of the world's woodlands.

17. As used in this passage, *exacerbated* (line 13) means

    (A) annoyed.
    (B) improved.
    (C) worsened.
    (D) embittered.
    (E) exasperated.

18. The author of this selection is most likely

    (A) a scientist looking for alternate fuel sources, especially solar and wind power.
    (B) an industrialist determined to corner the market on fossil fuels.
    (C) a public advocate trying to improve the ecosystem.
    (D) a Web site for vegetarians.
    (E) an animal-rights activist.

19. The word *thwart* (line 49) is used to mean

    (A) baffle.
    (B) hinder.
    (C) facilitate.
    (D) countenance.
    (E) increase.

20. In the last paragraph, it becomes apparent that the author believes

    (A) individuals can help reverse global warming even by taking small steps.
    (B) there is nothing we can do to prevent further global warming.
    (C) the problem of global warming has been overstated.
    (D) global warming and ozone depletion really are the same thing.
    (E) now it is up to the government to step in and stop deforestation and global warming.

ANSWER KEY AND EXPLANATIONS

1. C	5. E	9. A	13. D	17. C
2. C	6. A	10. A	14. B	18. C
3. E	7. B	11. C	15. A	19. B
4. C	8. E	12. A	16. D	20. A

1. **The correct answer is (C).** The second half of the sentence shows that *vastness* is the dominant quality of the proposed office complex.

2. **The correct answer is (C).** The sentence describes something that twentieth-century Japan wanted to do; therefore, it must be referring to a desirable combination of the best of the old and the new. Choice (C) makes sense because it refers to *assimilating*, that is, absorbing, what is good in modern life, while retaining what is *traditional*. A negative word like *outmoded*, choice (B), doesn't fit this context.

3. **The correct answer is (E).** Because the second half of the sentence contrasts "the affluent" with "those who cannot afford new outdoor furniture," we can see that the first blank should be filled with a word referring to class or economic differences. This narrows the possibilities to choices (C) and (E). Choice (C) doesn't work because an attempt to restrict someone's lifestyle wouldn't logically make them feel *pleased*.

4. **The correct answer is (C).** The two words in this answer choice nicely paraphrase the two points made later in the sentence: *impractical* relates to "difficult to institute," and "*detrimental to . . . unity*" supports "lead[ing] to bickering."

5. **The correct answer is (E).** The words "anomaly" and "although" both suggest that the second half of the sentence is built around a contrast between the role colorful plumage usually plays among birds and the role it actually plays in this particular species. Thus, the two words we want must be nearly opposite in meaning, as the two words in choice (E) are.

6. **The correct answer is (A).** The word "unlike" shows us that the two halves of the sentence contrast with each other. The idea of a *lifetime* commitment nicely contrasts with the idea of changing jobs several times.

7. **The correct answer is (B).** If musical talent runs in Andre's family, then it is logical to consider his gift inborn, inherited, or *innate*.

8. **The correct answer is (E).** A simple cause-and-effect relationship is required here; if the research contains "many obvious lapses," then accepting its conclusions is certainly *difficult*.

9. **The correct answer is (A).** All we need here is a word that summarizes the tone of the second half of the sentence. A word like "violence," "bloodthirstiness," or *brutality* works.

10. **The correct answer is (A).** If the Internet today offers "services" that are "marketed," then it is clearly a *commercial* (that is, for-profit) enterprise.

11. **The correct answer is (C).** You can infer the neutral tone from the unbiased quotation and the dispassionate list of cities and statistics.

12. **The correct answer is (A).** Make the inference from Barbara Ryan's quotation. There is no support for any of the other choices.

13. **The correct answer is (D).** This is a literal comprehension question. Every answer but choice (D) can be found in the passage.

14. **The correct answer is (B).** The technical details and scientific tone suggest that the passage was written to inform beekeepers about a menace that may be contaminating their hives. Choices (C), (D), and (E) have a more passionate, fiery tone; choice (A) is a complaint.

15. **The correct answer is (A).** The answer is directly stated in the second and third sentences.

16. **The correct answer is (D).** The answer is directly stated in the second paragraph.

17. **The correct answer is (C).** You can infer the definition from the context clues "destruction" and "desecrate."

18. **The correct answer is (C).** You can infer the answer from the specific details describing ways that people can help correct the problem and improve the ecosystem.

19. **The correct answer is (B).** You can infer the definition from the context clues "the progression of global warming."

20. **The correct answer is (A).** You can infer the answer from the specific details about the ways we can help as well as from the optimistic tone.

ANSWER SHEET PRACTICE TEST 4

1 Ⓐ Ⓑ Ⓒ Ⓓ Ⓔ   6 Ⓐ Ⓑ Ⓒ Ⓓ Ⓔ   11 Ⓐ Ⓑ Ⓒ Ⓓ Ⓔ   16 Ⓐ Ⓑ Ⓒ Ⓓ Ⓔ
2 Ⓐ Ⓑ Ⓒ Ⓓ Ⓔ   7 Ⓐ Ⓑ Ⓒ Ⓓ Ⓔ   12 Ⓐ Ⓑ Ⓒ Ⓓ Ⓔ   17 Ⓐ Ⓑ Ⓒ Ⓓ Ⓔ
3 Ⓐ Ⓑ Ⓒ Ⓓ Ⓔ   8 Ⓐ Ⓑ Ⓒ Ⓓ Ⓔ   13 Ⓐ Ⓑ Ⓒ Ⓓ Ⓔ   18 Ⓐ Ⓑ Ⓒ Ⓓ Ⓔ
4 Ⓐ Ⓑ Ⓒ Ⓓ Ⓔ   9 Ⓐ Ⓑ Ⓒ Ⓓ Ⓔ   14 Ⓐ Ⓑ Ⓒ Ⓓ Ⓔ   19 Ⓐ Ⓑ Ⓒ Ⓓ Ⓔ
5 Ⓐ Ⓑ Ⓒ Ⓓ Ⓔ   10 Ⓐ Ⓑ Ⓒ Ⓓ Ⓔ   15 Ⓐ Ⓑ Ⓒ Ⓓ Ⓔ   20 Ⓐ Ⓑ Ⓒ Ⓓ Ⓔ

Critical Reading Practice Test 4

20 Questions • 25 Minutes

> **Directions:** The incomplete sentences below are followed by five words or pairs of words. Choose that word or pair of words that when substituted for the blank space or spaces, best completes the meaning of the sentence. Mark the letter of your choice on your answer sheet.

Example:

In view of the extenuating circumstances and the defendant's youth, the judge recommended ----.

(A) conviction
(B) a defense
(C) a mistrial
(D) leniency
(E) life imprisonment

Ⓐ Ⓑ Ⓒ ● Ⓔ

1. Her character was completely ----; she was totally devoid of ----.

(A) prosaic .. dullness
(B) prudent .. affection
(C) passive .. inertia
(D) impassive .. emotion
(E) saintly .. virtue

2. To succeed in the training program requires great —; you have to endure many months of rigorous exercise.

(A) reluctance
(B) creativity
(C) diffidence
(D) insensitivity
(E) tenacity

3. Since eating that ---- amount of food I have become ----.

   (A) substantial .. unchanged
   (B) miniscule .. corpulent
   (C) gargantuan .. emaciated
   (D) prodigious .. bilious
   (E) impeccable .. fastidious

4. The performer was exceedingly ----; she could juggle three apples at once.

   (A) inept
   (B) contentious
   (C) complacent
   (D) adroit
   (E) astute

5. I am ---- about the job; although the atmosphere is pleasant, the work is boring.

   (A) ambivalent
   (B) exultant
   (C) timorous
   (D) laconic
   (E) reticent

6. Herbert had none of the social graces; he was appallingly ----.

   (A) unlimbered
   (B) underrated
   (C) unfettered
   (D) uncluttered
   (E) uncouth

7. The ---- shantytown was infested with vermin and ----with disease.

   (A) attractive .. riddled
   (B) spurious .. infected
   (C) squalid .. rife
   (D) tidy .. inoculated
   (E) lugubrious .. fraught

8. The gathering was anything but ----; the partygoers were in a(n) ---- mood.

   (A) aggressive .. pushy
   (B) modest .. humble
   (C) gregarious .. loquacious
   (D) mournful .. ebullient
   (E) hostile .. frenetic

9. The entering class was fairly ----; nearly all the students came
   from a ---- background.

   (A) hostile .. receptive
   (B) homogeneous .. similar
   (C) formidable .. fastidious
   (D) exemplary .. related
   (E) parochial .. redundant

Directions: Each reading passage below is followed by a set of questions. Read the passage and answer the accompanying questions, basing your answers on what is stated or implied in the passage. Mark the letter of your choice on your answer sheet.

Questions 10–15 are based on the following passage.

Oliver Goldsmith (1730–1774) wrote criticism, plays, novels, biographies, travelogues, and nearly every other conceivable kind of composition. This good-humored essay is from a series published in the Public Ledger and then in book form as The Citizen of the World *(1762).*

Were we to estimate the learning of the English by the number of books that are every day published among them, perhaps no country, not even China itself, could equal them in this particular. I have reckoned not less than twenty-three new books

(5)   published in one day, which, upon computation, makes eight thousand three hundred and ninety-five in one year. Most of these are not confined to one single science, but embrace the whole circle. History, politics, poetry, mathematics, metaphysics, and the philosophy of nature, are all comprised in a manual no

(10) larger than that in which our children are taught the letters. If then, we suppose the learned of England to read but an eighth part of the works which daily come from the press (and surely none can pretend to learning upon less easy terms), at this rate every scholar will read a thousand books in one year. From

(15) such a calculation, you may conjecture what an amazing fund of literature a man must be possessed of, who thus reads three new books every day, not one of which but contains all the good things that ever were said or written.

     And yet I know not how it happens, but the English are

(20) not, in reality so learned as would seem from this calculation. We meet but few who know all arts and sciences to perfection; whether it is that the generality are incapable of such extensive knowledge, or that the authors of those books are not adequate instructors. In China, the Emperor himself takes cognizance

(25) of all the doctors in the kingdom who profess authorship. In England, every man may be an author, that can write; for they have by law a liberty, not only of saying what they please, but of being also as dull as they please.

     Yesterday, as I testified to my surprise, to the man in black,

(30) where writers could be found in sufficient number to throw

off the books I saw daily crowding from the press. I at first
imagined that their learned seminaries might take this method
of instructing the world. But, to obviate this objection, my
companion assured me that the doctors of colleges never wrote,

(35)   and that some of them had actually forgot their reading. "But if
you desire," continued he, "to see a collection of authors, I fancy
I can introduce you to a club, which assembles every Saturday
at seven . . . ." I accepted his invitation; we walked together,
and entered the house some time before the usual hour for the

(40)   company assembling. My friend took this opportunity of letting
me into the characters of the principal members of the club . . .

"The first person," said he, "of our society is Doctor
Nonentity, a metaphysician. Most people think him a profound
scholar, but, as he seldom speaks, I cannot be positive in that

(45)   particular; he generally spreads himself before the fire, sucks
his pipe, talks little, drinks much, and is reckoned very good
company. I'm told he writes indexes to perfection: he makes
essays on the origin of evil, philosophical inquiries upon any
subject, and draws up an answer to any book upon 24 hours'

(50)   warning . . . ."

10. Goldsmith's disdainful attitude toward English authors is best
explicated in

  (A) lines 6–8.
  (B) lines 21–24.
  (C) lines 26–28.
  (D) lines 33–35.
  (E) lines 43–45.

11. Goldsmith believes that

  (A) we can tell how knowledgeable English authors are by
counting the number of books they publish.
  (B) the number of books published in England is not up to
standards set in China.
  (C) the number of books published in England says nothing
about English scholarship.
  (D) most English writers are better-educated than their Chinese
counterparts.
  (E) every scholar reads a thousand books a year.

12. Why does Goldsmith calculate the number of books published in England?

    (A) To impress his readers with English erudition
    (B) To make the point that anyone can be an author
    (C) As defense for his argument that England is better than China
    (D) To show that most English publications are foreign
    (E) As a comparison with publication quotas in other lands

13. The tone of paragraph 2 may best be described as

    (A) self-satisfied.
    (B) awestruck.
    (C) affectionate.
    (D) sardonic.
    (E) solemn.

14. Goldsmith first assumes that English writers come from

    (A) foreign lands.
    (B) seminaries.
    (C) China.
    (D) clubs.
    (E) the press.

15. The word *obviate* (line 33) means

    (A) clarify.
    (B) obscure.
    (C) turn.
    (D) negate.
    (E) facilitate.

Questions 16–20 are based on the following passage.

Pauline Johnson (1861–1913) was the daughter of Mohawk leader George Henry Martin; her mother was English. Johnson was known in her time as a poet and performer. For years she toured throughout Canada giving dramatic readings. Late in her life she turned to writing short stories. This excerpt is from A Red Girl's Reasoning, *first published in 1893.*

How interesting—do tell us some more of your old home, Mrs. McDonald; you so seldom speak of your life at the post, and we fellows so often wish to hear of it all," said Logan eagerly.

"Why do you not ask me of it, then?"

(5)   "Well—er, I'm sure I don't know; I'm fully interested in the Ind—in your people—your mother's people, I mean, but it always seems so personal, I suppose; and —a—a—"

"Perhaps you are, like all other white people, afraid to mention my nationality to me."

(10)   The captain winced, and Mrs. Stuart laughed uneasily. Joe McDonald was not far off, and he was listening, and chuckling, and saying to himself, "That's you, Christie, lay 'em out; it won't hurt 'em to know how they appear once in a while."

"Well, Captain Logan," she was saying, "what is it you would (15) like to hear—of my people, or my parents, or myself?"

"All, all, my dear," cried Mrs. Stuart clamorously. "I'll speak for him—tell us of yourself and your mother—your father is delightful, I am sure—but then he is only an ordinary Englishman, not half so interesting as a foreigner, or—or (20) perhaps I should say, a native."

Christie laughed. "Yes," she said, "my father often teases my mother now about how *very* native she was when he married her; then, how could she have been otherwise? She did not know a word of English, and there was not another English-speaking (25) person besides my father and his two companions within sixty miles."

"Two companions, eh? One a Catholic priest and the other a wine merchant, I suppose, and with your father in the Hudson Bay, they were good representatives of the pioneers in the New (30) World," remarked Logan waggishly.

"Oh, no, they were all Hudson Bay men. There were no rum-sellers and no missionaries in that part of the country then."

Mrs. Stuart looked puzzled. *"No missionaries?"* she repeated with an odd intonation.

(35)   Christie's insight was quick. There was a peculiar expression of interrogation in the eyes of her listeners, and the girl's blood leapt angrily up into her temples as she said hurriedly, "I know what you mean; I know what you are thinking. You are wondering how my parents were married—"

(40)   "Well—er, my dear, it seems peculiar—if there was no priest, and no magistrate, why—a—" Mrs. Stuart paused awkwardly.

"The marriage was performed by Indian rites," said Christie.

"Oh, do tell about it; is the ceremony very interesting and (45) quaint—are your chieftains anything like Buddhist priests?" It was Logan who spoke.

"Why, no," said the girl in amazement at that gentleman's ignorance. "There is no ceremony at all, save a feast. The two people just agree to live only with and for each other, and the (50) man takes his wife to his home, just as you do. There is no ritual to bind them; they need none; an Indian's word was his law in those days, you know."

Mrs. Stuart stepped backwards. "Ah!" was all she said. Logan removed his eye-glass and stared blankly at Christie.

(55) "And did McDonald marry you in this singular fashion?" he questioned.

"Oh, no, we were married by Father O'Leary. Why do you ask?"

"Because if he had, I'd have blown his brains out tomorrow."

(60) Mrs. Stuart's partner, who had heretofore been silent, coughed and began to twirl his cuff stud nervously, but nobody took notice of him. Christie had risen, slowly, ominously—risen, with the dignity and pride of an empress.

"Captain Logan," she said, "what do you dare to say to me?

(65) What do you dare to mean? Do you presume to think it would not have been lawful for Joe to marry me according to my people's rites? Do you for one instant dare to question that my parents were not as legally—"

"Don't, dear, don't," interrupted Mrs. Stuart hurriedly, "it is

(70) bad enough now, goodness knows; don't make—" Then she broke off blindly.

16. The word *post* (line 2) probably means

   (A) register.
   (B) trading headquarters.
   (C) mailroom.
   (D) assignment.
   (E) stake.

17. What is Joe McDonald's initial reaction to his wife's attitude toward the captain and Mrs. Stuart?

   (A) He supports her frankness.
   (B) He is horrified at her rudeness.
   (C) He is amused by her formality.
   (D) He wishes he were more like her.
   (E) He challenges her disrespectful behavior.

18. Why is Mrs. Stuart not particularly interested in hearing about Christie's father?

   (A) He is not an interesting man.
   (B) She cares little about tradespeople.
   (C) She, too, is from England.
   (D) He is not exotic enough for her taste.
   (E) He leads a life that is different from hers.

19. Mrs. Stuart's "odd intonation" (line 34) apparently results from
    (A) an inability to pronounce the words she is saying.
    (B) her alarm at Christie's words.
    (C) her anger at Logan's implications.
    (D) her ignorance and lack of vocabulary.
    (E) a sudden loss of the powers of speech.

20. As the story continues, Joe McDonald is appalled and angry at Christie for "shocking" Logan and Mrs. Stuart. Based on the story so far, how would you expect Christie to react to Joe's disapproval?
    (A) She would probably acquiesce and apologize to Joe.
    (B) She would ask Joe to intercede for her with Logan and Mrs. Stuart.
    (C) She would tell Logan and Mrs. Stuart that she made up the whole story.
    (D) She would humbly beg Mrs. Stuart's pardon.
    (E) She would deny that she had done anything wrong.

STOP

IF YOU FINISH BEFORE THE TIME IS UP,
GO BACK AND CHECK YOUR WORK.

ANSWER KEY AND EXPLANATIONS

1. D	5. A	9. B	13. D	17. A
2. E	6. E	10. C	14. B	18. D
3. D	7. C	11. C	15. D	19. B
4. D	8. D	12. B	16. B	20. E

1. **The correct answer is (D).** To be *impassive* (without feelings) is to be totally devoid of (lacking in) *emotion*.

2. **The correct answer is (E).** To endure many months of training you need great *tenacity,* or persistence.

3. **The correct answer is (D).** If you eat a *substantial* amount of food, you will not be *unchanged* (unaffected). If you eat a *miniscule* amount, you will not become *corpulent* (excessively fat). If you eat a *gargantuan* (suitable to a giant) amount, you will certainly not become *emaciated* (thin to the point of starvation). But if you eat a *prodigious* (unusually enormous) amount, you are very likely to become *bilious* (sick to the stomach).

4. **The correct answer is (D).** If the performer can juggle three apples at once, she is remarkably skillful, or *adroit*.

5. **The correct answer is (A).** A job that is both pleasant and boring is likely to arouse feelings that are mixed, or *ambivalent*.

6. **The correct answer is (E).** Having no "social graces" means to be rude, or crude. The obvious answer is *uncouth* (uncultured, crude, boorish).

7. **The correct answer is (C).** A shantytown is a collection of ramshackle dwellings that are often miserable, dirty, or *squalid*. Such places are likely to be *rife,* or filled, with disease.

8. **The correct answer is (D).** The "anything but" construction calls for words that are opposites. The only answer choice that offers a pair of opposites is (D), *mournful* (sad) and *ebullient* (joyful).

9. **The correct answer is (B).** Because the second clause of the sentence defines the first, the only possible answer must be a pair of synonyms. The only such pair is answer (B), *homogeneous* (alike) and *similar*.

10. **The correct answer is (C).** The statement in lines 26–28, that writers can write whatever they please and be as dull as they please, is Goldsmith's way of expressing his contempt for modern authors. Anyone can declare himself an author; few have anything intelligent to say.

11. **The correct answer is (C).** Goldsmith begins by saying "Were we to estimate the learning of the English by the number of books

that are published every day …" but goes on to conclude that "… the English are not, in reality so learned as would seem from this calculation."

12. **The correct answer is (B).** Goldsmith's point is that England publishes an astonishing number of books, but the number has little to do with the quality.

13. **The correct answer is (D).** The whole tone of the piece is ironic; Goldsmith is making his point through dry, *sardonic* wit.

14. **The correct answer is (B).** He states this in line 32, but quickly dispels the notion when his companion assures him that "doctors of colleges never wrote."

15. **The correct answer is (D).** Goldsmith suggests that seminaries might be publishing this glut of books to educate the world, but his friend voids that argument in the next sentence.

16. **The correct answer is (B).** Christie lived at the "post," and references to Hudson Bay make this the only sensible answer.

17. **The correct answer is (A).** Lines 10–13 demonstrate Joe's approval.

18. **The correct answer is (D).** An "ordinary Englishman" cannot be fascinating to Mrs. Stuart.

19. **The correct answer is (B).** Mrs. Stuart is eager to be shocked; Christie's words imply something shocking to her.

20. **The correct answer is (E).** Christie's frankness and pride are stressed throughout the passage. There is little to allow a reader to predict that she would apologize, lie, or rely on her husband. In fact, she leaves Joe when he refuses to support her in this.

ANSWER SHEET PRACTICE TEST 5

1 Ⓐ Ⓑ Ⓒ Ⓓ Ⓔ   6 Ⓐ Ⓑ Ⓒ Ⓓ Ⓔ   11 Ⓐ Ⓑ Ⓒ Ⓓ Ⓔ   16 Ⓐ Ⓑ Ⓒ Ⓓ Ⓔ
2 Ⓐ Ⓑ Ⓒ Ⓓ Ⓔ   7 Ⓐ Ⓑ Ⓒ Ⓓ Ⓔ   12 Ⓐ Ⓑ Ⓒ Ⓓ Ⓔ   17 Ⓐ Ⓑ Ⓒ Ⓓ Ⓔ
3 Ⓐ Ⓑ Ⓒ Ⓓ Ⓔ   8 Ⓐ Ⓑ Ⓒ Ⓓ Ⓔ   13 Ⓐ Ⓑ Ⓒ Ⓓ Ⓔ   18 Ⓐ Ⓑ Ⓒ Ⓓ Ⓔ
4 Ⓐ Ⓑ Ⓒ Ⓓ Ⓔ   9 Ⓐ Ⓑ Ⓒ Ⓓ Ⓔ   14 Ⓐ Ⓑ Ⓒ Ⓓ Ⓔ   19 Ⓐ Ⓑ Ⓒ Ⓓ Ⓔ
5 Ⓐ Ⓑ Ⓒ Ⓓ Ⓔ   10 Ⓐ Ⓑ Ⓒ Ⓓ Ⓔ   15 Ⓐ Ⓑ Ⓒ Ⓓ Ⓔ   20 Ⓐ Ⓑ Ⓒ Ⓓ Ⓔ

Critical Reading Practice Test 5

20 Questions • 25 Minutes

Directions: The incomplete sentences below are followed by five words or pairs of words. Choose that word or pair of words that when substituted for the blank space or spaces, best completes the meaning of the sentence. Mark the letter of your choice on your answer sheet.

Example:

In view of the extenuating circumstances and the defendant's youth, the judge recommended ----.

(A) conviction
(B) a defense
(C) a mistrial
(D) leniency
(E) life imprisonment

Ⓐ Ⓑ Ⓒ ● Ⓔ

1. When you are restive, you don't have much ----.

(A) restlessness
(B) animosity
(C) equanimity
(D) motion
(E) equilibrium

2. With speculative investments like oil wells and horse races, money is more easily made or lost; the gain is ---- with the risk.

(A) less
(B) greater
(C) equal
(D) better
(E) commensurate

3. To tremble in the face of a storm is to ----.

(A) glower
(B) cower
(C) shower
(D) tower
(E) flower

4. Eleanor steadfastly refused to change her stubborn ways; she remained ---- to the end.

(A) embattled
(B) regurgitating
(C) recalcitrant
(D) decalcified
(E) concomitant

5. Benjamin Franklin said that ---- is not always a virtue; there are times when you must speak up for yourself.

(A) pride
(B) forthrightness
(C) sham
(D) prudery
(E) modesty

6. They ---- their offer of aid when they became disillusioned with the project.

(A) expanded
(B) redoubled
(C) bolstered
(D) constrained
(E) rescinded

7. The firm's books were out of balance; there was a(n) ---- between the amount of physical inventory and the amount of calculated inventory.

(A) anachronism
(B) enigma
(C) discredit
(D) discrepancy
(E) dissension

8. As a ---- he was a disaster, for his students rarely understood his lectures; yet he was a ---- scholar.

    (A) dean .. banal
    (B) philosopher .. failed
    (C) teacher .. formidable
    (D) professor .. second-rate
    (E) speaker .. contemptuous

9. Far from the ---- crowds of the city, I find refuge at my ---- cabin on Big Lake.

    (A) pervasive .. dominant
    (B) aggressive .. listless
    (C) petrified .. motivating
    (D) overwhelming .. secluded
    (E) extensive .. scanty

Directions: Each reading passage below is followed by a set of questions. Read the passage and answer the accompanying questions, basing your answers on what is stated or implied in the passage. Mark the letter of your choice on your answer sheet.

Questions 10–16 are based on the following passage.

George Washington served as president of the Constitutional Convention in 1787, and he was then elected President of the United States in 1789. This is from his first address to Congress.

Such being the impressions under which I have, in obedience to the public summons, repaired to the present station, it would be peculiarly improper to omit, in this first official act, my fervent supplications to the Almighty Being, who rules
(5) over the universe, who presides in the councils of nations, and whose providential aids can supply every human defect, that his benediction may consecrate to the liberties and happiness of the people of the United States a government instituted by themselves for these essential purposes, and may enable
(10) every instrument employed in its administration to execute with success the functions allotted to his charge. In tendering this homage to the great Author of every public and private good, I assure myself that it expresses your sentiments not less than my own; nor those of my fellow-citizens at large,
(15) less than either. No people can be bound to acknowledge and adore the invisible hand, which conducts the affairs of men, more than the people of the United States. Every step, by which they have advanced to the character of an independent nation, seems to have been distinguished by some token of
(20) providential agency. And, in the important revolution just accomplished in the system of their united government, the tranquil deliberations and voluntary consent of so many distinct communities, from which the event has resulted, cannot be compared with the means by which most govern-
(25) ments have been established, without some return of pious gratitude along with a humble anticipation of the future blessings which the past seems to presage. These reflections, arising out of the present crisis, have forced themselves too strongly on my mind to be suppressed. You will join with me,
(30) I trust, in thinking that there are none, under the influence of which the proceedings of a new and free government can more auspiciously commence.

By the article establishing the executive department,
it is made the duty of the President "to recommend to your
(35)   consideration such measures as he shall judge necessary and
expedient." The circumstances, under which I now meet you,
will acquit me from entering into that subject farther than
to refer you to the great constitutional charter under which
we are assembled; and which, in defining your powers, desig-
(40)   nates the objects to which your attention is to be given. It will
be more consistent with those circumstances, and far more
congenial with the feelings which actuate me, to substitute, in
place of a recommendation of particular measures, the tribute
that is due to the talents, the rectitude, and the patriotism,
(45)   which adorn the characters selected to devise and adopt
them. In these honorable qualifications I behold the surest
pledges, that as, on one side, no local prejudices or attach-
ments, no separate views or party animosities, will misdirect
the comprehensive and equal eye, which ought to watch over
(50)   this great assemblage of communities and interests; so, on
another, that the foundations of our national policy will be
laid in the pure and immutable principles of private morality,
and the preeminence of a free government be exemplified by
all the attributes, which can win the affections of its citizens,
(55)   and command the respect of the world.

10. Washington's first official act is to

    (A)   refer Congress to the constitutional charter.
    (B)   pay tribute to the uprightness of the Founding Fathers.
    (C)   pray for divine guidance.
    (D)   lay the foundations of national policy in the province of
           private morality.
    (E)   obtain the voluntary consent of several communities.

11. According to Washington, "the invisible hand which conducts the
    affairs of men" (line 16)

    (A)   is that of the President.
    (B)   should be, but isn't, that of Congress.
    (C)   is the constitution.
    (D)   should be revered, especially by Americans.
    (E)   should be respected and adored by all peoples.

12. Acting as chief executive, Washington feels that it is appropriate to

   (A) follow faithfully the article establishing the executive department.
   (B) recommend to Congress consideration of certain measures.
   (C) pay tribute to those who "devise and adopt" particular measures.
   (D) announce that there shall be no interparty strife.
   (E) impose the morality of the United States on the world at large.

13. Washington foresees a national policy that will

   (A) preclude partisan interests.
   (B) impose American morality on the world.
   (C) "misdirect the comprehensive and equal eye."
   (D) be restricted to American interests.
   (E) put the United States in charge of the world.

14. When Washington says that "in obedience to the public summons" he has "repaired to the present station," he means that he

   (A) volunteered for his current duties.
   (B) has been elected to this office.
   (C) was hauled before this court to testify.
   (D) intends to correct the mistakes of his predecessors.
   (E) will step down as required by law.

15. The word *acquit* (line 37) is used to mean

   (A) act.
   (B) sentence.
   (C) excuse.
   (D) discontinue.
   (E) reject.

16. The "comprehensive and equal eye" that is to watch over Congress is

   (A) the eye of God.
   (B) the will of the people.
   (C) a "Big Brother" figure in government.
   (D) Congress's unbiased objectivity.
   (E) the power of the press.

Questions 17–20 are based on the following passage.

He was born a slave, but T. Thomas Fortune (1856–1928) went on to become a journalist, editor, and civil rights activist, founding several early black newspapers and a civil rights organization that predated W. E. B. DuBois' Niagara Movement (later the NAACP). Like many black leaders of his time, Fortune was torn between the radical leanings of DuBois and the more conservative ideology of Booker T. Washington. This 1884 essay, The Negro and the Nation, *dates from his more militant period.*

The war of the Rebellion settled only one question: It forever settled the question of chattel slavery in this country. It forever choked the life out of the infamy of the Constitutional right of one man to rob another, by purchase of his person, or of his
(5)   honest share of the produce of his own labor. But this was the only question permanently and irrevocably settled. Nor was this the all-absorbing question involved. The right of a state to secede from the so-called Union remains where it was when the treasonable shot upon Fort Sumter aroused the people to all
(10)   the horrors of internecine war. And the measure of protection which the national government owes the individual members of states, a right imposed upon it by the adoption of the Fourteenth Amendment to the Constitution, remains still to be affirmed.

It was not sufficient that the federal government should
(15)   expend its blood and treasure to unfetter the limbs of four millions of people. There can be a slavery more odious, more galling, than mere chattel slavery. It has been declared to be an act of charity to enforce ignorance upon the slave, since to inform his intelligence would simply be to make his unnatural lot all the
(20)   more unbearable. Instance the miserable existence of Æsop, the great black moralist. But this is just what the manumission of the black people of this country has accomplished. They are more absolutely under the control of the Southern whites; they are more systematically robbed of their labor; they are more
(25)   poorly housed, clothed and fed, than under the slave régime; and they enjoy, practically, less of the protection of the laws of the state or of the federal government. When they appeal to the federal government they are told by the Supreme Court to go to the state authorities—as if they would have appealed to the one
(30)   had the other given them that protection to which their sovereign citizenship entitles them!

Practically, there is no law in the United States which extends its protecting arm over the black man and his rights. He is, like the Irishman in Ireland, an alien in his native land.

(35) There is no central or auxiliary authority to which he can appeal for protection. Wherever he turns he finds the strong arm of constituted authority powerless to protect him. The farmer and the merchant rob him with absolute immunity, and irresponsible ruffians murder him without fear of punishment, undeterred by (40) the law, or by public opinion—which connives at, if it does not inspire, the deeds of lawless violence. Legislatures of states have framed a code of laws which is more cruel and unjust than any enforced by a former slave state.

The right of franchise has been practically annulled in every (45) one of the former slave states, in not one of which, today, can a man vote, think, or act as he pleases. He must conform his views to the views of the men who have usurped every function of government—who, at the point of the dagger, and with shotgun, have made themselves masters in defiance of every law or (50) precedent in our history as a government. They have usurped government with the weapons of the cowards and assassins, and they maintain themselves in power by the most approved practices of the most odious of tyrants. These men have shed as much innocent blood as the bloody triumvirate of Rome. Today, (55) red-handed murderers and assassins sit in the high places of power, and bask in the smiles of innocence and beauty.

17. The only solution the Civil War provided, according to Fortune, was to the problem of
    (A) mutually destructive war.
    (B) protection.
    (C) slavery.
    (D) secession.
    (E) constitutional rights.

18. The word *manumission* (line 21) means
    (A) emancipation.
    (B) duty.
    (C) possessions.
    (D) forgiveness.
    (E) transportation.

19. Now that slavery has been abolished, Fortune believes, black people
    (A) are chattel.
    (B) have fewer rights than before.
    (C) are protected by laws.
    (D) can succeed in the white man's world.
    (E) inspire lawless violence.

20. Fortune uses the example of the Irishman to show that
    (A) famine is not alien to people in the United States.
    (B) one can be treated as a foreigner in the land of one's birth.
    (C) some people have a native land; others have none.
    (D) one can be born to slavery but rise above it.
    (E) people may be treated more fairly in a monarchy than in a democracy.

STOP

IF YOU FINISH BEFORE THE TIME IS UP,
GO BACK AND CHECK YOUR WORK.

ANSWER KEY AND EXPLANATIONS

1. C	5. E	9. D	13. A	17. C
2. E	6. E	10. D	14. B	18. A
3. B	7. D	11. D	15. C	19. B
4. C	8. C	12. C	16. D	20. B

1. **The correct answer is (C).** When you are "restive" (nervous, upset), you may have at the same time *restlessness, animosity, motion,* or *equilibrium,* but you cannot have *equanimity* (evenness, peace of mind, or tranquility).

2. **The correct answer is (E).** In speculation, a gain is not necessarily *greater* or *less* or *better* with risk. It may *occasionally* be *equal* with the risk, but it is most usually *commensurate* (corresponding in extent of degree) with it.

3. **The correct answer is (B).** "To tremble in the face of a storm" is to show fear or discomfort in a special way. *Glower* (to stare or scowl with sullen anger) does not connote fear or trembling; neither do *shower, tower,* or *flower.* To *cower* is to crouch, as from fear or cold, or to shrink and tremble.

4. **The correct answer is (C).** *Embattled* (fighting), *regurgitating* (bringing partly digested food back to the mouth), *decalcified* (having calcium removed from the system), and *concomitant* (accompanying, attendant) do not in any way suggest a steadfast refusal to submit to change. The only possible choice is *recalcitrant* (refusing to obey authority, stubbornly defiant).

5. **The correct answer is (E).** The context of this sentence suggests that not speaking up for yourself is *not* always good; in other words, the missing term has something to do with self-effacement. Only *modesty* can fill this gap properly.

6. **The correct answer is (E).** The sentence describes people who are disillusioned with a project. They are therefore most likely to *rescind,* or withdraw, their offer of aid.

7. **The correct answer is (D).** If the "books were out of balance," there had to be some sort of differential between the two inventories. Only the last two choices pertain to any differential. *Dissension,* however, is a difference in feelings; *discrepancy* (inconsistency) fits the context.

8. **The correct answer is (C).** "Yet" indicates that the second clause will have a meaning that contrasts with that of the first clause. In the first clause, someone is a disaster. The only choice for the second

blank that contrasts that idea is *formidable,* meaning that he was a first-rate scholar.

9. **The correct answer is (D).** The logic of this sentence is based on contrast; the clues are "crowds," "refuge," and "cabin." In choices (A) and (B), the first substitution works, but the second is meaningless. In choices (C) and (E), neither word makes sense in context.

10. **The correct answer is (D).** The last six lines constitute the only part of the speech that could be called an "official act." Choice (E) was part of the "revolution just accomplished." Choices (A) and (C) are simply a referral and a prayer. Choice (B) is a trap: he is paying tribute not to the Founding Fathers but to the legislators in his audience.

11. **The correct answer is (D).** Every step they have taken "seems to have been distinguished by some token of providential agency."

12. **The correct answer is (C).** He gets nowhere near (E). He sees "surest pledges"—but certainly can't "announce"—that there "shall be no interparty strife," (D). He doesn't mention any need to "follow faithfully" that article; he simply refers to it, (A). And rather than recommend "certain measures," (B), he prefers to "pay tribute," (C).

13. **The correct answer is (A).** He says nothing like (E) or (D), and the morality he hopes for is *not* "American," (B), but private, and *not* to be imposed on anybody. And because of the "honorable qualifications" of his audience, he sees *nothing* that will "misdirect the comprehensive and equal eye," (C). The one thing among these choices he truly does foresee is that there will be "no … party animosities," (A).

14. **The correct answer is (B).** Washington is politely intimating that he would never be where he is had "the public summons" not called him to this "station." He has been summoned by the will of the people.

15. **The correct answer is (C).** Washington says that present circumstances mean that he need not "enter into [the] subject" of recommending measures to Congress; he is excused from that duty.

16. **The correct answer is (D).** A careful reading of line 49 shows that Washington is concerned that Congress must be unbiased and impartial, guided by the "principles of private morality." If "local prejudices" or "party animosities" interfere, Congress's "equal eye" will be "misdirected."

17. **The correct answer is (C).** The first sentence contains this answer; the paragraph goes on to explain what was *not* settled by the war.

18. **The correct answer is (A).** You can deduce this answer by reading the whole paragraph carefully. Fortune talks about "a slavery more

odious … than chattel slavery." Even after being liberated, or *emancipated,* black people remain in chains.

19. **The correct answer is (B).** Paragraphs 2 and 3 are entirely in support of this.

20. **The correct answer is (B).** No law protects the black man; he is, "like the Irishman in Ireland, an alien in his native land" (line 34).

APPENDIX

A Helpful Word List

A Helpful Word List

A

abbreviate (verb) to make briefer, to shorten. *Because time was running out, the speaker had to abbreviate his remarks.* **abbreviation** (noun).

Word Origin:
Latin; *brevis* = short. Also found in English *brevity*.

abrasive (adjective) irritating, grinding, rough. *The manager's rude, abrasive way of criticizing the workers was bad for morale.* **abrasion** (noun).

abridge (verb) to shorten, to reduce. *The Bill of Rights is designed to prevent Congress from abridging the rights of Americans.* **abridgment** (noun).

absolve (verb) to free from guilt, to exonerate. *The criminal jury absolved the man of the murder of his ex-wife.* **absolution** (noun).

abstain (verb) to refrain, to hold back. *After his heart attack, he was warned by the doctor to abstain from smoking, drinking, and overeating.* **abstinence** (noun), **abstemious** (adjective).

accentuate (verb) to emphasize, to stress. *The overcast skies and chill winds accentuated our gloomy mood.*

acrimonious (adjective) biting, harsh, caustic. *The election campaign became acrimonious, as the candidates traded insults and accusations.* **acrimony** (noun).

Word Origin:
Latin: acer = *sharp*. Also found in English *acerbity, acrid, exacerbate*.

adaptable (adjective) able to be changed to be suitable for a new purpose. *Some scientists say that the mammals outlived the dinosaurs because they were more adaptable to a changing climate.* **adapt** (verb), **adaptation** (noun).

adulation (noun) extreme admiration. *Few young actors have received greater adulation than did Marlon Brando after his performance in* A Streetcar Named Desire. **adulate** (verb), **adulatory** (adjective).

adversary (noun) an enemy or opponent. *When the former Soviet Union became an American ally, the United States lost its last major adversary.*

adversity (noun) misfortune. *It's easy to be patient and generous when things are going well; a person's true character is revealed under adversity.* **adverse** (adjective).

aesthetic (adjective) relating to art or beauty. *Mapplethorpe's photos may be attacked on moral grounds, but no one questions their aesthetic value—they are beautiful.* **aestheticism** (noun).

affected (adjective) false, artificial. *At one time, Japanese women were taught to speak in an affected, high-pitched voice, which was thought girlishly attractive.* **affect** (verb or noun), **affectation** (noun).

aggressive (adjective) forceful, energetic, and attacking. *A football player needs a more aggressive style of play than a soccer player.* **aggression** (noun).

alacrity (noun) promptness, speed. *Thrilled with the job offer, he accepted with alacrity—"Before they can change their minds!" he thought.*

allege (verb) to state without proof. *Some have alleged that the actor was murdered, but all the evidence points to suicide.* **allegation** (noun).

alleviate (verb) to make lighter or more bearable. *Although no cure for AIDS has been found, doctors are able to alleviate the sufferings of those with the disease.* **alleviation** (noun).

ambiguous (adjective) having two or more possible meanings. *The phrase, "Let's table that discussion" is ambiguous; some think it means, "Let's discuss it now," while others think it means, "Let's save it for later."* **ambiguity** (noun).

ambivalent (adjective) having two or more contradictory feelings or attitudes; uncertain. *She was ambivalent toward her impending marriage; at times she was eager to go ahead, while at other times she wanted to call it off.* **ambivalence** (noun).

amiable (adjective) likable, agreeable, friendly. *He was an amiable lab partner, always smiling, on time, and ready to work.* **amiability** (noun).

amicable (adjective) friendly, peaceable. *Although they agreed to divorce, their settlement was amicable and they remained friends afterward.*

amplify (verb) to enlarge, expand, or increase. *Uncertain as to whether they understood, the students asked the teacher to amplify his explanation.* **amplification** (noun).

anachronistic (adjective) out of the proper time. *The reference, in Shakespeare's* Julius Caesar, *to "the clock striking twelve" is anachronistic, since there were no striking timepieces in ancient Rome.* **anachronism** (noun).

Word Origin:
Latin: *levis* = light. Also found in English *levitate, levity.*

Word Origin:
Latin: *amare* = love. Also found in English *amicable, amity, amorous.*

Word Origin:
Greek: *chronos* = time. Also found in English *chronic, chronicle, chronograph, chronology, synchronize.*

anarchy (noun) absence of law or order. *For several months after the Nazi government was destroyed, there was no effective government in parts of Germany and anarchy ruled.* **anarchic** (adjective).

anomaly (noun) something different or irregular. *The dwarf planet Pluto, orbiting next to the giants Jupiter, Saturn, and Neptune, has long appeared to be an anomaly.* **anomalous** (adjective).

antagonism (noun) hostility, conflict, opposition. *As more and more reporters investigated the Watergate scandal, antagonism between Nixon and the press increased.* **antagonistic** (adjective), **antagonize** (verb).

antiseptic (adjective) fighting infection; extremely clean. *A wound should be washed with an antiseptic solution. The all-white offices were bare and almost antiseptic in their starkness.*

apathy (noun) lack of interest, concern, or emotion. *American voters are showing increasing apathy over politics; fewer than half voted in the last election.* **apathetic** (adjective).

arable (adjective) able to be cultivated for growing crops. *Rocky New England has relatively little arable farmland.*

arbiter (noun) someone able to settle a dispute; a judge or referee. *The public is the ultimate arbiter of commercial value: It decides what sells and what doesn't.*

arbitrary (adjective) based on random or merely personal preference. *Both computers cost the same and had the same features, so in the end I made an arbitrary decision about which to buy.*

arcane (adjective) little-known, mysterious, obscure. *Eliot's* Waste Land *is filled with arcane lore, including quotations in Latin, Greek, French, German, and Sanskrit.* **arcana** (noun, plural).

ardor (noun) a strong feeling of passion, energy, or zeal. *The young revolutionary proclaimed his convictions with an ardor that excited the crowd.* **ardent** (adjective).

arid (adjective) very dry; boring and meaningless. *The arid climate of Arizona makes farming difficult. Some find the law a fascinating topic, but for me it is an arid discipline.* **aridity** (noun).

ascetic (adjective) practicing strict self-discipline for moral or spiritual reasons. *The so-called Desert Fathers were hermits who lived an ascetic life of fasting, study, and prayer.* **asceticism** (noun).

assiduous (verb) working with care, attention, and diligence. *Although Karen is not a naturally gifted math student, by assiduous study she managed to earn an A in trigonometry.* **assiduity** (noun).

> **Word Origin:**
> Latin: *arbiter* = judge. Also found in English *arbitrage, arbitrary, arbitrate.*

astute (adjective) observant, intelligent, and shrewd. *Alan's years of experience in Washington and his personal acquaintance with many political insiders make him an astute commentator on politics.*

atypical (adjective) not typical; unusual. *In* The Razor's Edge, *Bill Murray, best known as a comic actor, gave an atypical dramatic performance.*

audacious (adjective) bold, daring, adventurous. *Her plan to cross the Atlantic single-handed in a twelve-foot sailboat was audacious, if not reckless.* **audacity** (noun).

audible (adjective) able to be heard. *Although she whispered, her voice was picked up by the microphone, and her words were audible throughout the theater.* **audibility** (noun).

auspicious (adjective) promising good fortune; propitious. *The news that a team of British climbers had reached the summit of Everest seemed an auspicious sign for the reign of newly crowned Queen Elizabeth II.*

authoritarian (adjective) favoring or demanding blind obedience to leaders. *Despite Americans' belief in democracy, the American government has supported authoritarian regimes in other countries.* **authoritarianism** (noun)

> **Word Origin:**
> Latin: *audire* = to hear. Also found in English *audition, auditorium, auditory.*

B

belated (adjective) delayed past the proper time. *She called her mother on January 5th to offer her a belated "Happy New Year."*

belie (verb) to present a false or contradictory appearance. *Julie's youthful appearance belies her long, distinguished career in show business.*

benevolent (adjective) wishing or doing good. *In old age, Carnegie used his wealth for benevolent purposes, donating large sums to found libraries and schools.* **benevolence** (noun).

berate (verb) to scold or criticize harshly. *The judge angrily berated the two lawyers for their unprofessional behavior.*

bereft (adjective) lacking or deprived of something. *Bereft of parental love, orphans sometimes grow up insecure.*

bombastic (adjective) inflated or pompous in style. *Old-fashioned bombastic political speeches don't work on television, which demands a more intimate style of communication.* **bombast** (noun).

> **Word Origin:**
> Latin: *bene* = well. Also found in English *benediction, benefactor, beneficent, beneficial, benefit, benign.*

bourgeois (adjective) middle-class or reflecting middle-class values. *The Dadaists of the 1920s produced art deliberately designed to offend bourgeois art collectors, with their taste for respectable, refined, uncontroversial pictures.* **bourgeois** (noun).

buttress (noun) something that supports or strengthens. *The endorsement of the American Medical Association is a powerful buttress for the claims made about this new medicine.* **buttress** (verb).

C

camaraderie (noun) a spirit of friendship. *Spending long days and nights together on the road, the members of a traveling theater group develop a strong sense of camaraderie.*

candor (noun) openness, honesty, frankness. *In his memoir, the former defense secretary describes his mistakes with remarkable candor.* **candid** (adjective).

capricious (adjective) unpredictable, willful, whimsical. *The pop star has changed her image so many times that each new transformation now appears capricious rather than purposeful.* **caprice** (noun).

carnivorous (adjective) meat-eating. *The long, dagger-like teeth of the Tyrannosaurus rex make it obvious that this was a carnivorous dinosaur.* **carnivore** (noun).

carping (adjective) unfairly or excessively critical; querulous. *The newspaper is famous for its demanding critics, but none is harder to please than the carping McNamera, said to have single-handedly destroyed many acting careers.* **carp** (verb).

catalytic (adjective) bringing about, causing, or producing some result. *The conditions for revolution existed in America by 1765; the disputes about taxation that arose later were the catalytic events that sparked the rebellion.* **catalyze** (verb).

caustic (adjective) burning, corrosive. *No one was safe when the satirist H.L. Mencken unleashed his caustic wit.*

censure (noun) blame, condemnation. *The news that the senator had harassed several women brought censure from many feminists.* **censure** (verb).

chaos (noun) disorder, confusion, chance. *The first few moments after the explosion were pure chaos: no one was sure what had happened, and the area was filled with people running and yelling.* **chaotic** (adjective).

Word Origin:
Latin: *vorare* = to eat. Also found in English *devour, omnivorous, voracious.*

Word Origin:
Greek: *kaustikos* = burning. Also found in English *holocaust.*

Word Origin:

Latin: *circus* = circle. Also found in English *circumference, circumnavigate, circumscribe, circumspect, circumvent.*

Word Origin:

Latin: *cognoscere* = to know. Also found in English *cognition, cognitive, incognito, recognize.*

circuitous (adjective) winding or indirect. *We drove to the cottage by a circuitous route so we could see as much of the surrounding countryside as possible.*

circumlocutory (adjective) speaking in a roundabout way; wordy. *Legal documents are often circumlocutory, making them difficult to understand.* **circumlocution** (noun).

circumscribe (verb) to define by a limit or boundary. *Originally, the role of the executive branch of government was clearly circumscribed, but that role has greatly expanded over time.* **circumscription** (noun).

circumvent (verb) to get around. *When Jerry was caught speeding, he tried to circumvent the law by offering the police officer a bribe.*

clandestine (adjective) secret, surreptitious. *As a member of the underground, Balas took part in clandestine meetings to discuss ways of sabotaging the Nazi forces.*

cloying (adjective) overly sweet or sentimental. *The deathbed scenes in the novels of Dickens are famously cloying: as Oscar Wilde said, "One would need a heart of stone to read the death of Little Nell without laughing."*

cogent (adjective) forceful and convincing. *The committee members were won over to the project by the cogent arguments of the chairman.* **cogency** (noun).

cognizant (adjective) aware, mindful. *Cognizant of the fact that it was getting late, the master of ceremonies cut short the last speech.* **cognizance** (noun).

cohesive (adjective) sticking together, unified. *An effective military unit must be a cohesive team, all its members working together for a common goal.* **cohere** (verb), **cohesion** (noun).

collaborate (verb) to work together. *To create a truly successful movie, the director, writers, actors, and many others must collaborate closely.* **collaboration** (noun), **collaborative** (adjective).

colloquial (adjective) informal in language; conversational. *Some expressions from Shakespeare, such as the use of "thou" and "thee," sound formal today but were colloquial English in Shakespeare's time.*

competent (adjective) having the skill and knowledge needed for a particular task; capable. *Any competent lawyer can draw up a will.* **competence** (noun).

complacent (adjective) smug, self-satisfied. *During the 1970s, American automakers became complacent, believing that they would continue to be successful with little effort.* **complacency** (noun).

composure (noun) calm, self-assurance. *The president managed to keep his composure during his speech even when the TelePrompTer broke down, leaving him without a script.* **composed** (adjective).

conciliatory (adjective) seeking agreement, compromise, or reconciliation. *As a conciliatory gesture, the union leaders agreed to postpone a strike and to continue negotiations with management.* **conciliate** (verb), **conciliation** (noun).

concise (adjective) expressed briefly and simply; succinct. *Less than a page long, the Bill of Rights is a concise statement of the freedoms enjoyed by all Americans.* **concision** (noun).

> **Word Origin:**
> Latin: *caedere* = to cut. Also found in English *decide, excise, incision, precise.*

condescending (adjective) having an attitude of superiority toward another; patronizing. *"What a cute little car!" she remarked in a condescending style. "I suppose it's the nicest one someone like you could afford!"* **condescension** (noun).

condolence (noun) pity for someone else's sorrow or loss; sympathy. *After the sudden death of the princess, thousands of messages of condolence were sent to her family.* **condole** (verb).

> **Word Origin:**
> Latin: *dolere* = to feel pain. Also found in English *dolorous, indolent.*

confidant (noun) someone entrusted with another's secrets. *No one knew about Janee's engagement except Sarah, her confidant.* **confide** (verb), **confidential** (adjective).

conformity (noun) agreement with, or adherence to, custom or rule. *In my high school, conformity was the rule: everyone dressed the same, talked the same, and listened to the same music.* **conform** (verb), **conformist** (adjective or noun).

consensus (noun) general agreement among a group. *Among Quakers, voting traditionally is not used; instead, discussion continues until the entire group forms a consensus.*

consolation (noun) relief or comfort in sorrow or suffering. *Although we miss our dog very much, it is a consolation to know that she died quickly, without suffering.* **console** (verb).

consternation (noun) shock, amazement, dismay. *When a voice in the back of the church shouted out, "I know why they should not be married!" the entire gathering was thrown into consternation.*

consummate (verb) to complete, finish, or perfect. *The deal was consummated with a handshake and the payment of the agreed-upon fee.* **consummate** (adjective), **consummation** (noun).

contaminate (verb) to make impure. *Chemicals dumped in a nearby forest had seeped into the soil and contaminated the local water supply.* **contamination** (noun).

Word Origin:

Latin: *tempus* = time.
Also found in English
*temporal, temporary,
temporize.*

contemporary (adjective or noun) modern, current; from the same time. *I prefer old-fashioned furniture rather than contemporary styles. The composer Vivaldi was roughly contemporary with Bach.*

contrite (adjective) sorry for past misdeeds. *The public is often willing to forgive celebrities who are involved in some scandal, as long as they appear contrite.* **contrition** (noun).

conundrum (noun) a riddle, puzzle, or problem. *The question of why an all-powerful, all-loving God allows evil to exist is a conundrum many philosophers have pondered.*

convergence (noun) the act of coming together in unity or similarity. *A remarkable example of evolutionary convergence can be seen in the shark and the dolphin, two sea creatures that developed from different origins to become very similar in form.* **converge** (verb).

Word Origin:

Latin: *volvere* = to roll.
Also found in English
*devolve, involve, revo-
lution, revolve, voluble.*

convoluted (adjective) twisted, complicated, intricate. *Tax law has become so convoluted that it's easy for people to accidentally violate it.* **convolute** (verb), **convolution** (noun).

corroborating (adjective) supporting with evidence; confirming. *A passerby who had witnessed the crime gave corroborating testimony about the presence of the accused person.* **corroborate** (verb), **corroboration** (noun).

corrosive (adjective) eating away, gnawing, or destroying. *Years of poverty and hard work had a corrosive effect on her beauty.* **corrode** (verb), **corrosion** (noun).

credulity (noun) willingness to believe, even with little evidence. *Con artists fool people by taking advantage of their credulity.* **credulous** (adjective).

criterion (noun) a standard of measurement or judgment. (The plural is criteria.) *In choosing a design for the new taxicabs, reliability will be our main criterion.*

Word Origin:

Greek: *krinein* = to
choose. Also found in
English *criticize, critique.*

critique (noun or verb) a critical evaluation. *The editor gave a detailed critique of the manuscript, explaining its strengths and its weaknesses.*

culpable (adjective) deserving blame, guilty. *Although he committed the crime, he should not be considered culpable for his actions because he was mentally ill.* **culpability** (noun).

cumulative (adjective) made up of successive additions. *Smallpox was eliminated only through the cumulative efforts of several generations of doctors and scientists.* **accumulation** (noun), **accumulate** (verb).

curtail (verb) to shorten. *Because of the military emergence, all soldiers on leave were ordered to curtail their absences and return to duty.*

D

debase (verb) to lower in quality, character, or esteem. *The quality of TV journalism has been debased by the many new tabloid-style talk shows.*

debunk (verb) to expose as false or worthless. *The magician loves to debunk psychics, mediums, clairvoyants, and others who claim supernatural powers.*

decorous (adjective) having good taste; proper, appropriate. *The once reserved and decorous style of the British monarchy began to change when the chic, flamboyant young Diana Spencer joined the family.* **decorum** (noun).

decry (verb) to criticize or condemn. *Cigarette ads aimed at youngsters have led many to decry the marketing tactics of the tobacco industry.*

deduction (noun) a logical conclusion, especially a specific conclusion based on general principles. *Based on what is known about the effects of greenhouse gases on atmospheric temperature, scientists have made several deductions about the likelihood of global warming.* **deduce** (verb).

> **Word Origin:**
> Latin: *ducere* = to lead. Also found in English *ductile, induce, produce, reduce.*

delegate (verb or noun) to give authority or responsibility. *The president delegated the vice-president to represent the administration at the peace talks.*

deleterious (adjective) harmful. *About thirty years ago, scientists proved that working with asbestos could be deleterious to one's health, producing cancer and other diseases.*

> **Word Origin:**
> Latin: *delere* = to destroy. Also found in English *delete.*

delineate (verb) to outline or describe. *Naturalists had long suspected the fact of evolution, but Darwin was the first to delineate a process—natural selection—through which evolution could occur.*

demagogue (noun) a leader who plays dishonestly on the prejudices and emotions of his followers. *Senator Joseph McCarthy was a demagogue who used the paranoia of the anti-Communist 1950s as a way of seizing fame and power in Washington.* **demagoguery** (noun).

demure (adjective) modest or shy. *The demure heroines of Victorian fiction have given way to today's stronger, more opinionated, and more independent female characters.*

denigrate (verb) to criticize or belittle. *The firm's new president tried to explain his plans for improving the company without seeming to denigrate the work of his predecessor.* **denigration** (noun).

depose (verb) to remove from office, especially from a throne. *Iran was formerly ruled by a monarch called the Shah, who was deposed in 1976.*

derelict (adjective) negligent of one's duty. *The train crash was blamed on a switchman who was derelict, having fallen asleep while on duty.* **dereliction** (noun).

derivative (adjective) taken from a particular source. *When a person first writes poetry, her poems are apt to be derivative of whatever poetry she most enjoys reading.* **derivation** (noun), **derive** (verb).

desolate (adjective) empty, lifeless, and deserted; hopeless, gloomy. *Robinson Crusoe was shipwrecked and had to learn to survive alone on a desolate island. The murder of her husband left Mary Lincoln desolate.* **desolation** (noun).

destitute (adjective) very poor. *Years of rule by a dictator who stole the wealth of the country had left the people of the Philippines destitute.* **destitution** (noun).

deter (verb) to discourage from acting; to inhibit. *The best way to deter crime is to ensure that criminals will receive swift and certain punishment.* **deterrence** (noun), **deterrent** (adjective).

detractor (noun) someone who belittles or disparages. *The singer has many detractors who consider his music boring, inane, and sentimental.* **detract** (verb).

deviate (verb) to depart from a standard or norm. *Having agreed upon a spending budget for the company, we mustn't deviate from it; if we do, we may run out of money soon.* **deviation** (noun).

devious (adjective) tricky, deceptive. *The stockbroker's devious financial tactics were designed to enrich his firm while confusing or misleading government regulators.*

didactic (adjective) intended to teach, instructive. *The children's TV show* Sesame Street *is designed to be both entertaining and didactic.*

diffident (adjective) hesitant, reserved, shy. *Someone with a diffident personality should pursue a career that involves little public contact.* **diffidence** (noun).

diffuse (verb) to spread out, to scatter. *The red dye quickly became diffused through the water, turning it a very pale pink.* **diffusion** (noun).

digress (verb) to wander from the main path or the main topic. *My high school biology teacher loved to digress from science into personal anecdotes about his college adventures.* **digression** (noun), **digressive** (adjective).

dilatory (adjective) delaying, procrastinating. *The lawyer used various dilatory tactics, hoping that his opponent would get tired of waiting for a trial and drop the case.*

diligent (adjective) working hard and steadily. *Through diligent efforts, the townspeople were able to clear away the debris from the flood in a matter of days.* **diligence** (noun).

diminutive (adjective) unusually small, tiny. *Children are fond of Shetland ponies because their diminutive size makes them easy to ride.*

discern (verb) to detect, notice, or observe. *I could discern the shape of a whale off the starboard bow, but it was too far away to determine its size or species.* **discernment** (noun).

disclose (verb) to make known; to reveal. *Election laws require candidates to disclose the names of those who contribute money to their campaigns.* **disclosure** (noun).

discomfit (verb) to frustrate, thwart, or embarrass. *Discomfited by the interviewer's unexpected question, Peter could only stammer in reply.* **discomfiture** (noun).

disconcert (verb) to confuse or embarrass. *When the hallway bells began to ring halfway through her lecture, the speaker was disconcerted and didn't know what to do.*

discredit (verb) to cause disbelief in the accuracy of some statement or the reliability of a person. *Although many people still believe in UFOs, the reports of "alien encounters" have been thoroughly discredited among scientists.*

discreet (adjective) showing good judgment in speech and behavior. *Be discreet when discussing confidential business matters—don't talk among strangers on the elevator, for example.* **discretion** (noun).

discrepancy (noun) a difference or variance between two or more things. *The discrepancies between the two witnesses' stories show that one of them must be lying.* **discrepant** (adjective).

disdain (noun) contempt, scorn. *The millionaire was disliked by many people because she treated "little people" with such disdain.* **disdain** (verb), **disdainful** (adjective).

> **Word Origin:**
> Latin: *credere* = to believe. Also found in English *credential, credible, credit, credo, credulous, incredible.*

disingenuous (adjective) pretending to be candid, simple, and frank. *When the Texas billionaire ran for president, many considered his "just plain folks" style disingenuous.*

disparage (verb) to speak disrespectfully about, to belittle. *Many political ads today both praise their own candidate and disparage his or her opponent.* **disparagement** (noun), **disparaging** (adjective).

disparity (noun) difference in quality or kind. *There is often a disparity between the kind of high-quality television people say they want and the low-brow programs they actually watch.* **disparate** (adjective).

disregard (verb or noun) to ignore, to neglect. *When you die, your survivors may disregard your wishes about how your property should be handled if you don't write a will.*

disruptive (adjective) causing disorder, interrupting. *When the senator spoke at our college, angry demonstrators picketed, heckled, and engaged in other disruptive activities.* **disrupt** (verb), **disruption** (noun).

dissemble (verb) to pretend, to simulate. *When the police questioned her about the crime, she dissembled innocence.*

dissipate (verb) to spread out or scatter. *The windows and doors were opened, allowing the smoke that had filled the room to dissipate.* **dissipation** (noun).

dissonance (noun) mix of discordant sounds; lack of agreement between ideas. *Most modern music is characterized by dissonance, which many listeners find hard to enjoy. There is a noticeable dissonance between two common beliefs of most conservatives: their faith in unfettered free markets and their preference for traditional social values.* **dissonant** (adjective).

Word Origin:
Latin: *sonare* = to sound. Also found in English *consonance, sonar, sonic, sonorous.*

diverge (verb) to move in different directions. *Frost's poem* The Road Less Traveled *tells of the choice he made when "Two roads diverged in a yellow wood."* **divergence** (noun), **divergent** (adjective).

diversion (noun) a distraction or pastime. *During the two hours he spent in the doctor's waiting room, his hand-held computer game was a welcome diversion.* **divert** (verb).

divination (noun) the art of predicting the future. *In ancient Greece, people wanting to know their fate would visit the priests at Delphi, who were supposedly skilled at divination.* **divine** (verb).

divisive (adjective) causing disagreement or disunity. *Throughout history, race has been the most divisive issue in American society.*

divulge (verb) to reveal. *The people who count the votes for the Oscar awards are under strict orders not to divulge the names of the winners.*

dogmatic (adjective) holding firmly to a particular set of beliefs with little or no basis. *Believers in Marxist doctrine tend to be dogmatic, ignoring evidence that contradicts their beliefs.* **dogmatism** (noun).

dominant (adjective) great in importance or power. *The historian suggests that the existence of the frontier had a dominant influence on American culture.* **dominate** (verb), **domination** (noun).

dubious (adjective) doubtful, uncertain. *Despite the chairman's attempts to convince the committee members that his plan would succeed, most of them remained dubious.* **dubiety** (noun).

durable (adjective) long-lasting. *Denim is a popular material for work clothes because it is strong and durable.*

duress (noun) compulsion or restraint. *Fearing that the police might beat him, he confessed to the crime, not willingly but under duress.*

> *Word Origin*:
> Latin: *durare* = to last.
> Also found in English *durance, duration, endure.*

E

eclectic (adjective) drawn from many sources; varied, heterogeneous. *The Mellon family art collection is an eclectic one, including works ranging from ancient Greek sculptures to modern paintings.* **eclecticism** (noun).

efficacious (adjective) able to produce a desired effect. *Though thousands of people today are taking herbal supplements to treat depression, researchers have not yet proved them efficacious.* **efficacy** (noun).

effrontery (noun) shameless boldness. *The sports world was shocked when a pro basketball player had the effrontery to choke his head coach during a practice session.*

effusive (adjective) pouring forth one's emotions very freely. *Having won the Oscar for Best Actress, Sally Field gave an effusive acceptance speech in which she marveled, "You like me! You really like me!"* **effusion** (noun).

egoism (noun) excessive concern with oneself; conceit. *Robert's egoism was so great that all he could talk about was the importance—and the brilliance—of his own opinions.* **egoistic** (adjective).

egregious (adjective) obvious, conspicuous, flagrant. *It's hard to imagine how the editor could allow such an egregious error to appear.*

> *Word Origin:*
> Latin: *grex* = herd.
> Also found in English *aggregate, congregate, gregarious.*

elated (adjective) excited and happy; exultant. *When the Green Bay Packers' last, desperate pass was dropped, the elated fans of the Denver Broncos began to celebrate.* **elate** (verb), **elation** (noun).

elliptical (adjective) very terse or concise in writing or speech; difficult to understand. *Rather than speak plainly, she hinted at her meaning through a series of nods, gestures, and elliptical half-sentences.*

> **Word Origin:**
> Latin: *ludere* = to play. Also found in English *delude, illusion, interlude, ludicrous.*

elusive (adjective) hard to capture, grasp, or understand. *Though everyone thinks they know what "justice" is, when you try to define the concept precisely, it proves to be quite elusive.*

embezzle (verb) to steal money or property that has been entrusted to your care. *The church treasurer was found to have embezzled thousands of dollars by writing phony checks on the church bank account.* **embezzlement** (noun).

emend (verb) to correct. *Before the letter is mailed, please emend the two spelling errors.* **emendation** (noun).

emigrate (verb) to leave one place or country to settle elsewhere. *Millions of Irish emigrated to the New World in the wake of the great Irish famines of the 1840s.* **emigrant** (noun), **emigration** (noun).

eminent (adjective) noteworthy, famous. *Vaclav Havel was an eminent author before being elected president of the Czech Republic.* **eminence** (noun).

emissary (noun) someone who represents another. *In an effort to avoid a military showdown, Carter was sent as an emissary to Korea to negotiate a settlement.*

emollient (noun) something that softens or soothes. *She used a hand cream as an emollient on her dry, work-roughened hands.* **emollient** (adjective).

empathy (noun) imaginative sharing of the feelings, thoughts, or experiences of another. *It's easy for a parent to have empathy for the sorrow of another parent whose child has died.* **empathetic** (adjective).

empirical (adjective) based on experience or personal observation. *Although many people believe in ESP, scientists have found no empirical evidence of its existence.* **empiricism** (noun).

emulate (verb) to imitate or copy. *The British band Oasis admitted their desire to emulate their idols, the Beatles.* **emulation** (noun).

encroach (verb) to go beyond acceptable limits; to trespass. *By quietly seizing more and more authority, Robert Moses continually encroached on the powers of other government leaders.* **encroachment** (noun).

enervate (verb) to reduce the energy or strength of someone or something. *The stress of the operation left her feeling enervated for about two weeks.*

engender (verb) to produce, to cause. *Countless disagreements over the proper use of national forests have engendered feelings of hostility between ranchers and environmentalists.*

enhance (verb) to improve in value or quality. *New kitchen appliances will enhance your house and increase the amount of money you'll make when you sell it.* **enhancement** (noun).

enmity (noun) hatred, hostility, ill will. *Long-standing enmity, like that between the Protestants and Catholics in Northern Ireland, is difficult to overcome.*

enthrall (verb) to enchant or charm. *When the Swedish singer Jenny Lind toured America in the nineteenth century, audiences were enthralled by her beauty and talent.*

ephemeral (adjective) quickly disappearing; transient. *Stardom in pop music is ephemeral; most of the top acts of ten years ago are forgotten today.*

equanimity (noun) calmness of mind, especially under stress. *Roosevelt had the gift of facing the great crises of his presidency—the Depression, the Second World War—with equanimity and even humor.*

eradicate (verb) to destroy completely. *American society has failed to eradicate racism, although some of its worst effects have been reduced.*

espouse (verb) to take up as a cause; to adopt. *No politician in America today will openly espouse racism, although some behave and speak in racially prejudiced ways.*

euphoric (adjective) feeling extreme happiness and well-being; elated. *One often feels euphoric during the earliest days of a new love affair.* **euphoria** (noun).

evanescent (adjective) vanishing like a vapor; fragile and transient. *As she walked by, the evanescent fragrance of her perfume reached me for just an instant.*

exacerbate (verb) to make worse or more severe. *The roads in our town already have too much traffic; building a new shopping mall will exacerbate the problem.*

> *Word Origin*:
> Latin: *anima* = mind, spirit. Also found in English *animate*, *magnanimous*, *pusillanimous*, *unanimous*.

Word Origin:
Latin: *asper* = rough. Also found in English *asperity*.

exasperate (verb) to irritate or annoy. *Because she was trying to study, Sharon was exasperated by the yelling of her neighbors' children.*

exculpate (verb) to free from blame or guilt. *When someone else confessed to the crime, the previous suspect was exculpated.* **exculpation** (noun), **exculpatory** (adjective).

exemplary (adjective) worthy to serve as a model. *The Baldrige Award is given to a company with exemplary standards of excellence in products and service.* **exemplar** (noun), **exemplify** (verb).

exonerate (verb) to free from blame. *Although he was suspected at first of being involved in the bombing, later evidence exonerated him.* **exoneration** (noun), **exonerative** (adjective).

expansive (adjective) broad and large; speaking openly and freely. *The LBJ Ranch is located on an expansive tract of land in Texas. Over dinner, she became expansive in describing her dreams for the future.*

expedite (verb) to carry out promptly. *As the flood waters rose, the governor ordered state agencies to expedite their rescue efforts.*

expertise (noun) skill, mastery. *The software company was eager to hire new graduates with programming expertise.*

expiate (verb) to atone for. *The president's apology to the survivors of the notorious Tuskegee experiments was his attempt to expiate the nation's guilt over their mistreatment.* **expiation** (noun).

Word Origin:
Latin: *proprius* = own. Also found in English *appropriate, property, proprietary, proprietor.*

expropriate (verb) to seize ownership of. *When the Communists came to power in China, they expropriated most businesses and turned them over to government-appointed managers.* **expropriation** (noun).

extant (adjective) currently in existence. *Of the seven ancient "Wonders of the World," only the pyramids of Egypt are still extant.*

extenuate (verb) to make less serious. *Karen's guilt is extenuated by the fact that she was only twelve when she committed the theft.* **extenuating** (adjective), **extenuation** (noun).

extol (verb) to greatly praise. *At the party convention, speaker after speaker rose to extol their candidate for the presidency.*

extricate (verb) to free from a difficult or complicated situation. *Much of the humor in the TV show* I Love Lucy *comes in watching Lucy try to extricate herself from the problems she creates by fibbing or trickery.* **extricable** (adjective).

extrinsic (adjective) not an innate part or aspect of something; external. *The high price of old baseball cards is due to extrinsic factors, such as the nostalgia felt by baseball fans for the stars of their youth, rather than the inherent beauty or value of the cards themselves.*

exuberant (adjective) wildly joyous and enthusiastic. *As the final seconds of the game ticked away, the fans of the winning team began an exuberant celebration.* **exuberance** (noun).

F

facile (adjective) easy; shallow or superficial. *The one-minute political commercial favors a candidate with facile opinions rather than serious, thoughtful solutions.* **facilitate** (verb), **facility** (noun).

fallacy (noun) an error in fact or logic. *It's a fallacy to think that "natural" means "healthful"; after all, the deadly poison arsenic is completely natural.* **fallacious** (adjective).

felicitous (adjective) pleasing, fortunate, apt. *The sudden blossoming of the dogwood trees on the morning of Matt's wedding seemed a felicitous sign of good luck.* **felicity** (noun).

feral (adjective) wild. *The garbage dump was inhabited by a pack of feral dogs, which had escaped from their owners and become completely wild.*

fervent (adjective) full of intense feeling; ardent, zealous. *In the days just after his religious conversion, his piety was at its most fervent.* **fervid** (adjective), **fervor** (noun).

flagrant (adjective) obviously wrong; offensive. *Nixon was forced to resign the presidency after a series of flagrant crimes against the U.S. Constitution.* **flagrancy** (noun).

flamboyant (adjective) very colorful, showy, or elaborate. *At Mardi Gras, partygoers compete to show off the most wild and flamboyant outfits.*

florid (adjective) flowery, fancy; reddish. *The grand ballroom was decorated in a florid style. Years of heavy drinking had given him a florid complexion.*

foppish (adjective) describing a man who is foolishly vain about his dress or appearance. *The foppish character of the 1890s wore bright-colored spats and a top hat; in the 1980s, he wore fancy suspenders and a shirt with a contrasting collar.* **fop** (noun).

> *Word Origin*:
> Latin: *facere* = to do. Also found in English *facility, factor, facsimile, faculty.*

formidable (adjective) awesome, impressive, or frightening. *According to his plaque in the Baseball Hall of Fame, pitcher Tom Seaver turned the New York Mets "from lovable losers into formidable foes."*

fortuitous (adjective) lucky, fortunate. *Although the mayor claimed credit for the falling crime rate, it was really caused by several fortuitous trends.*

fractious (adjective) troublesome, unruly. *Members of the British Parliament are often fractious, shouting insults and sarcastic questions during debates.*

fragility (noun) the quality of being easy to break; delicacy, weakness. *Because of their fragility, few stained glass windows from the early Middle Ages have survived.* **fragile** (adjective).

fraternize (verb) to associate with on friendly terms. *Although baseball players aren't supposed to fraternize with their opponents, players from opposing teams often chat before games.* **fraternization** (noun).

frenetic (adjective) chaotic, frantic. *The floor of the stock exchange, filled with traders shouting and gesturing, is a scene of frenetic activity.*

frivolity (noun) lack of seriousness; levity. *The frivolity of the Mardi Gras carnival is in contrast to the seriousness of the religious season of Lent, which follows.* **frivolous** (adjective).

frugal (adjective) spending little. *With our last few dollars, we bought a frugal dinner: a loaf of bread and a piece of cheese.* **frugality** (noun).

fugitive (noun or adjective) someone trying to escape. *When two prisoners broke out of the local jail, police were warned to keep an eye out for the fugitives.*

 G

gargantuan (adjective) huge, colossal. *The building of the Great Wall of China was one of the most gargantuan projects ever undertaken.*

genial (adjective) friendly, gracious. *A good host welcomes all visitors in a warm and genial fashion.*

grandiose (adjective) overly large, pretentious, or showy. *Among Hitler's grandiose plans for Berlin was a gigantic building with a dome several times larger than any ever built.* **grandiosity** (noun).

> *Word Origin*:
> Latin: *frater* = brother. Also found in English *fraternal, fraternity, fratricide.*

gratuitous (adjective) given freely or without cause. *Since her opinion was not requested, her harsh criticism of his singing seemed a gratuitous insult.*

gregarious (adjective) enjoying the company of others; sociable. *Marty is naturally gregarious, a popular member of several clubs and a sought-after lunch companion.*

guileless (adjective) without cunning; innocent. *Deborah's guileless personality and complete honesty make it hard for her to survive in the harsh world of politics.*

gullible (adjective) easily fooled. *When the sweepstakes entry form arrived bearing the message, "You may be a winner!" my gullible neighbor tried to claim a prize.* **gullibility** (noun).

H

hackneyed (adjective) without originality, trite. *When someone invented the phrase, "No pain, no gain," it was clever, but now it is so commonly heard that it seems hackneyed.*

haughty (adjective) overly proud. *The fashion model strode down the runway, her hips thrust forward and a haughty expression, like a sneer, on her face.* **haughtiness** (noun).

hedonist (noun) someone who lives mainly to pursue pleasure. *Having inherited great wealth, he chose to live the life of a hedonist, traveling the world in luxury.* **hedonism** (noun), **hedonistic** (adjective).

heinous (adjective) very evil, hateful. *The massacre by Pol Pot of over a million Cambodians is one of the twentieth century's most heinous crimes.*

hierarchy (noun) a ranking of people, things, or ideas from highest to lowest. *A cabinet secretary ranks just below the president and vice president in the hierarchy of the executive branch.* **hierarchical** (adjective).

hypocrisy (noun) a false pretense of virtue. *When the sexual misconduct of the television preacher was exposed, his followers were shocked at his hypocrisy.* **hypocritical** (adjective).

I

iconoclast (noun) someone who attacks traditional beliefs or institutions. *The comedian enjoys his reputation as an iconoclast, though people in power often resent his satirical jabs.* **iconoclasm** (noun), **iconoclastic** (adjective).

idiosyncratic (adjective) peculiar to an individual; eccentric. *She sings pop music in an idiosyncratic style, mingling high-pitched whoops and squeals with throaty gurgles.* **idiosyncrasy** (noun).

idolatry (noun) the worship of a person, thing, or institution as a god. *In Communist China, Chairman Mao was the subject of idolatry; his picture was displayed everywhere, and millions of Chinese memorized his sayings.* **idolatrous** (adjective).

impartial (adjective) fair, equal, unbiased. *If a judge is not impartial, then all of her rulings are questionable.* **impartiality** (noun).

impeccable (adjective) flawless. *The crooks printed impeccable copies of the Super Bowl tickets, making it impossible to distinguish them from the real things.*

impetuous (adjective) acting hastily or impulsively. *Ben's resignation was an impetuous act; he did it without thinking, and he soon regretted it.* **impetuosity** (noun).

impinge (verb) to encroach upon, touch, or affect. *You have a right to do whatever you want, as long as your actions don't impinge on the rights of others.*

implicit (adjective) understood without being openly expressed; implied. *Although most clubs had no rules excluding blacks and Jews, many had an implicit understanding that no blacks or Jews would be allowed to join.*

impute (verb) to credit or give responsibility to; to attribute. *Although Sarah's comments embarrassed me, I don't impute any ill will to her; I think she didn't realize what she was saying.* **imputation** (noun).

inarticulate (adjective) unable to speak or express oneself clearly and understandably. *A skilled athlete may be an inarticulate public speaker, as demonstrated by many post-game interviews.*

incisive (adjective) expressed clearly and directly. *Franklin settled the debate with a few incisive remarks that summed up the issue perfectly.*

Word Origin:
Latin: *articulus* = joint, division. Also found in English *arthritis, articulate.*

incompatible (adjective) unable to exist together; conflicting. *Many people hold seemingly incompatible beliefs: for example, supporting the death penalty while believing in the sacredness of human life.* **incompatibility** (noun).

inconsequential (adjective) of little importance. *When the stereo was delivered, it was a different shade of gray than I expected, but the difference was inconsequential.*

incontrovertible (adjective) impossible to question. *The fact that Sheila's fingerprints were the only ones on the murder weapon made her guilt seem incontrovertible.*

incorrigible (adjective) impossible to manage or reform. *Lou is an incorrigible trickster, constantly playing practical jokes no matter how much his friends complain.*

incremental (adjective) increasing gradually by small amounts. *Although the initial cost of the Medicare program was small, the incremental expenses have grown to be very large.* **increment** (noun).

incriminate (adjective) to give evidence of guilt. *The Fifth Amendment to the Constitution says that no one is required to reveal information that would incriminate him in a crime.* **incriminating** (adjective).

incumbent (noun or adjective) someone who occupies an office or position. *It is often difficult for a challenger to win a seat in Congress from the incumbent.* **incumbency** (noun).

indeterminate (adjective) not definitely known. *The college plans to enroll an indeterminate number of students; the size of the class will depend on the number of applicants and how many accept offers of admission.* **determine** (verb).

indifferent (adjective) unconcerned, apathetic. *The mayor's small proposed budget for education suggests that he is indifferent to the needs of our schools.* **indifference** (noun).

indistinct (adjective) unclear, uncertain. *We could see boats on the water, but in the thick morning fog their shapes were indistinct.*

indomitable (adjective) unable to be conquered or controlled. *The world admired the indomitable spirit of Nelson Mandela; he remained courageous despite years of imprisonment.*

induce (verb) to cause. *The doctor prescribed a medicine that is supposed to induce a lowering of the blood pressure.* **induction** (noun).

ineffable (adjective) difficult to describe or express. *He gazed in silence at the sunrise over the Taj Mahal, his eyes reflecting an ineffable sense of wonder.*

inevitable (adjective) unable to be avoided. *Once the Japanese attacked Pearl Harbor, American involvement in World War II was inevitable.* **inevitability** (noun).

inexorable (adjective) unable to be deterred; relentless. *It's difficult to imagine how the mythic character of Oedipus could have avoided his evil destiny; his fate appears inexorable.*

ingenious (adjective) showing cleverness and originality. *The Post-it® Note is an ingenious solution to a common problem—how to mark papers without spoiling them.* **ingenuity** (noun).

inherent (adjective) naturally part of something. *Compromise is inherent in democracy, since everyone cannot get his way.* **inhere** (verb), **inherence** (noun).

innate (adjective) inborn, native. *Not everyone who takes piano lessons becomes a fine musician, which shows that music requires innate talent as well as training.*

innocuous (adjective) harmless, inoffensive. *I was surprised that Andrea took offense at such an innocuous joke.*

inoculate (verb) to prevent a disease by infusing with a disease-causing organism. *Pasteur found he could prevent rabies by inoculating patients with the virus that causes the disease.* **inoculation** (noun).

insipid (adjective) flavorless, uninteresting. *Most TV shows are so insipid that you can watch them while reading without missing a thing.* **insipidity** (noun).

insolence (noun) an attitude or behavior that is bold and disrespectful. *Some feel that news reporters who shout questions at the president are behaving with insolence.* **insolent** (adjective).

insular (adjective) narrow or isolated in attitude or viewpoint. *New Yorkers are famous for their insular attitudes; they seem to think that nothing important has ever happened outside of their city.* **insularity** (noun).

insurgency (noun) uprising, rebellion. *The angry townspeople had begun an insurgency bordering on downright revolution; they were collecting arms, holding secret meetings, and refusing to pay certain taxes.* **insurgent** (adjective).

integrity (noun) honesty, uprightness; soundness, completeness. *"Honest Abe" Lincoln is considered a model of political integrity. Inspectors examined the building's support beams and foundation and found no reason to doubt its structural integrity.*

interlocutor (noun) someone taking part in a dialogue or conversation. *Annoyed by the constant questions from someone in the crowd, the speaker challenged his interlocutor to offer a better plan.*

interlude (noun) an interrupting period or performance. *The two most dramatic scenes in King Lear are separated, strangely, by a comic interlude starring the king's jester.*

interminable (adjective) endless or seemingly endless. *Addressing the United Nations, Castro announced, "We will be brief"—then delivered an interminable four-hour speech.*

intransigent (adjective) unwilling to compromise. *Despite the mediator's attempts to suggest a fair solution, the two parties were intransigent, forcing a showdown.* **intransigence** (noun).

intrepid (adjective) fearless and resolute. *Only an intrepid adventurer is willing to undertake the long and dangerous trip by sled to the South Pole.* **intrepidity** (noun).

intrusive (adjective) forcing a way in without being welcome. *The legal requirement of a search warrant is supposed to protect Americans from intrusive searches by the police.* **intrude** (verb), **intrusion** (noun).

intuitive (adjective) known directly, without apparent thought or effort. *An experienced chess player sometimes has an intuitive sense of the best move to make, even if she can't explain it.* **intuit** (verb), **intuition** (noun).

inundate (verb) to flood; to overwhelm. *As soon as playoff tickets went on sale, eager fans inundated the box office with orders.*

invariable (adjective) unchanging, constant. *When writing a book, it was her invariable habit to rise at 6 and work at her desk from 7 to 12.* **invariability** (noun).

inversion (noun) a turning backward, inside out, or upside down; a reversal. *Latin poetry often features inversion of word order; for example, the first line of Vergil's Aeneid: "Arms and the man I sing."* **invert** (verb), **inverted** (adjective).

inveterate (adjective) persistent, habitual. *It's very difficult for an inveterate gambler to give up the pastime.* **inveteracy** (noun).

invigorate (verb) to give energy to, to stimulate. *As her car climbed the mountain road, Lucinda felt invigorated by the clear air and the cool breezes.*

invincible (adjective) impossible to conquer or overcome. *For three years at the height of his career, boxer Mike Tyson seemed invincible.*

Word Origin:
Latin: *loqui* = to speak. Also found in English *colloquial, colloquy, eloquent, grandiloquent, locution, loquacious.*

Word Origin:
Latin: *trepidus* = alarmed. Also found in English *trepidation.*

Word Origin:
Latin: *varius* = various. Also found in English *prevaricate, variable, variance, variegated, vary.*

inviolable (adjective) impossible to attack or trespass upon. *In the president's remote hideaway at Camp David, guarded by the Secret Service, his privacy is, for once, inviolable.*

irrational (adjective) unreasonable. *Charles knew that his fear of insects was irrational, but he was unable to overcome it.* **irrationality** (noun).

irresolute (adjective) uncertain how to act, indecisive. *When McGovern first said he supported his vice presidential candidate "one thousand percent," then dropped him from the ticket, it made McGovern appear irresolute.* **irresolution** (noun).

J

jeopardize (verb) to put in danger. *Terrorist attacks jeopardize the fragile peace in the Middle East.* **jeopardy** (noun).

juxtapose (verb) to put side by side. *It was strange to see the old-time actor Charlton Heston and rock icon Bob Dylan juxtaposed at the awards ceremony.* **juxtaposition** (noun).

L

languid (adjective) without energy; slow, sluggish, listless. *The hot, humid weather of late August can make anyone feel languid.* **languish** (verb), **languor** (noun).

latent (adjective) not currently obvious or active; hidden. *Although he had committed only a single act of violence, the psychiatrist who examined him said he had probably always had a latent tendency toward violence.* **latency** (noun).

laudatory (adjective) giving praise. *The ads for the movie are filled with laudatory comments from critics.*

lenient (adjective) mild, soothing, or forgiving. *The judge was known for his lenient disposition; he rarely imposed long jail sentences on criminals.* **leniency** (noun).

lethargic (adjective) lacking energy; sluggish. *Visitors to the zoo are surprised that the lions appear so lethargic, but in the wild lions sleep up to eighteen hours a day.* **lethargy** (noun).

liability (noun) an obligation or debt; a weakness or drawback. *The insurance company had a liability of millions of dollars after the town was destroyed by a tornado. Slowness afoot is a serious liability in an aspiring basketball player.* **liable** (adjective).

Word Origin:
Latin: *laus* = praise. Also found in English *applaud, laud, laudable, plaudit.*

lithe (adjective) flexible and graceful. *The ballet dancer was almost as lithe as a cat.*

longevity (noun) length of life; durability. *The reduction in early deaths from infectious diseases is responsible for most of the increase in human longevity over the past two centuries.*

lucid (adjective) clear and understandable. *Hawking's* A Short History of the Universe *is a lucid explanation of modern scientific theories about the origin of the universe.* **lucidity** (noun).

lurid (adjective) shocking, gruesome. *While the serial killer was on the loose, the newspapers were filled with lurid stories about his crimes.*

M

malediction (noun) curse. *In the fairy tale* Sleeping Beauty, *the princess is trapped in a death-like sleep because of the malediction uttered by an angry witch.*

malevolence (noun) hatred, ill will. *Critics say that Iago, the villain in Shakespeare's* Othello, *seems to exhibit malevolence with no real cause.* **malevolent** (noun).

malinger (verb) to pretend illness to avoid work. *During the labor dispute, hundreds of employees malingered, forcing the company to slow production and costing it millions in profits.*

malleable (adjective) able to be changed, shaped, or formed by outside pressures. *Gold is a very useful metal because it is so malleable. A child's personality is malleable and deeply influenced by the things her parents say and do.* **malleability** (noun).

mandate (noun or verb) order, command. *The new policy on gays in the military went into effect as soon as the president issued his mandate about it.* **mandatory** (adjective).

maturation (noun) the process of becoming fully grown or developed. *Free markets in the former Communist nations are likely to operate smoothly only after a long period of maturation.* **mature** (adjective and verb), **maturity** (noun).

mediate (verb) to reconcile differences between two parties. *During the baseball strike, both the players and the club owners were willing to have the president mediate the dispute.* **mediation** (noun).

Word Origin:
Latin: *malus* = bad.
Also found in English *malefactor, malevolence, malice, malicious.*

Word Origin:
Latin: *mandare* = entrust, order. Also found in English *command, demand, remand.*

Word Origin:
Latin: *medius* = middle. Also found in English *intermediate, media, medium.*

mediocrity (noun) the state of being moderate or poor in quality. *The New York Mets, who'd finished in ninth place in 1968, won the world's championship in 1969, going from horrible to great in a single year and skipping mediocrity.* **mediocre** (adjective).

mercurial (adjective) changing quickly and unpredictably. *The mercurial personality of Robin Williams, with his many voices and styles, made him perfect for the role of the ever-changing genie in* Aladdin.

meticulous (adjective) very careful with details. *Repairing watches calls for a craftsperson who is patient and meticulous.*

mimicry (noun) imitation, aping. *The continued popularity of Elvis Presley has given rise to a class of entertainers who make a living through mimicry of "The King."* **mimic** (noun and verb).

misconception (noun) a mistaken idea. *Columbus sailed west under the misconception that he would reach the shores of Asia that way.* **misconceive** (verb).

mitigate (verb) to make less severe; to relieve. *Wallace certainly committed the assault, but the verbal abuse he'd received helps to explain his behavior and somewhat mitigates his guilt.* **mitigation** (noun).

modicum (noun) a small amount. *The plan for your new business is well designed; with a modicum of luck, you should be successful.*

mollify (verb) to soothe or calm; to appease. *Carla tried to mollify the angry customer by promising him a full refund.*

morose (adjective) gloomy, sullen. *After Chuck's girlfriend dumped him, he lay around the house for a couple of days, feeling morose.*

mundane (adjective) everyday, ordinary, commonplace. *Moviegoers in the 1930s liked the glamorous films of Fred Astaire because they provided an escape from the mundane problems of life during the Great Depression.*

munificent (adjective) very generous; lavish. *The billion-dollar donation to the United Nations is probably the most munificent act of charity in history.* **munificence** (noun).

mutable (adjective) likely to change. *A politician's reputation can be highly mutable, as seen in the case of Harry Truman—mocked during his lifetime, revered afterward.*

Word Origin:
Latin: *modus* = measure. Also found in English *immoderate, moderate, modest, modify, modulate.*

Word Origin:
Latin: *mutare* = to change. Also found in English *immutable, mutant, mutation.*

N

narcissistic (adjective) showing excessive love for oneself; egoistic. *Andre's room, decorated with photos of himself and the sports trophies he has won, suggests a narcissistic personality.* **narcissism** (noun).

nocturnal (adjective) of the night; active at night. *Travelers on the Underground Railroad escaped from slavery to the North by a series of nocturnal flights. The eyes of nocturnal animals must be sensitive in dim light.*

nonchalant (adjective) appearing to be unconcerned. *Unlike the other players on the football team, who pumped their fists when their names were announced, John ran on the field with a nonchalant wave.* **nonchalance** (noun).

nondescript (adjective) without distinctive qualities; drab. *The bank robber's clothes were nondescript; none of the witnesses could remember their color or style.*

notorious (adjective) famous, especially for evil actions or qualities. *Warner Brothers produced a series of movies about notorious gangsters such as John Dillinger and Al Capone.* **notoriety** (noun).

novice (noun) beginner, tyro. *Lifting your head before you finish your swing is a typical mistake committed by a novice at golf.*

nuance (noun) a subtle difference or quality. *At first glance, Monet's paintings of water lilies look much alike, but the more you study them, the more you appreciate the nuances of color and shading that distinguish them.*

nurture (verb or noun) to nourish or help to grow. *The money given by the National Endowment for the Arts helps nurture local arts organizations throughout the country.*

> *Word Origin*:
> Latin: *novus* = new.
> Also found in English *innovate, novelty, renovate.*

O

obdurate (adjective) unwilling to change; stubborn, inflexible. *Despite the many pleas he received, the governor was obdurate in his refusal to grant clemency to the convicted murderer.*

objective (adjective) dealing with observable facts rather than opinions or interpretations. *When a legal case involves a shocking crime, it may be hard for a judge to remain objective in her rulings.*

oblivious (adjective) unaware, unconscious. *Karen practiced her oboe with complete concentration, oblivious to the noise and activity around her.* **oblivion** (noun), **obliviousness** (noun).

> *Word Origin*:
> Latin: *durus* = hard.
> Also found in English *durable, endure.*

obscure (adjective or verb) little known; hard to understand. *Mendel was an obscure monk until decades after his death, when his scientific work was finally discovered. Most people find the writings of James Joyce obscure; hence the popularity of books that explain his books.* **obscurity** (noun).

obsessive (adjective) haunted or preoccupied by an idea or feeling. *His concern with cleanliness became so obsessive that he washed his hands twenty times every day.* **obsess** (verb), **obsession** (noun).

obsolete (adjective) no longer current; old-fashioned. *W. H. Auden said that his ideal landscape would include water wheels, wooden grain mills, and other forms of obsolete machinery.* **obsolescence** (noun).

obstinate (adjective) stubborn, unyielding. *Despite years of effort, the problem of drug abuse remains obstinate.* **obstinacy** (noun).

obtrusive (adjective) overly prominent. *Philip should sing more softly; his bass is so obtrusive that the other singers can barely be heard.* **obtrude** *(verb),* **obtrusion** (noun).

ominous (adjective) foretelling evil. *Ominous black clouds gathered on the horizon, for a violent storm was fast approaching.* **omen** (noun).

onerous (adjective) heavy, burdensome. *The hero Hercules was ordered to clean the Augean Stables, one of several onerous tasks known as "the labors of Hercules."* **onus** (noun).

opportunistic (adjective) eagerly seizing chances as they arise. *When Princess Diana died suddenly, opportunistic publishers quickly released books about her life and death.* **opportunism** (noun).

opulent (adjective) rich, lavish. *The mansion of newspaper tycoon Hearst is famous for its opulent decor.* **opulence** (noun).

ornate (adjective) highly decorated, elaborate. *Baroque architecture is often highly ornate, featuring surfaces covered with carving, sinuous curves, and painted scenes.*

ostentatious (adjective) overly showy, pretentious. *To show off his wealth, the millionaire threw an ostentatious party featuring a full orchestra, a famous singer, and tens of thousands of dollars worth of food.*

ostracize (verb) to exclude from a group. *In Biblical times, those who suffered from the disease of leprosy were ostracized and forced to live alone.* **ostracism** (noun).

P

pallid (adjective) pale; dull. *Working all day in the coal mine had given him a pallid complexion. The new musical offers only pallid entertainment: the music is lifeless, the acting dull, the story absurd.*

parched (adjective) very dry; thirsty. *After two months without rain, the crops were shriveled and parched by the sun.* **parch** (verb).

pariah (noun) outcast. *Accused of robbery, he became a pariah; his neighbors stopped talking to him, and people he'd considered friends no longer called.*

partisan (adjective or noun) reflecting strong allegiance to a particular party or cause. *The vote on the president's budget was strictly partisan: every member of the president's party voted yes, and all others voted no.*

pathology (noun) disease or the study of disease; extreme abnormality. *Some people believe that high rates of crime are symptoms of an underlying social pathology.* **pathological** (adjective).

> **Word Origin:**
> Greek: *pathos* = suffering. Also found in English *apathy, empathy, pathetic, pathos, sympathy.*

pellucid (adjective) very clear; transparent; easy to understand. *The water in the mountain stream was cold and pellucid. Thanks to the professor's pellucid explanation, I finally understand relativity theory.*

penitent (adjective) feeling sorry for past crimes or sins. *Having grown penitent, he wrote a long letter of apology, asking forgiveness.*

penurious (adjective) extremely frugal; stingy. *Haunted by memories of poverty, he lived in penurious fashion, driving a twelve-year-old car and wearing only the cheapest clothes.* **penury** (noun).

perceptive (adjective) quick to notice, observant. *With his perceptive mind, Holmes was the first to notice the importance of this clue.* **perceptible** (adjective), **perception** (noun).

perfidious (adjective) disloyal, treacherous. *Although he was one of the most talented generals of the American Revolution, Benedict Arnold is remembered today as a perfidious betrayer of his country.* **perfidy** (noun).

> **Word Origin:**
> Latin: *fides* = faith. Also found in English *confide, confidence, fidelity, infidel.*

perfunctory (adjective) unenthusiastic, routine, or mechanical. *When the play opened, the actors sparkled, but by the thousandth night their performance had become perfunctory.*

permeate (verb) to spread through or penetrate. *Little by little, the smell of gas from the broken pipe permeated the house.*

persevere (verb) to continue despite difficulties. *Although several of her teammates dropped out of the marathon, Laura persevered.* **perseverance** (noun).

perspicacity (noun) keenness of observation or understanding. *Journalist Murray Kempton was famous for the perspicacity of his comments on social and political issues.* **perspicacious** (adjective).

peruse (verb) to examine or study. *Mary-Jo perused the contract carefully before she signed it.* **perusal** (noun).

pervasive (adjective) spreading throughout. *As news of the disaster reached the town, a pervasive sense of gloom could be felt everywhere.* **pervade** (verb).

phlegmatic (adjective) sluggish and unemotional in temperament. *It was surprising to see Tom, who is normally so phlegmatic, acting excited.*

placate (verb) to soothe or appease. *The waiter tried to placate the angry customer with the offer of a free dessert.* **placatory** (adjective).

plastic (adjective) able to be molded or reshaped. *Because it is highly plastic, clay is an easy material for beginning sculptors to use.*

plausible (adjective) apparently believable. *The idea that a widespread conspiracy to kill President Kennedy has been kept secret for over thirty years hardly seems plausible.* **plausibility** (noun).

polarize (adjective) to separate into opposing groups or forces. *For years, the abortion debate polarized the American people, with many people voicing extreme views and few trying to find a middle ground.* **polarization** (noun).

portend (verb) to indicate a future event; to forebode. *According to folklore, a red sky at dawn portends a day of stormy weather.*

potentate (noun) a powerful ruler. *Before the Russian Revolution, the Tsar was one of the last hereditary potentates of Europe.*

pragmatism (noun) a belief in approaching problems through practical rather than theoretical means. *Roosevelt's approach toward the Great Depression was based on pragmatism: "Try something," he said; "If it doesn't work, try something else."* **pragmatic** (adjective).

preamble (noun) an introductory statement. *The preamble to the Constitution begins with the famous words, "We the people of the United States of America …"*

precocious (adjective) mature at an unusually early age. *Picasso was so precocious as an artist that, at nine, he is said to have painted far better pictures than his teacher.* **precocity** (noun).

Word Origin:
Latin: *ambulare* = to walk. Also found in English *ambulatory*, *circumambulate*, *perambulate*.

predatory (adjective) living by killing and eating other animals; exploiting others for personal gain. *The tiger is the largest predatory animal native to Asia. The corporation has been accused of predatory business practices that prevent other companies from competing with them.* **predation** (noun), **predator** (noun).

predilection (noun) a liking or preference. *To relax from his presidential duties, Kennedy had a predilection for spy novels featuring James Bond.*

predominant (adjective) greatest in numbers or influence. *Although hundreds of religions are practiced in India, the predominant faith is Hinduism.* **predominance** (noun), **predominate** (verb or adjective).

prepossessing (adjective) attractive. *Smart, lovely, and talented, she has all the prepossessing qualities that mark a potential movie star.*

presumptuous (adjective) going beyond the limits of courtesy or appropriateness. *The senator winced when the presumptuous young staffer addressed him as "Chuck."* **presume** (verb), **presumption** (noun).

pretentious (adjective) claiming excessive value or importance. *For an ordinary shoe salesman to call himself a "Personal Foot Apparel Consultant" seems awfully pretentious.* **pretension** (noun).

procrastinate (verb) to put off, to delay. *If you habitually procrastinate, try this technique: never touch a piece of paper without either filing it, responding to it, or throwing it out.* **procrastination** (noun).

profane (adjective or verb) impure, unholy. *It seems inappropriate to have such profane activities as in-line skating and disco dancing in a church.* **profanity** (noun).

proficient (adjective) skillful, adept. *A proficient artist, Louise quickly and accurately sketched the scene.* **proficiency** (noun).

proliferate (verb) to increase or multiply. *Over the past fifteen years, high-tech companies have proliferated in northern California, Massachusetts, and other regions.* **proliferation** (noun).

prolific (adjective) producing many offspring or creations. *With over three hundred books to his credit, Isaac Asimov was one of the most prolific writers of all time.*

prominence (noun) the quality of standing out; fame. *Kennedy's victory in the West Virginia primary gave him a position of prominence among the Democratic candidates for president.* **prominent** (adjective).

> *Word Origin*:
> Latin: *dominare* = to rule. Also found in English *dominate, domineer, dominion, indomitable.*

promulgate (verb) to make public, to declare. *Lincoln signed the proclamation that freed the slaves in 1862, but he waited several months to promulgate it.*

propagate (verb) to cause to grow; to foster. *John Smithson's will left his fortune for the founding of an institution to propagate knowledge, without saying whether that meant a university, a library, or a museum.* **propagation** (noun).

propriety (noun) appropriateness. *Some people had doubts about the propriety of Clinton's discussing his underwear on MTV.*

prosaic (adjective) everyday, ordinary, dull. *Paul's Case tells the story of a boy who longs to escape from the prosaic life of a clerk into a world of wealth, glamour, and beauty.*

protagonist (noun) the main character in a story or play; the main supporter of an idea. *Leopold Bloom is the protagonist of James Joyce's great novel* Ulysses.

> **Word Origin:**
> Latin: *vocare* = to call. Also found in English *evoke, invoke, revoke, vocal, vocation.*

provocative (adjective) likely to stimulate emotions, ideas, or controversy. *The demonstrators began chanting obscenities, a provocative act that they hoped would cause the police to lose control.* **provoke** (verb), **provocation** (noun).

proximity (noun) closeness, nearness. *Neighborhood residents were angry over the proximity of the sewage plant to the local school.* **proximate** (adjective).

> **Word Origin:**
> Latin: *proximus* = near, next. Also found in English *approximate.*

prudent (adjective) wise, cautious, and practical. *A prudent investor will avoid putting all of her money into any single investment.* **prudence** (noun), **prudential** (adjective).

pugnacious (adjective) combative, bellicose, truculent. *Ty Cobb, the pugnacious outfielder for the Detroit Tigers, got into more than his fair share of brawls, both on and off the field.* **pugnacity** (noun).

> **Word Origin:**
> Latin: *pungere* = to jab, to prick. Also found in English *pugilist, punctuate, puncture, pungent.*

punctilious (adjective) very concerned about proper forms of behavior and manners. *A punctilious dresser like James would rather skip the party altogether than wear the wrong color tie.* **punctilio** (noun).

pundit (noun) someone who offers opinions in an authoritative style. *The Sunday afternoon talk shows are filled with pundits, each with his or her own theory about this week's political news.*

punitive (adjective) inflicting punishment. *The jury awarded the plaintiff one million dollars in punitive damages, hoping to teach the defendant a lesson.*

purify (verb) to make pure, clean, or perfect. *The new plant is supposed to purify the drinking water provided to everyone in the nearby towns.* **purification** (noun).

Q

quell (verb) to quiet, to appease. *It took a huge number of police to quell the rioting.*

querulous (adjective) complaining, whining. *The nursing home attendant needed a lot of patience to care for the three querulous, unpleasant residents on his floor.*

R

rancorous (adjective) expressing bitter hostility. *Many Americans are disgusted by recent political campaigns, which seem more rancorous than ever before.* **rancor** (noun).

rationale (noun) an underlying reason or explanation. *At first, it seemed strange that several camera companies would freely share their newest technology; but their rationale was that offering one new style of film would benefit them all.*

raze (verb) to completely destroy; demolish. *The old Coliseum building will soon be razed to make room for a hotel.*

reciprocate (verb) to make a return for something. *If you'll babysit for my kids tonight, I'll reciprocate by taking care of yours tomorrow.* **reciprocity** (noun).

reclusive (adjective) withdrawn from society. *During the last years of her life, actress Greta Garbo led a reclusive existence, rarely appearing in public.* **recluse** (noun).

reconcile (verb) to make consistent or harmonious. *Roosevelt's greatness as a leader could be seen in his ability to reconcile the demands and values of the varied groups that supported him.* **reconciliation** (noun).

recriminate (verb) to accuse, often in response to an accusation. *Divorce proceedings sometimes become bitter, as the two parties recriminate each other over the causes of the breakup.* **recrimination** (noun), **recriminatory** (adjective).

recuperate (verb) to regain health after an illness. *Although she left the hospital two days after her operation, it took her a few weeks to fully recuperate.* **recuperation** (noun), **recuperative** (adjective).

redoubtable (adjective) inspiring respect, awe, or fear. *Johnson's knowledge, experience, and personal clout made him a redoubtable political opponent.*

refurbish (verb) to fix up; to renovate. *It took three days' work by a team of carpenters, painters, and decorators to completely refurbish the apartment.*

refute (adjective) to prove false. *The company invited reporters to visit their plant in an effort to refute the charges of unsafe working conditions.* **refutation** (noun).

relevance (noun) connection to the matter at hand; pertinence. *Testimony in a criminal trial may be admitted only if it has clear relevance to the question of guilt or innocence.* **relevant** (adjective).

remedial (adjective) serving to remedy, cure, or correct some condition. *Affirmative action can be justified as a remedial step to help minority members overcome the effects of past discrimination.* **remediation** (noun), **remedy** (verb).

remorse (noun) a painful sense of guilt over wrongdoing. *In Poe's story* The Tell-Tale Heart, *a murderer is driven insane by remorse over his crime.* **remorseful** (adjective).

remuneration (noun) pay. *In a civil lawsuit, the attorney often receives part of the financial settlement as his or her remuneration.* **remunerate** (verb), **remunerative** (adjective).

renovate (verb) to renew by repairing or rebuilding. *The television program* This Old House *shows how skilled craftspeople renovate houses.* **renovation** (noun).

renunciation (noun) the act of rejecting or refusing something. *King Edward VII's renunciation of the British throne was caused by his desire to marry an American divorcee, something he couldn't do as king.* **renounce** (verb).

replete (adjective) filled abundantly. *Graham's book is replete with wonderful stories about the famous people she has known.*

reprehensible (adjective) deserving criticism or censure. *Although the athlete's misdeeds were reprehensible, not all fans agree that he deserves to be excluded from the Baseball Hall of Fame.* **reprehend** (verb), **reprehension** (noun).

repudiate (verb) to reject, to renounce. *After it became known that the congressman had been a leader of the Ku Klux Klan, most politicians repudiated him.* **repudiation** (noun).

reputable (adjective) having a good reputation; respected. *Find a reputable auto mechanic by asking your friends for recommendations based on their own experiences.* **reputation** (noun), **repute** (noun).

resilient (adjective) able to recover from difficulty. *A pro athlete must be resilient, able to lose a game one day and come back the next with confidence and enthusiasm.* **resilience** (noun).

resplendent (adjective) glowing, shining. *In late December, midtown New York is resplendent with holiday lights and decorations.* **resplendence** (noun).

responsive (adjective) reacting quickly and appropriately. *The new director of the Internal Revenue Service has promised to make the agency more responsive to public complaints.* **respond** (verb), **response** (noun).

restitution (noun) return of something to its original owner; repayment. *Some Native American leaders are demanding that the U.S. government make restitution for the lands taken from them by white settlers.*

revere (verb) to admire deeply, to honor. *Millions of people around the world revered Mother Teresa for her saintly generosity.* **reverence** (noun or verb), **reverent** (adjective).

rhapsodize (verb) to praise in a wildly emotional way. *That critic is such a huge fan of Toni Morrison that she will surely rhapsodize over the writer's next novel.* **rhapsodic** (adjective).

S

sagacious (adjective) discerning, wise. *Only a leader as sagacious as Nelson Mandela could have united South Africa so successfully and peacefully.* **sagacity** (noun).

salvage (verb or noun) to save from wreck or ruin. *After the earthquake destroyed her home, she was able to salvage only a few of her belongings.* **salvageable** (adjective).

sanctimonious (adjective) showing false or excessive piety. *The sanctimonious prayers of the TV preacher were interspersed with requests that the viewers send him money.* **sanctimony** (noun).

scapegoat (noun) someone who bears the blame for others' acts; someone hated for no apparent reason. *Although Buckner's error was only one reason the Red Sox lost, many fans made him the scapegoat, booing him mercilessly.*

Word Origin:
Latin: *putare* = to reckon. Also found in English *compute, dispute, impute, putative.*

Word Origin:
Latin: *sanctus* = holy. Also found in English *sanctify, sanction, sanctity, sanctuary.*

scrupulous (adjective) acting with extreme care; painstaking. *Disney theme parks are famous for their scrupulous attention to small details.* **scruple** (noun).

scrutinize (verb) to study closely. *The lawyer scrutinized the contract, searching for any sentence that could pose a risk for her client.* **scrutiny** (noun).

secrete (verb) to emit; to hide. *Glands in the mouth secrete saliva, a liquid that helps in digestion. The jewel thieves secreted the necklace in a tin box buried underground.*

sedentary (adjective) requiring much sitting. *When Officer Samson was given a desk job, she had trouble getting used to sedentary work after years on the street.*

> *Word Origin*:
> Latin: *sedere* = to sit. Also found in English *sedate, sedative, sediment.*

sequential (adjective) arranged in an order or series. *The courses for the chemistry major are sequential; you must take them in order, since each course builds on the previous ones.* **sequence** (noun or verb).

serendipity (noun) the ability to make lucky accidental discoveries. *Great inventions sometimes come about through deliberate research and hard work, sometimes through pure serendipity.* **serendipitous** (adjective).

servile (adjective) like a slave or servant; submissive. *The tycoon demanded that his underlings behave in a servile manner, agreeing quickly with everything he said.* **servility** (noun).

simulated (adjective) imitating something else; artificial. *High-quality simulated gems must be examined under a magnifying glass to be distinguished from real ones.* **simulate** (verb), **simulation** (noun).

> *Word Origin*:
> Latin: *simulare* = to resemble. Also found in English *semblance, similarity, simulacrum, simultaneous, verisimiltude.*

solace (verb or noun) to comfort or console. *There was little the rabbi could say to solace the husband after his wife's death.*

spontaneous (adjective) happening without plan or outside cause. *When the news of Kennedy's assassination broke, people everywhere gathered in a spontaneous effort to share their shock and grief.* **spontaneity** (noun).

spurious (adjective) false, fake. *The so-called Piltdown Man, supposed to be the fossil of a primitive human, turned out to be spurious, although who created the hoax is still uncertain.*

squander (verb) to use up carelessly, to waste. *Those who had made donations to the charity were outraged to learn that its director had squandered millions on fancy dinners and first-class travel.*

stagnate (verb) to become stale through lack of movement or change. *Having had no contact with the outside world for generations, Japan's culture gradually stagnated.* **stagnant** (adjective), **stagnation** (noun).

staid (adjective) sedate, serious, and grave. *This college is no "party school"; the students all work hard, and the campus has a reputation for being staid.*

stimulus (noun) something that excites a response or provokes an action. *The arrival of merchants and missionaries from the West provided a stimulus for change in Japanese society.* **stimulate** (verb).

stoic (adjective) showing little feeling, even in response to pain or sorrow. *A soldier must respond to the death of his comrades in stoic fashion, because the fighting will not stop for his grief.* **stoicism** (noun).

strenuous (adjective) requiring energy and strength. *Hiking in the foothills of the Rockies is fairly easy, but climbing the higher peaks can be strenuous.*

submissive (adjective) accepting the will of others; humble, compliant. *At the end of Ibsen's play* A Doll's House, *Nora leaves her husband and abandons the role of submissive housewife.*

substantiated (adjective) verified or supported by evidence. *The charge that Nixon had helped to cover up crimes was substantiated by his comments about it on a series of audio tapes.* **substantiate** (verb), **substantiation** (noun).

sully (verb) to soil, stain, or defile. *Nixon's misdeeds as president did much to sully the reputation of the American government.*

superficial (adjective) on the surface only; without depth or substance. *Her wound was superficial and required only a light bandage. His superficial attractiveness hides the fact that his personality is lifeless and his mind is dull.* **superficiality** (noun).

superfluous (adjective) more than is needed, excessive. *Once you've won the debate, don't keep talking; superfluous arguments will only bore and annoy the audience.*

suppress (verb) to put down or restrain. *As soon as the unrest began, thousands of helmeted police were sent into the streets to suppress the riots.* **suppression** (noun).

surfeit (noun or verb) an excess. *Most American families have a surfeit of food and drink on Thanksgiving Day.*

surreptitious (adjective) done in secret. *Because Iraq has avoided weapons inspections, many believe it has a surreptitious weapons development program.*

surrogate (noun or verb) a substitute. *When the congressman died in office, his wife was named to serve the rest of his term as a surrogate.*

sustain (verb) to keep up, to continue; to support. *Because of fatigue, he was unable to sustain the effort needed to finish the marathon.*

T

tactile (adjective) relating to the sense of touch. *The thick brush strokes and gobs of color give the paintings of Van Gogh a strongly tactile quality.* **tactility** (noun).

talisman (noun) an object supposed to have magical effects or qualities. *Superstitious people sometimes carry a rabbit's foot, a lucky coin, or some other talisman.*

tangential (adjective) touching lightly; only slightly connected or related. *Having enrolled in a class on African-American history, the students found the teacher's stories about his travels in South America only of tangential interest.* **tangent** (noun or adjective).

> **Word Origin:**
> Latin: *tangere* = to touch. Also found in English *contact, contiguous, tangent, tangible.*

tedium (noun) boredom. *For most people, watching the Weather Channel for 24 hours would be sheer tedium.* **tedious** (adjective).

temerity (noun) boldness, rashness, excessive daring. *Only someone who didn't understand the danger would have the temerity to try to climb Everest without a guide.* **temerarious** (adjective).

temperance (noun) moderation or restraint in feelings or behavior. *Most professional athletes practice temperance in their personal habits; too much eating or drinking, they know, can harm their performance.* **temperate** (adjective).

tenacious (adjective) clinging, sticky, or persistent. *Tenacious in pursuit of her goal, she applied for the grant unsuccessfully four times before it was finally approved.* **tenacity** (noun).

> **Word Origin:**
> Latin: *tenere* = to hold. Also found in English *retain, tenable, tenant, tenet, tenure.*

tentative (adjective) subject to change; uncertain. *They made tentative plans to meet for dinner next week, but neither of them could confirm before checking their schedules.*

terminate (verb) to end, to close. *The Olympic Games terminate with a grand ceremony attended by athletes from every participating country.* **terminal** (noun or adjective), **termination** (noun).

terrestrial (adjective) of the earth. *The movie* Close Encounters of the Third Kind *tells the story of the first contact between beings from outer space and terrestrial humans.*

therapeutic (adjective) curing or helping to cure. *Hot-water spas were popular in the nineteenth century among the sickly, who believed that soaking in the water had therapeutic effects.* **therapy** (noun).

timorous (adjective) fearful, timid. *The cowardly lion approached the throne of the wizard with a timorous look on his face.*

toady (noun or verb) someone who flatters a superior in hopes of gaining favor; a sycophant. *"I can't stand a toady!" declared the movie mogul. "Give me someone who'll tell me the truth—even if it costs him his job!"*

tolerant (adjective) accepting, enduring. *San Franciscans have a tolerant attitude about lifestyles: "Live and let live" seems to be their motto.* **tolerate** (verb), **toleration** (noun).

toxin (noun) poison. *DDT is a powerful toxin once used to kill insects but now banned in the United States because of the risk it poses to human life.* **toxic** (adjective).

tranquillity (noun) freedom from disturbance or turmoil; calm. *She moved from New York City to rural Vermont seeking the tranquillity of country life.* **tranquil** (adjective).

transgress (verb) to go past limits; to violate. *If Iraq has developed biological weapons, then it has transgressed the United Nation's rules against weapons of mass destruction.* **transgression** (noun).

transient (adjective) passing quickly. *Long-term visitors to this hotel pay at a different rate than transient guests who stay for just a day or two.* **transience** (noun).

transitory (adjective) quickly passing. *Public moods tend to be transitory; people may be anxious and angry one month, but relatively content and optimistic the next.* **transition** (noun).

translucent (adjective) letting some light pass through. *Blocks of translucent glass let daylight into the room while maintaining privacy.*

transmute (verb) to change in form or substance. *In the middle ages, the alchemists tried to discover ways to transmute metals such as iron into gold.* **transmutation** (noun).

treacherous (adjective) untrustworthy or disloyal; dangerous or unreliable. *Nazi Germany proved to be a treacherous ally, first signing a peace pact with the Soviet Union, then invading. Be careful crossing the rope bridge; parts are badly frayed and treacherous.* **treachery** (noun).

tremulous (adjective) trembling or shaking; timid or fearful. *Never having spoken in public before, he began his speech in a tremulous, hesitant voice.*

trite (adjective) boring because of over-familiarity; hackneyed. *Her letters were filled with trite expressions, like "All's well that ends well" and "So far so good."*

truculent (adjective) aggressive, hostile, belligerent. *Hitler's truculent behavior in demanding more territory for Germany made it clear that war was inevitable.* **truculence** (noun).

truncate (verb) to cut off. *The manuscript of the play appeared truncated; the last page ended in the middle of a scene, halfway through the first act.*

turbulent (adjective) agitated or disturbed. *The night before the championship match, Martina was unable to sleep, her mind turbulent with fears and hopes.* **turbulence** (noun).

Word Origin:
Latin: *turba* = confusion. Also found in English *disturb, perturb, turbid*.

U

unheralded (adjective) little known, unexpected. *In a year of big-budget, much-hyped mega-movies, this unheralded foreign film has surprised everyone with its popularity.*

unpalatable (adjective) distasteful, unpleasant. *Although I agree with the candidate on many issues, I can't vote for her, because I find her position on capital punishment unpalatable.*

unparalleled (adjective) with no equal; unique. *His victory in the Masters golf tournament by a full twelve strokes was an unparalleled accomplishment.*

unstinting (adjective) giving freely and generously. *Eleanor Roosevelt was much admired for her unstinting efforts on behalf of the poor.*

untenable (adjective) impossible to defend. *The theory that this painting is a genuine Van Gogh became untenable when the artist who actually painted it came forth.*

untimely (adjective) out of the natural or proper time. *The untimely death of a youthful Princess Diana seemed far more tragic than Mother Teresa's death of old age.*

unyielding (adjective) firm, resolute, obdurate. *Despite criticism, he was unyielding in his opposition to capital punishment; he vetoed several death penalty bills as governor.*

usurper (noun) someone who takes a place or possession without the right to do so. *Kennedy's most devoted followers tended to regard later presidents as usurpers, holding the office they felt he or his brothers should have held.* **usurp** (verb), **usurpation** (noun).

utilitarian (adjective) purely of practical benefit. *The design of the Model T car was simple and utilitarian, lacking the luxuries found in later models.*

utopia (noun) an imaginary, perfect society. *Those who founded the Oneida community dreamed that it could be a kind of utopia—a prosperous state with complete freedom and harmony.* **utopian** (adjective or noun).

V

validate (verb) to officially approve or confirm. *The election of the president is validated when the members of the Electoral College meet to confirm the choice of the voters.* **valid** (adjective), **validity** (noun).

variegated (adjective) spotted with different colors. *The brilliant, variegated appearance of butterflies makes them popular among collectors.* **variegation** (noun).

venerate (verb) to admire or honor. *In Communist China, Chairman Mao Zedong was venerated as an almost god-like figure.* **venerable** (adjective), **veneration** (noun).

verdant (adjective) green with plant life. *Southern England is famous for its verdant countryside filled with gardens and small farms.* **verdancy** (noun).

vestige (noun) a trace or remainder. *Today's tiny Sherwood Forest is the last vestige of a woodland that once covered most of England.* **vestigial** (adjective).

vex (verb) to irritate, annoy, or trouble. *Unproven for generations, Fermat's last theorem was one of the most famous, and most vexing, of all mathematical puzzles.* **vexation** (noun).

vicarious (adjective) experienced through someone else's actions by way of the imagination. *Great literature broadens our minds by giving us vicarious participation in the lives of other people.*

vindicate (verb) to confirm, justify, or defend. *Lincoln's Gettysburg Address was intended to vindicate the objectives of the Union in the Civil War.*

> **Word Origin**:
> *virtus* = strength. Also found in English *virtue*.

virtuoso (noun) someone very skilled, especially in an art. *Vladimir Horowitz was one of the great piano virtuosos of the twentieth century.* **virtuosity** (noun).

vivacious (adjective) lively, sprightly. *The role of Maria in "The Sound of Music" is usually played by a charming, vivacious young actress.* **vivacity** (noun).

volatile (adjective) quickly changing; fleeting, transitory; prone to violence. *Public opinion is notoriously volatile; a politician who is very popular one month may be voted out of office the next.* **volatility** (noun).

W

whimsical (adjective) based on a capricious, carefree, or sudden impulse or idea; fanciful, playful. *The book is filled with the kind of goofy jokes that are typical of the author's whimsical sense of humor.* **whim** (noun).

Z

zealous (adjective) filled with eagerness, fervor, or passion. *A crowd of the candidate's most zealous supporters greeted her at the airport with banners, signs, and a marching band.* **zeal** (noun), **zealot** (noun), **zealotry (noun).**